Also By Zohar Love, DD.

PROSPERITY FROM YOUR SOUL: The Metaphysics of co-Creating Your Ideal Life

A Lifestyle of PROSPERITY FROM YOUR SOUL: A Guide to Living a Prosperity-Magnetizing Lifestyle

Coming Soon

Books:
Reiki – The Light of Your Soul: USUI REIKI RYOHO—月 井 霊 気 療 法 As Originally Taught by Mikao Usui Sensei

Innovative Modalities:
RezoDance: healing movement imbued with reiki energy and Nature elements to affect complete balance, and harness the freedom of spirit to affect freedom of mind and body.

Rezossage: holistic massage modality that treats the whole person, and affects deep changes in a nurturing way. Deep tissue massage without pain!

Retreat Courses:
Level 1 – Prosperity From Your Soul: Combining the metaphysical understandings of the book Prosperity From Your Soul, with reiki training, and RezoDance empowerment, leading you through the Seven Stages of tuning into your Ideal Lifeplan, and devising a specific plan of action to manifest it. A weeklong retreat.

Level 2 – Soul Communications & Soul Mates: Learn to employ True communications in all of your relationships, from the business place to your Soulmates, and by that, magnetize a higher degree of happiness, health, and True abundance into your life. A weeklong retreat course, which includes Second Degree reiki training, as well as a Kindness Massage training.

Level 3 – Reiki Mastership & RezoDance Facilitators Course: Become empowered as a reiki master, and learn the art of hosting and facilitating RezoDance sessions. A weeklong retreat, which empowers and prepares participants to open their own reiki school and RezoDance studio.

Level 4 – Rezossage Course: A yearlong 650-hour course, which teaches the art of Rezossage.

Seven Stages to co-Creating

Prosperity From Your Soul

A Step-by-Step Guide to Reclaiming Your Ideal Life

Zohar Love

BALBOA
PRESS

A DIVISION OF HAY HOUSE

Balboa Press books may be ordered through booksellers or by contacting:

Balboa Press
A Division of Hay House
1663 Liberty Drive
Bloomington, IN 47403
www.balboapress.com
1 (877) 407-4847

ISBN: 978-1-5043-3391-7 (sc)
ISBN: 978-1-5043-3392-4 (e)

Print information available on the last page.

Balboa Press rev. date: 07/14/2015

Contents

Introduction

In *Prosperity From Your Soul*, we've talked about the unique Lifeplan that each one of us has, which is Ideal, from the perspective of the Soul, for Its growth and the fulfillment of Its mission in life. And when we follow that Plan, financial prosperity, as well as health, happiness, love, and every other blessing that we Truly wish for, automatically manifest in our lives as natural byproducts of the True Abundance of Soul.

In *Prosperity From Your Soul*, you and I have walked together the path of deeply understanding the metaphysics of co-Creating your Ideal Life. We've talked about how powerful a co-Creator of our lives we each are, and have understood that all we need to do in order to co-Create more prosperous lives for ourselves is become more *conscious* co-Creators. We've discussed why the Universe *needs* us to co-Create this reality with Her-Him, and the mechanism by which this process of co-Creation takes place on every level and in each moment of life. More than that, I hope that reading Prosperity From Your Soul has helped you develop an aware of your thoughts, beliefs, attitudes, feelings, and actions that are supportive of co-Creating prosperity, versus the ones that need to change in order to magnetize True abundance into your life. One point that is important to remember in all this is that nothing happens in life without the assertion of free will at one level or another, and the clearer you are on what it is that You Truly want—the more aligned your will is with the Will of your Soul, the more powerfully and timely abundance will manifest in your life.

What we haven't yet achieved together is tune into the fine details of *your specific* Ideal Lifeplan—the plan that your Soul has laid out for you for this lifetime for the achievement of optimal Soul growth, and as byproducts, the co-Creation of health, happiness, and prosperity. So what needs to happen now in order for you to merge your "now" reality with the reality of your Ideal Lifepath is: you need to align yourself with the consciousness and energetic vibration of your Soul. Being tuned into the *consciousness* of your Soul will enable you to become privy to the specifics of your Ideal Lifeplan, and devise a plan of action to start merging the current reality of your life with your Ideal one; while dwelling in the *energetic vibration* of your Soul will help you live a life that is inspired by your Soul, which will inevitably lead you to merge with your Ideal Lifepath—the life path that enacts your Soul's Ideal Lifeplan, and magnetizes all-inclusive prosperity into your life.

In this book, I would like to guide you through that path. We will walk a meditational, Soul-searching journey together, to help you awaken the powerful co-Creator dormant within you. Through the meditations in this book, you will shed off the layers of all that have, until now, obstructed the True You from shining through, tune into the Ideal Life that your Soul has in store for you, and devise a specific plan of action to merge your current life with your Ideal Lifepath of all-inclusive prosperity. As we have discussed in *Prosperity From Your Soul*, the A-B-C of your plan—the steps that you devise—may not be steps A through Z of your Ideal Lifeplan. They may only be steps A through G of the Plan. But remember that the Universe is meeting you more than halfway, and It is going to keep showing you more steps and bring you auspicious synchronicities that will easily carry you across the bridge from your "now" to your Ideal.

You naturally co-Create your life as a continuous flow of moments, feelings, and thoughts, which turn into actions and events, all of which fit like a perfect tapestry within the flow of your life's Creation. In order to facilitate the co-Creation of prosperity, you need to restore your original state of harmony with the perfect synchronistic flow of events that was meant to be your most auspicious life. This essentially means becoming more conscious of what it is that you are inviting/co-Creating into your life, and navigating your life in each moment in the direction of the most auspicious Lifeplan that your Soul has laid out. To give you step-by-step instruction on becoming a conscious co-Creator of your life, and to guide you to *consciously* navigate your life towards your Ideal one, I've been guided to divide the co-Creative process into seven stages:

The Seven Stages of co-Creation

The first, almost unspoken, step of co-Creation is to awaken to the realization that it is within your power to co-Create a healthier, happier, more prosperous life for yourself, and that you are worthy of it. *Prosperity From Your Soul* was targeted at helping this awakening bubble inside you, and crystalize into a realization that you are a beloved and deserving child of your Creator, and are therefore worthy of every wonderful thing. I hope that through reading it, you have started to grow deep roots of self-Love and worthiness, as those feelings are necessary to co-Create the life that you Truly want.

To fully support you in your process, before beginning the seven-stage process, Chapters 1 and 2 include some tools to learn to better communicate with your all Soul Self, and some basic meditational tools to help you find stillness within your mind and heart. For it is within the stillness of your heart that you may find your God-centered Soul Self—the all-knowing, all-powerful co-Creator whose spark dwells within you, and who is just waiting to shower you with Light-Love, and Its resultant health, happiness, prosperity, and joy. Of particular importance is Zohar Breath Meditation, detailed in Chapter 2, which is a powerful tool to connect with your Soul Self. Zohar Breath Meditation lays the foundation for many of the more involved meditations in this book.

Once you've realized that you are capable and worthy of co-Creating more, and have a basic grasp of meditation, there are seven stages to becoming a successful co-Creator of your most Ideal Lifepath. Here is the gist of this seven-stage process that I've been guided to give you:

Stage 1 – Eliminating Negativity & Dissolving Roadblocks:

The first stage of bringing your Ideal Lifepath into manifestation is removing the crust of doubt and fear from around your inner spark of Godlikeness. I look at it like the crust of a lychee fruit—the crust being rough, hard, and sometimes even ugly; and the fruit inside being a beautiful white, soft, sweet, and very juicy fruit. By virtue of our humanness, we all carry some mental blocks, and the energetic imprints of at least some childhood trauma, disappointment, fear, self-defeating programing, or just plain old stress. Like the hard crust of a lychee fruit, those blocks and energetic debris are just the crust around our wonderful True Selves. And as you'll find out experientially in this book, once you have meditationally removed these blocks and their energetic imprints, objective blocks will also lift off from the circumstances of your life, as if by magic. It is this openness that then allows both inspired ideas, and the means for their co-Creation, to flow into your life freely and abundantly.

So in this first Stage, we will devote some time to consciously eliminating all lower vibrational energies and energetic blocks from your psyche and energetic bodies. It is a purification process, which will clear, open, and balance all of your meridians, chakras and Light Bodies, in order to allow you to freely receive the Universe's natural flow of abundance that was always meant to be yours. In Chapter 3 we will eliminate the first layer of negativity—stress; and in Chapter 4 we will more actively dissolve any deeper blocks you might be carrying. Chapter 4 includes some pretty profound meditational tools for cutting cords, letting go of negative cellular memories, and removal of karma and psychic debris, just to name a few. What is nice about the meditational processes of Chapters 3 and 4 is that they help you remove those roadblocks from your path to prosperity without dragging you through the mud of having to re-experience any of the difficult themes. The meditations use positive visualizations, combined with breath patterns, to harness the power of your free will to remove these blocks. And it works like magic, because you *are* a powerful co-Creator of your life, who was given free will at every level of your existence.

Stage 2 – Tapping the Infinite Funnel of Abundance Through Gratitude & Kindness:

This stage is really about erecting the four pillars of prosperity: self-validation, gratitude, kindness, and love. Keeping your thoughts, feelings, and actions focused on joy and gratitude helps to actively connect your crown chakra with the Divine, thereby raising your vibration into likeness and resonance with the potential riches of your Soul. And as we have discussed in *Prosperity From Your Soul*, kindness connects you to all of life through the highest vibration. Kindness and generosity to yourself and others harness love energy to connect you with your reality through an open heart-chakra. This in turn creates a sort of vacuum that magnetizes more blessings into your life through your crown chakra, through which joy and gratitude have already connected you to the Creative realms of the Divine. As you act from an openhearted space of joy, love, kindness and generosity, your feelings enlarge your being to resonate with All-There-Is, and your kind actions ground all these blessings into your life, thereby connecting you to the Infinite Funnel of Abundance, all of which translates to Infinite Abundance flowing into your life.

In chapter 5, we will do some meditations to help you erect the four pillars of prosperity. We will work on meditationally connecting you with deep feelings of kindness and generosity. We will do some healing meditations to help you tune into self-worthiness and validation. And we will do a Gratitude Meditation, which is instrumental when you realize that feeling gratitude is one of the keys to becoming a more successful co-Creator.

Stage 3 – The Essence of Your Soul:

The key to co-Creating your most prosperous Lifepath is to align the will of your here-now self with that of your Soul Self. One of the key elements of your Ideal Lifeplan is your Ideal Lifework, which is an occupation that capitalizes on your Truest gifts and passions. But since your Truest gifts, deepest passions, and most heartfelt yearnings were all implanted in you by your Soul Self, than before you can tune into your Ideal Lifeplan of prosperity, you need to become intimate with your Soul Self, Its very essence, and deeply understand what gifts and passions It has given you. This re-acquaintance with your Soul Self, Its gifts, and Its passions, lays the foundation for tuning into your Ideal Lifeplan in the next stage. Chapter 6 will guide you through this important stage.

Stage 4 – Your Ideal Lifeplan:

Once you know what your True gifts and passions are, it is time to tune into your life mission, the Ideal-you, and the details of your Ideal Lifeplan.

In chapter 7, we will also meditate to categorize (not judge) all the elements in your life, in terms of which of them are parts of your Ideal Lifepath, and which elements need to change in order to facilitate co-Creating your Ideal Life. And of course, we will meditate to tune into your Ideal Lifeplan.

Stage 5 – Focusing the Plan:

Tuning into some ethereal dreamy plan is not enough. At this point, in order to truly attract what you want to manifest into your life, you need to bring your energetic vibration into likeness and resonance with it. One potent way to do that is to meditationally have a complete Internal Experience of living the life that you want—involving all the smells, visions, sounds, tastes, and textures you'd be sensing, as well as all of the daily feelings you'd be experiencing once you bring your Ideal Life into manifestation. Of course, in order to co-Create your Ideal Lifepath, this Internal Experience needs to be dipped in joy.

In Chapter 7, we will do a meditation called Your Ideal Daily Routine Internal Experience, to focus your vision and have a complete internal experience of living your Ideal Lifepath. The meditations in Chapter 7 will powerfully shift your energetic vibration into likeness and resonance with your Ideal Lifepath of prosperity. You might be amazed at the synchronicities that will start showing up in your life once you start doing these Internal Experience meditations daily.

Stage 6 – Devising a Plan of Action:

To bring things into focus, the end of Chapter 7 contains a meditation that will help channel the understandings of your previous meditations into a specific plan of action that you can actually start following in your here-now reality. This plan is about taking actions inspired by your Soul, to bring the Soul's highest visions into physical manifestation. Of course as you already know, you won't have to go it alone, as the Universe will meet you more than half way.

Stage 7 – Walking the Path of a Conscious co-Creator:

Stage 7 is about more than just making lists. It is about actually walking the path of a conscious co-Creator, and is the stage that you'll be in the longest. It begins in Chapter 8 of this book, which will give you some important tools to help you stay on the path of a conscious co-Creator, vibrationally, and with your thoughts, feelings and actions. As a potent co-Creative tool, Chapter 8 will guide you to find the Balance of Grace—the balance between being vivacious and upbeat yet peaceful; and between actively pursuing your goals yet leaving room for the Universe to meet you halfway. Finding the Balance of Grace daily will allow you to *continuously* magnetize prosperity to you, and will *keep* you on your Ideal Lifepath, once you've merged with it. Chapter 8 will also teach you how to set your vision free—free to resonate with the Universe, fetch the object of your desire for you, and bring it into manifestation in your life.

Within this seven-stage process, Stages 1 through 3 are a continuous flow: you should always keep yourself cleansed form any negativity; you should always dwell in a vibration of love, joy, gratitude and kindness; and you should always be connected to the True essence of your Soul. Stages 4 through 6 usually only happen during a shift—while you're figuring out a new Lifepath of abundance, or during any subsequent course corrections. But once you've figured it out and once it has all started to happen for you, everything will just keep flowing synchronistically with the Universe. As long as you keep finding the Balance of Grace and setting your vision free daily, you'll keep walking your Ideal Lifepath of all-inclusive prosperity.

To help further guide you through this important stage of actually walking the path of a conscious co-Creator, the next book in this series—*A Lifestyle of Prosperity From Your Soul*—includes lifestyle practices that lay the physical foundation for bringing forth enhanced amounts of Creative energy through your Infinite Funnel of Abundance. The idea in *A Lifestyle of Prosperity From your Soul* is and to first keep your body-temple—the vessel that your Soul has chosen for experiencing this human lifetime—energetically light and capable of accepting the enhanced amount prosperity-bringing Creative energy, and in good enough shape to handle the activities that may be required by your new auspicious Lifepath; as well as to make room in your life for new auspicious things to come to you. So the third book of this series will help you shift your lifestyle into one that helps bring your Soul consciousness and Creative resources into your everyday life.

This book can be used in two ways: If you've signed up for the Level 1 – Prosperity From Your Soul Course, reading through these processes ahead of time will help prepare you for the course. During the course, you will be empowered with some reiki attunements, and lovingly guided through this seven-stage process by your course facilitator. The course processes are also empowered by daily RezoDance sessions, which is fantastic tool of focusing your consciousness, uplifting your energetic vibration, freeing your body, and of course, manifesting prosperity. It is a very powerful course, designed to give you the ultimate support on your path to becoming a conscious co-Creator.

But even if you are not taking the course at this time, using the systematic and extensive guidance in this book will help you connect with your all knowing Soul Self, tune into the details of your Ideal Lifeplan, and devise a plan of action to manifest it. Know that even if I am not physically with you to hold your hand through your process of becoming a conscious co-Creator, I am very much rooting for your success. But more importantly, know that your powerful Soul is rooting for your success, and that the empowerment to reclaim your Ideal Lifepath has always been within you as a blessed child of your Creator.

Chapter 1

Everyday Communications with Your Soul

Your Soul—as a direct extension of Its Creator—is the powerful co-Creator of your Life! Because your Soul is in cahoots with God, Its resources are endless, and Its wisdom to guide your life is always lit by Divine Light, which by definition is dipped in joy, bliss, and endless unconditional Love for you. Even if you didn't read the first *Prosperity From Your Soul* book, you already know deep within the inner chamber of your heart that you are immensely beloved, and that your Soul and Its Creator want you to have the best, most auspicious life possible—filled with not only financial prosperity, but also health, happiness, love, and all of the blessings that your heart Truly desires. **The "trick" to co-Creating a lifetime of health, happiness and prosperity is to develop an intimate relationship with your Soul, which allows you to not only tap into Its wisdom, but also bring forth the Infinite resources that your Soul has been given mandate to manifest for you.**

So it becomes obvious that to co-Create a lifetime of all-inclusive prosperity, you need to develop an intimate relationship with your Soul, and let It be the guiding Light of your life. It is true that a certain aspect of your Soul is always within you, or else you would not be breathing, living, or reading these lines. Your magnificent and humungous Soul actually exists on a multitude of dimensions, from Divine Oneness, through the Heavenly realm, and all the way to your here-now reality. The majority of your Soul normally dwells in the Heavenly and Divine realms even during your lifetime, as that is where the Soul feels most at HOME. But your Soul is never completely detached from you. It is always actively involved in orchestrating your life, giving you clues, signs and loving support. Your task—your first task in becoming a more conscious co-Creator of a successful life—is to learn to understand the guidance that your Soul is giving you.

As you start co-Creating your life according to Your (Soul's) wishes, the most pressing issue is going to be tuning into, and interpreting the road signs that your Soul and the Universe are already giving you. And yes—the Universe is set up to give you unlimited love, support, resources, and signs to help guide you towards your Ideal Lifepath. The reason that I put the forte on communications with your Soul is that all Universal road signs, occurrences, and blessings come through your Soul, because by Universal law, nothing can happen in your life without is taking, whether that's synchronistic events, nature signs, internal communications, or any divination tools, the communication always passes through the filter of your Soul's approval. To better understand this, realize that Universal communications with you is not so much really a communication, as much as it is a harmonious Oneness—a flow, if you will, of your life with the most auspicious Divine Plan for you. This is because at the Heavenly realms in which the majority of your Soul dwells, your Soul is in a high degree of Oneness with your Spirit Guide, your Angel (or any other celestial beings who might be working with you to better your life), and with Divine Oneness. While you are constantly accompanied by your loving guardian Angel and Spirit Guide, it really is your Soul that is in charge of guiding you through the intricate paths of life towards your Ideal Lifepath.

Guidance from your Soul and from your Spirit Guides and Angels can take many forms. Your Angels and Guides, through your Soul, are constantly cheering you on and giving you loving guidance. And I have by no means listed here all the forms through which this guidance comes; as that would be impossible to list, since Soul communications are a private, for-your-eyes-only kind of a thing. This chapter will help you become aware of the possible forms of communications that your Soul may employ, so that you can open up to receive Its road signs, so to speak. I have listed here the signs from external to internal, and from the most obvious, which most people receive, to the more subtle, which takes some practice to perceive.

External Road Signs

In the truest sense, there really is nothing outside your Self, since your Soul is in Oneness with All-There-Is. However, to help you navigate your life towards your Ideal Lifepath and to help decipher the road signs that your Soul is already giving you day-by-day, it is helpful to divide the signs into external and internal signs.

Synchronicity:

The most prominent external road sign, which can help you know whether or not you are on your Ideal Lifepath, is to notice whether or not your life is flowing synchronistically with the harmonious flow of the Universe. Synchronicity is something most people have heard of, which is why I started with it as the first road sign. But what exactly is synchronicity?

Simply put, there are no coincidences in life. Have you ever started on one path based on logic, and found that all doors are closing in your face? And have you ever then changed your path to one inspired by your higher intuition, and found all doors just miraculously opening before you, and everything just beautifully unfolding for you as a perfect flow? The second case is synchronicity, or what I've been guided to call the path of Prosperity From Your Soul. When you travel through your Ideal Lifepath to fulfill your highest life-mission, your path is designed to flow synchronistically with everyone else who crosses your path in a perfect harmony—one feeding and supporting the other perfectly, as if everything is orchestrated by a higher guiding hand. That is how things are designed to be.

At any point in life, at some level of our consciousness, we each know whether or not we are on the path of Prosperity From Your Soul. In the deep inner chambers of our hearts, we each know whether we are tuning into a low-vibrational version of ourselves, or a higher one. And we know how certain thoughts and actions make us feel. We also know how the Universe is interacting with us: we either feel that everything is going difficult with stumbling blocks at every step; or we feel that everything is flowing synchronistically easy, and gifts just fall into our laps. How the Universe interacts with us at each point is a great telltale of how aligned our current path is with our Ideal Lifeplan.

However, note that the synchronistically auspicious way doesn't always stem from the most immediately logical choice. It will make perfect sense in retrospect, since hindsight is always twenty-twenty. But your Soul, as a direct extension of Its Creator, always has the highest perspective. It knows how things are going to turn out at each point, because the highest consciousness of your Soul lives in a realm in which there is no such thing as time, which has allowed your Soul to preview your life extensively before coming into this incarnation. So if you've made a choice that resulted in one failure after another, it's time for reassessment, as it is very possible that this choice is not in accordance with your Ideal Lifeplan. If, on the other hand, you've made a choice and you suddenly notice that everything is flowing easily and joyfully into your life, then you are in synchronistic flow with the Universe, and you can conclude that you are walking the path of your Ideal Lifeplan—the most auspicious path meant for you to walk, or at least walking towards it.

This level of signage from the Universe doesn't even have to be anything major in your life. It could be something trivial. For example, last week as I was preparing to go to the Conscious Life Expo, I was updating the information of my business cards and printing more cards on my home printer. I was tired and my brain was in kind of a fog at the time, so I probably wasn't thinking clearly about the changes that I was making to the cards. At any rate, I put one sheet of expensive business card paper in my printer, and the paper got stuck, one time after another. On that particular evening, I was being bullheaded. I insisted, and managed to print three pages of business cards, despite the fact that the paper kept getting stuck in the printer. I decided to take a little break, drink some water, and take some deep breaths. And once I did, I discovered that I had made a mistake on the verbiage of the cards. As soon as I corrected the mistake, the paper no longer got stuck in the printer. So this wasn't a major life event. My Soul was simply trying to prevent me from wasting the expensive paper on the mistaken cards.

In the same way, you might experience many mishaps in your everyday life. Your credit card may get stuck trying to pay for gas, only to find out once you lift your eyes that down the road, there is another gas station where the price of gas is fifty cents per gallon cheaper.

A very common occurrence is being rerouted because of road construction. Most people get in such a hurry that they frown on having to slow down or take an alternate route to where they are going. And it is true that every road construction affects everyone who's stuck at the same traffic jam with you. But why is this reroute or slowdown happening *to you* specifically? Say that during the traffic jam, music just "randomly" comes on the radio, which puts you in a happy and serene mood. In that case, is it possible that the Universe is telling you to slow down and smell the flowers? Or say that the constructions forced you to take a different route to your destination, along which you found a store that sells something for which you have been looking for a long time. You understand that in that case, the reroute wasn't an accident, right? The same goes for the line at the cafeteria during your lunch break. Maybe you're not happy "wasting" your lunch break on standing the long line. But on that particular day, your conversation with the person in front of you on line gave you a brilliant idea that relates to your next business endeavor, which is part of your Ideal Lifepath.

Another example of "inconveniences" that end up being auspicious synchronicities is: A few years ago, my friends were looking for the old restaurant where they had their first date some years prior, so they can go there to celebrate their anniversary. When they found the restaurant, they called for reservations and found out that it had recently closed. At first, they were very disappointed. But an instinct—as if an Angel touched my friend's shoulder—told him to ask about the old restaurant equipment. My friends' dream was to open a bakery, but they didn't think they had enough money for it. As it turned out, the old couple who had closed the restaurant was selling their old kitchen equipment for a tenth of its normal price. So the "inconvenience" of finding the restaurant closed helped my friends fulfill their dream.

Meeting people, especially when you or feel guided to participate in a particular event, is usually a synchronistic thing. When you feel a strong urge to go to a certain place at a certain time, when you get there, you'll usually find yourself magnetized to interact with certain people. And when you talk to them, the connection will usually prove to be mutually inspiring, or mutually beneficial. Sometimes you'll just overhear two people talking, and something in what they say will just "click" inside your mind: it'll be the answer to a question you've been asking; or it'll inspire an idea in you; or it'll remind you of something important.

I once had a book fall on my head in a bookstore. A number of years earlier, someone in a New Age store had told me that I should do kundalini meditation. Since he didn't elaborate and I didn't know what kundalini meditation really was, the advice went into one ear and out the other. A few years later, as I was strolling through a bookstore, naturally looking through the New Age section, the book that fell on my head was an instructional book on how to do kundalini yoga and meditation. Since I was already aware that such events are synchronistic signs from the Universe, I bought the book, read it, and started to practice kundalini yoga. This book falling on my head actually led me to many years of doing kundalini yoga, and eventually becoming a kundalini yoga teacher. Today, my daily spiritual practice includes mostly reiki and RezoDance (both of which you can learn in *Level 1 – Prosperity From Your Soul* retreat), and not so much kundalini yoga any more. But in retrospect, I recognize that my years of doing and teaching kundalini yoga were instrumental in helping me evolve to where I am today.

Synchronistic events don't have to be as dramatic as a book actually falling on your head. Maybe you're reading a book and a certain paragraph catches your eye, or gets stuck in your head. In that case, you need to stop and think about the paragraph, or perhaps bookmark the page and highlight the paragraph so that you can think about it more deeply later. That paragraph is somehow significant to you in your current lifepath.

Synchronistic events can be profound when your life really needs a redirect. But when you walk the path of your Ideal Life, synchronicity becomes an everyday harmonious flow with the blessings of the Universe.

Angelic Signs:

One of the most potent tools for co-Creating your wishes is asking for the help of Angels, ascended Masters, Spirit Guides, or any other deity you believe in. Realize, though, that as co-Creators of our reality, we are all One with our Creator, who is also the raw energy for the Creation, the process of Creation, and that which is Created, all at the same time. So Angels and other Light beings are not really separate from us or from God. Archangels are really the many aspects, or emanations through which God shows Her-His Grace to us. Angels and Archangels are Beings whose job it is to promote peace and Love. They have the role of helping us co-Create our Ideal Lifepaths. But it isn't that one particular Archangel is with you at one time or another while the others are not. Since Archangels are really the many faces of God, that inevitably means that they are One with the Divine Whole. And since at the same time you too are an integral part of your Creator, they are all with you at all times. The real question is which aspect of God you tune into (summon the power of) at each moment, as you work with one particular Archangel or another.

Angels are also here to inspire us; to help us feel how great we are; to remind us that the Creator and us are not separate; and to show us that all is possible in the name of Love-Light, as long as it doesn't violate free will! And when I say Angels, it does not necessarily have to conform to the form that Judeo-Christian traditions have intuited. It could be any Divine deity that you believe in and feel comfortable with.

However, as wonderful as Angelic help is, free will is a fundamental rule of Creation. Thus, Angels are not permitted to interfere in your life unless you ask for their help, or unless your life is at risk. This necessitates *asking* for Angelic help before you can get it. And while secretly wishing that some divine deity would swoop in and help you does constitute wishing for help, the more specifically you ask for Angelic help, the more timely and profoundly you'll get it. Once you've specifically asked for Angelic help, our spiritual Universe is set up to give you unlimited support.

How do you know when your Angels/Guides are near? There are simple signs:

The most immediate sign is that you suddenly feel calm, good, inspired, at peace, hopeful, or healed. You suddenly get a feeling that everything is going to be alright. That feeling is usually because Angels are surrounding you and healing you.

Your Angels and Spirit Guides can easily influence the subtle vibration of the air. This can be felt in a variety of ways. You may subtly feel the warmth of loving healing hands on top of yours. You may suddenly smell an unexplained beautiful fragrance in the air, usually a flowery smell.

Some people actually see flashes of light around the corner of their eyes. Many times I've taken pictures with my digital camera, and found unexplained white orbs of Light in the picture. I've even seen a few times them with my naked eye, but I had to off-focus my eyes and look hazily in order to perceive them. As soon as I engaged my logical mind and focused my view more sharply, I could no longer see the Light orbs. Some people, who are more gifted than I, can see the Angels externally on a regular basis, albeit most people perceive the presence of Angels internally.

Angels are also apt at manipulate electronics. So one way that your Angels and Guides can communicate with you is through music, especially if you have a form of music playing at random. I often put my iPod playing all yogic music at random, and ask my Angels to be in charge of the music. They always deliver. One of my most profound inspirational moments happened as a result of my Spirit Guide manipulating my Pandora Radio station. I was blessing a new deck of oracle cards that featured the Angels of Atlantis, when the station suddenly played a song from Secret Garden that always plays my heartstrings. I had to close my eyes to fully feel the music, and when I did, I had a vision of being surrounded by twelve Archangels radiating healing Light and Love towards me, after which I felt profoundly healed.

Numbers can have a special significance for us. Doreen Virtue—a psychic author whose guidance I have come to trust—has a significant section in her book *Healing With the Angels* on the general significance of numbers, and how they can be understood as signs from one's Angels. You can certainly look up the significance of particular numbers sequences that keep reappearing in your life. But as much as I highly value the angelic messages that Doreen Virtue relates in her books, the significance of any numbers sequence might be personal. For example, when talking about the numbers' sequence 111 or 11:11, Doreen says in her book, "Monitor your thoughts carefully, and be sure to only think about what you want, not what you don't want. This sequence is a sign that there is a gate of opportunity opening up, and your thoughts are manifesting into form at record speed…" I have no doubt that in some, maybe even in most instances, that is the meaning of this numbers sequence. But for me personally, for example, when my eyes get stuck on a clock with the digits 11:11, I always get the feeling of a portal, like I've just transferred to a fresh new reality, or like communications with the highest realms are possible at that moment. For you, the same numbers sequence may have a different personal meaning.

Nature Signs:

If you are very connected to the Earth-mother, than you may do well listening to Universal signs that come through nature. The best book written about the subject is called *Animal Speak,* by Ted Andrew, which details the meaning of many animal totems as well as nature signs. Some examples are: horses signify power and freedom; cats signify magic, mystery and independence; and eagles signify illumination of Spirit, healing and creation. Using nature signs does not, in any way, constitute paganism, or a worship of trees. Nature signs are merely an expression of the spirits of nature as expressions of Great Spirit (the Divine Creator). Remember that animals do not have a Neshama, but only a Nefesh and a Ruach. So they do not have individual Higher Selves, but are governed by the higher consciousness of the One. Thus, they can be used by Divine Intelligence to reach you in a way that can be interpreted much easier than dreams or visions. And everyone can receive nature signs; you don't have to be a bird whisperer in order to use them. You can even seek nature signs more actively, as suggested Ted Andrews.

On one winter afternoon during the time that I was reading *Animal Speak,* I got lost hiking a mountain trail in Malibu. It was the day after rain, so there was no one on the trail whom I could ask for directions, and nightfall was approaching. I then remembered some of the methods suggested in the book and decided to try it: Although I initially felt pretty ridiculous with myself talking to the Spirit of nature, I mentally told the spirit of nature to send me navigational signs through the singing of birds (there needs to be a pre-agreed upon sign). Even though I didn't notice any birds singing along my trail before, sure enough, after I set that intent, when I got to the next fork in the trail, I heard a bird singing up ahead and to the right of the fork in the trail. I decided that at that point, I was so lost that I had nothing to lose by following that guidance. So I turned right. For a while after that fork, I couldn't hear any birds, and started to worry. To my surprise, again as I approached the next intersection, I heard birds chirping joyfully, only this time, they were on the left side of the intersection. So I decided to follow the birds again. To make a long story short, the birds continued to direct me along the next few forks in the trail until a short while later, I got back to my car safely just before dark. Coincidence? Probably not!

Divination Tools

So far, we have talked about road signs that your Soul and the Universe are constantly giving you all the time, which you only have to develop an awareness of in order to understand. But you may also actively seek guidance from your Soul and from your Angels/Guides by using various divination tools:

Pre-Agreed Upon Signs:

Since you and God are One, and since you are the co-Creator of your reality, you can pretty much agree with the Universe not just on nature signs but on any other kind of sign. I once told God, "please, give me a sign: If I really am supposed to have my books published, then I want to see a circle with an arrow as part of its line, in the physical universe, within forty-eight hours from now."

And you know what? The Universe totally delivered. The next day, on arrival to San Jose airport, I saw a crop circle (not the supernatural kind, but a totally normal type) with an arrow as part of the circle. But since the arrow wasn't perfect, I doubted its validity as a sign. So I conversed with God again, and asked for a clearer sign. The next day, while I was installing a new program into my computer, its logo, lo and behold, was a circle with an arrow as part of the line. Now I know that most skeptics would say that the thought of asking for that shape as a sign could have originated from subconsciously knowing about the program's logo, or about the crop circle seen on the approach to San Jose airport. But would it hurt us all to be a little less skeptical and a little more optimistic? What did I really lose by choosing to believe that my books were going to be published? Nothing. And what did I gain by believing? Hope that I would get to help others through these books; getting myself enthusiastic about finishing the process of organizing the channeled materials into books; and getting myself into vibrational resonance with the reality in which my books are published, which I believe helped magnetize right publisher into my life. If nothing else, I gave myself a chance to manifest a happy self-fulfilling prophecy.

Dowsing & Muscle-Testing:

A certain deep level of our subconscious is always tuned into our Soul-level Truth, even when our conscious minds are only privy to here-now level of information. One method of extracting information from your deep subconscious is dowsing or muscle testing. By some accounts, people have been using dowsing to tune into higher level of information for thousands of years. According to Harvey Howells[3], there are cave drawings dating back to 6000 B.C. that show people using dowsing tools to search for underground water and minerals. In his book *Dowsing For Everyone,* Howells details how he learnt to dowse, and eventually taught others to use dowsing tools to intuit underground water, including knowing in advance (before drilling and without any scientific instruments) the quality, pressure and depth of the water, using either a pendulum, L-shaped rods, the Y-rod of antiquity, or in some cases, bare hands.

Generally the way dowsing works is: if you hold a pendulum by its string as still as you can, and as the pendulum starts swinging "on its own," you are getting a dowsing response. Once your pendulum swings, you can ask a few of questions to which you know the answers, in order to calibrate the direction of the "yes" and "no." Good questions for calibration are to ask about your name. For example: "Is my name Zohar?" "Is my name George?" one of which being the correct answer. Keep in mind that for some people, the "yes" and "no" responses are clockwise versus counterclockwise swings, and for others it is an up-down versus right-left swing. Once you know the directions of your "yes" and "no," you can ask other questions. I usually like to start the questions with: "Is it in my highest-best interest to…" or, "from the highest perspective, is such and such true," to qualify that I am intending to tune into higher-level Truth. In its simplest form, this is considered dowsing.

Muscle testing works in much the same way: because at the core of your being you are always tuned into Truth, your muscles will "test" weak when non-truth is being spoken (verbally or silently), and strong when Truth is spoken. In the same way, when a substance that does not serve your highest wellbeing is thought of or is within your auric sphere, your muscles will test weak; whereas when a substance that does serve your highest wellbeing is thought of or brought into your auric sphere, your muscles will test strong.

The traditional way to do muscle-testing is with two people: the person being tested stands with one arm extended straight out, either to the side or in front. When a question is asked, the helping person tries to overpower the tested person and push his/her arm down. If he/she succeeds, than the tested person's muscles are weak, which means the answer is "no;" if the tested person's arm remains up, that's a "yes" answer.

I've found a way to muscle-test myself using two hands: I make loop clenching my index finger and thumb of my left hand. The muscles clenching the closed loop are the tested muscles. Therefore, I do my best to keep the loop closed. Then with the right hand's index finger, I test the strength of the left hand's loop, by trying to separate the left hand's thumb and index finger. If I succeed in separating them, than my muscles are weak in response to the question asked, which means that the statement is non-truth; if the loop stays clenched, it means that my muscles are strong in response to the question asked, which means it was a true statement.

However, the problem with both dowsing and muscle testing is that higher-level Truth is not the only thing residing in our subconscious. Unfortunately, our subconscious is also given to the primal Nefesh (animal spirit), which is often tainted by fear. In fact, much of our subconscious holds our human conditionings that result from our scars of disappointment in life, and all kinds of self-defeating and programs. Our subconscious also holds the answers we want to hear, which is not always the same as the higher-level Truth. So to tune into Soul-level of information, one must sort through all the other junk before getting to our inner cell of Godlikeness that holds Truth. That makes it difficult to know what level of information is received from the dowsing method: I mean, how do I know, on any given day, whether my dowsing/muscle-testing is tuning into Truth, or just spiting out what's on my immediate subconscious?

I have to admit that I myself have never had consistently accurate results from dowsing. I have used a pendulum, L-rods, and muscle testing, and I always get a dowsing response. But upon testing the results against verifiable hard facts (such as the outside temperature, the expiration date of a license, etc.), I have arrived at the conclusion that my dowsing is, more often than not, giving me the answers I want to hear, tuning into the immediate subconscious from a very here-now perspective. Perhaps for that reason, I do not feel adequate to instruct you on dowsing in any detail. But I have been guided to at least share with you the existence of dowsing as an option that you can learn. It is possible that dowsing is just not a part of *my* path, but that *you* could become a successful dowser, and get accurate results. The American Society of Dowsers has published a twenty-nine-page booklet called *Letter To Robin* (downloadable for free on the internet), which explains the process of dowsing more in depth. Apparently, one needs to arrive at a "program," or agreement with one's "dowsing system," which I understand as an agreement between your conscious mind, your subconscious, and your higher guiding forces, such as your Soul and your Angels and Spirit Guides, to disallow lower-level interference, and allow only the highest level of information to come through. This program is said by experience dowsers to raise the accuracy of the dowsing considerably. For me, it didn't do so. But perhaps for you it will.

The second problem with dowsing and muscle testing is that the accuracy of your dowsing depends, to a great degree, on how detailed and appropriate your questions are. This point was driven home by Howells in his example of gas in the car: If you ask, "does my car need gas," the answer will always be "yes" because principally, your car has an internal combustion engine, which requires gasoline and air (also a gas) to run. Plus, it depends on how far your destination is. If your car has a quarter of a tank, and you are trying to drive 300 miles, than the answer is "yes." But if you are trying to drive five miles and you have a half tank, than the answer is "no." The most accurate question in that example would be, "does my car have sufficient fuel to reach XYZ destination?" So already we see that dowsing tunes into information in a very literal sense, which could be a minus if we are trying to tune into the real spirit of an issue.

The main problem with dowsing and muscle testing is that for the most part, your information channel is confined to "yes" and "no" answers. It's true that you can "program" into your dowsing system an agreement to swing in different clock directions corresponding degrees and percentages. It's also true that you can ask the L-rods to point to where someone or something is, and it'll point in that direction. Mr. Howell details one event in which he accurately dowsed his son's location, by asking the L-rods to point to the compass direction where his son was, and then narrowed down the number of miles from home with "yes" and "no" questions—information that he later verified with his son, and found to be correct for the moment that he was dowsing. However, when it comes to co-Creating prosperity, there is such a wide range of possibilities, within which your Ideal Lifepath is so unique and specifically tailored to you, that tuning into it requires more than "yes" and "no" answers.

The bigger question is: where are those questions coming from? I have a friend who, for many years, claimed that her third-eye is blocked, and that she cannot receive any visions or clairaudience messages. However, this woman is a highly skilled dowser, who performs many different types of healings and readings for people. One night, she was facilitating a shamanic journey for me. Since I had to be in a deep meditative state for this journey, my eyes were closed, so I could not see my friend's part in it. Unlike other shamans who enjoy vivid dreams and visions, my friend claimed that all the information she was receiving came solely through pendulum "yes" and "no" answers to silent questions that she was asking. But as she started recounting the details of one of my past lives, she was speaking almost fluently, albeit somewhat slow, as if she was reading a paragraph: "The year is 1721... you were a seven year old girl in a small village in Spain... " Then she proceeded to tell me all the events of that lifetime in extreme detail. I ask you as I asked her: How does one get that level of detail in that short a time, just from "yes" and "no" questions? I mean, unless her mind was working as quickly as a computer running through all the possibilities that have ever existed on earth, there would have had to be another mechanism at work, putting the right questions into her mind, dare I say higher intuition?

So in order to get accurate information from dowsing, you have to form the right questions and disallow any low-vibrational interference. And to do that, you must clear your mind of all clutter, filter through all of your limiting programing, completely still the mind, and tune into higher intuition. So my question to you is: if you could do all that, you'd be able to tune into firsthand information coming directly from your Soul, than why the heck would you need to dowse?

Oracle Cards:

Oracle cards are not the same as tarot cards, and there is no witchery involved in them. They are simply card decks with various artworks and pre-printed messages, which you shuffle and open "at random," the idea being that in order to give you specific messages, your Soul can control the "randomness" of the cards you pick. But all this depends on allowing your *deepest* intuition to guide you which cards to choose.

There are many ways to do a reading, and each deck of oracle cards is usually accompanied with a little booklet, detailing the methods of readings intended with these cards, as well as the possible messages of each card. In general, though, after doing a brief clearing and blessing (see Clearing & Protection later this chapter), you shuffle the cards, and then spread them faced down, so that you would not see the messages in the cards. Then you would pick three cards that you feel magnetized to open, and read their messages. You can actually open as many cards as you feel guided to open, but usually a three-card reading is interpreted: the first card is for the past or root of the issue, the second card is for the present or the right decision make, and the third card represents the future or outcome, if you follow the decision indicated in the second card. You can also open as many cards as you have issues in your present life, one card to shed light on each issue, or one card for each aspect of the same issue.

The beautiful thing is that anyone can buy a deck of oracle cards for usually about twenty dollars, bless them with prayerful intent, and perform their own reading. And the readings that you could do for yourself has the potential to be much more accurate than the reading that any "psychic" could do for you, since the highest level of information—from your Soul Self—is a for-your-eyes-only kind of a thing. There are as many oracle cards styles as there are belief systems, from Archangel oracle cards, to fairies, to earth-signs, to Tibetan koans… and everything in between. For many years, I have used many different styles of oracle cards, to teach people who come to me for reiki sessions and spiritual consultations how to do their own readings.

However, besides the limitation of confining messages to the forty-four cards of the decks, the main problem again with oracle card readings is that the accuracy of your results depends on how in tune you are with your Soul Self. I've done and taught enough readings to know that despite the fact that the cards are faced down—despite the fact that you physically can't see their faces when you select, the selection of cards is never really random. Since we are all psychic, your intuitive subconscious is privy to what's on the faces of those cards, and is going to guide you to "randomly" the pick the cards that are right for the level of consciousness that is ruling at that moment. The question is: which level of consciousness is ruling? Is it the lower fearful Nefesh (animal spirit), or the Neshama (Higher Self)?

For instance, let's say that you are about to launch a project that you've been working on for a while. And because you've invested so many of your resources on planning your project (time, money, effort), you have also become very emotionally invested in it. But let's say that at the last minute you have doubts and you want to tune into higher level of information for guidance. Most oracle card decks, no matter what flavor they're in, have at least one card that raises caution, and a few different cards that could be interpreted as a "go ahead" green light. So you bless the cards, shuffle, turn the cards face down, and then pick three cards. But at this point, since you don't know what part of your subconscious is leading the reading, there are several possible meanings to each possibility. If you pulled out the "go ahead" green light card, it could indeed be driven by the guidance of your Soul, knowing that your project would be successful. But it could just as easily be driven by the overzealousness of your here-now self to see the project through, even if it's not in your highest-best interest, just because you're so invested in it. In the same way, picking the "caution" card could be influenced by your here-now self's fear of moving forward, as part of your subconscious self-defeating programing; or it could indeed be a message from your Soul. How do you then know whether the information coming through the cards is controlled by your lower here-now self, or from your Soul Self?

Again, the only solution that I can give you is to sound that information against the Joy Meter and the God Meter—listen to the innermost resonance within you: is it a dissonant sound, or is it a harmonious song of joy? Another tool is Zohar Breath, or any other meditation that helps you tune into your innermost cell of Godlikeness. But then again, if you are capable of doing Zohar

Breath Meditation and tuning into your Akashic Records for information, why would you want to mess with oracle cards?

Automatic Writing:

Automatic writing is a way of channeling very specific information from your Soul Self. Most of the information contained in this *Prosperity From Your Soul* book series came to me through automatic writing. Most of my automatic writing came when over a period of a few years, I was awakened in the middle of the night (usually at two or three am) with a strong urge to write. When I was writing, I had no idea what I was writing, as the information did not pass through my conscious mind. It came *through* me. And usually when I finished writing, I would go back to sleep. Upon waking up in the morning, I had a vague memory that I did wake up and write something in the middle of the night. And when I read what I had written, I'd usually think: "Holy s#!t. Did I write this? This is too wise and profound for little old me to have written." And that's the type of information that usually comes through automatic writing, when you are really tuned into the wisdom of your Soul.

The type of automatic writing that we will do throughout this book is going to be a bit more controlled. We will soar into the heights of your Soul's consciousness through Zohar Breath Meditation, receive insights from your Soul, and then record them through automatic writing.

Automatic writing can be achieved by simply taking a few relaxing deep breath, letting your mind go, and writing or doodling whatever comes to you straight onto the paper. The idea is to tune out the cognitive mind, so that whatever you write/doodle comes directly from your subconscious onto the paper.

Without Zohar Breath Meditation, automatic writing can be an everyday tool for you to tune into what's going on inside you. The level of consciousness that you tune into (lower self, Higher Self) depends on the intent that you set. In your everyday life, you may wish to use automatic writing to help you tune into the immediate subconscious, for example if you want to understand what's subconsciously bugging you and why you are stressed on a particular week. Zohar Breath Meditation will set the stage, so that the Source of information coming through your automatic writing will actually be the wisdom of your Soul.

Internal Road Signs

In the next chapter, we will do Zohar Breath Meditation, which we will later develop into the skill to have complete conversations between your here-now self and your Soul Self—an important tool for walking your Ideal Lifepath of prosperity. One thing that can aid in categorizing the source of visions and whispers that you will meditationally see/hear inside your mind is learning to tell whether they are just the brainfucking mind noise coming from your lower human side, or if they are indeed coming from your Soul Self. In fact, as you are now starting your new path of Prosperity From Your Soul, it would be helpful to have a method of knowing which of your everyday life decisions are inspired by your here-now self, and which are indeed inspired by your all-knowing Soul Self.

The most profound internal signs that your Soul has given you are feelings. Feelings are said to be the primary senses of the Soul, because they help you gage what is going on at the higher levels without having to define it yet. However, when we talk about feelings, let's first understand what kind of feelings we are talking about. There are lower-level human emotions, which reflect your general human condition; and there are, on the other hand, the pure senses of the Soul. Recall from *Prosperity From Your Soul* that joy is the one thing that both your here-now self and your Soul Self agree on. Not the devious little enjoyment of a Big Mac, or of showing somebody off, which you'll surely regret later—those are your lower-level human emotions, but a deep inner joy that resonates musically in every fiber of your being. A thought, a feeling, or a notion is coming from your Soul if it just feels right in the bigger sense, and you can't quite explain why it does.

Another internal sign that you are tuned into the consciousness of your Soul is the peace, stillness, and clarity of mind that you feel. When you are tuned into the here-now level of your subconscious, your mind will usually be very busy; you'll be thinking of your shopping lists, errands, work issues, financial issues, last night's movie… and everything else under the sun. That's what I call the brainfucking noise. Accordingly, when you get messages from your here-now subconscious mind, they are usually in the form of a jumbled up cluster of thought. In contrast, when you are truly tuned into the consciousness of your Soul, your mind will be still and quiet. It is the kind of stillness that makes you feel absolutely at peace—at peace with whom you are at that moment, with your life, and with everything that is. In the most profound Zohar Breath Meditations, you will reach a height of Oneness in which you will want for nothing, and feel like a direct extension of Divine Love-Light-Peace. And that is how you know that you are dwelling in the vibration of your Soul. Within that peaceful contentedness, your Soul's messages will always be crystal clear.

The final internal sign that a message is coming from your Soul is the quality of the message received. I mean, your loving Soul would not be telling you to jump off a roof, curse at someone, or do anything unkind to yourself or others. One way to evaluate the quality of the message is to notice how you feel about following the advice of the message. If you think of following the advice of a message, do you get a knot in the pit of your stomach, or do you feel a profound inner joy? The best way to tell that a message is coming from your Soul Self is the scope of knowledge that it relates. When you are in a profound Zohar Breath Meditation—tuned into the heart of your Akashic Records, your Soul's messages always convey the higher aspects of any issue, such as the core reason or purpose of the issue in your life, in light of all of your Soul's history since Its inception, and the highest-vibrational solution for it.

Dreams:

Dreams are a very good way for your Soul, your Angels and your Spirit Guides to communicate with you. From a spiritual perspective, sleep is a golden opportunity to do the type of work that is difficult to do during waking hours. The possibilities of doing spiritual work during this time, when both your physical body and your logical mind are still, are endless. In fact, whether you acknowledge it or not, *we all do spiritual work during our dreamtime.*

As I say this, you may wonder how this idea jives with some of the troubled dreams you may have had. Maybe you've dreamed that you were constantly being chased by people, or that you were falling, or that you were poor and alone, for example. Well, you can relax, because even those "bad dreams" are spiritually important too, and are <u>not</u>, in any way, bad omens. Quite the contrary. Bad dreams bring to the surface low-vibrational themes, such as fear, worry, abuse, self-doubt, and other issues that need resolving. And this is actually a good thing, because it gives you the opportunity to resolve these issues during your dream state, and saves you from having to experience those disharmonious themes in your wakeful life. The process of bringing things into the surface is sometimes ongoing. Moreover, it's not always about anything in particular, which needs to be worked out. Sometimes it is just about purging of stress and other negative heavy emotions, which need to be expressed and purged out somehow. And isn't it better to do so through a dream, rather than through blowing up at your spouse or your boss in your wakeful reality?

Many times, troubled dreams are actually experiences that your Soul has signed you up for, in order to facilitate Soul growth. Let's say, for instance, that your Soul wanted you to experience imprisonment (either physically or mentally-emotionally), in order to drive you to reclaim your freedom. Wouldn't you rather experience that imprisonment in dream state than in your wakeful reality? The experience still facilitates the same Soul growth—you'd still wake up in the morning with a strong drive to assert your freedom. The only difference is that experiencing it in a dream allows you to end the misfortune simply by waking up. The way to release yourself from the disharmony of the dream is the same process you engage in to release yourself form unfortunate wakeful experiences: contemplate the message/lesson of the dream (ask yourself what learning or Soul growth were facilitated by this experience), and then just bless it (be grateful you could learn the lesson and leave behind the discord/misfortune), and let it go.

Dreams are also an excellent way to dissolve cords of entanglements with people in your lives. Many times you find your communications with a particular individual strained, and you have no idea why. Sometimes even doing repeated Cord Cutting Meditations (chapter 4) only serve to detach the entanglement cords temporarily, only to find that the cords have reattached after a week or a month. If you are blessed enough to go during dreamtime onto a journey into the source of your issue with that person, it can help resolve the karmic lessons that are at the base of the issue, and as a result, permanently improve your relationship with this person. Of course, as explained in *Prosperity From Your Soul*, resolving karmic issues is important to your overall harmony in life, because it allows you to then stay heart-centered on your Ideal Lifepath of prosperity without being swayed by others' low vibrations.

Dreams can be positive telltales: Have you ever had dreams that just *felt* so very real? Or maybe you've had a dream in which you were feeling supreme peace, and knew that you were guided and protected by Something. Those dreams are indeed messages from your Soul. And in a way, they are real in the sense that they are real experiences, which create an impact on your emotional and energetic self, even if you didn't physically fly to China or slay the dragon.

In interpreting the message of those dreams, it isn't necessarily the content of the dream that drives the realization that it is a form of communication from your Soul, but the feeling. For example, over the years, I have had a few dreams in which I dreamed that I was going to die. But in each of those dreams, I felt very serene with the knowing of my impending death. In fact, I felt so peaceful and elated during the dreams, that I was actually looking forward to this transition. And each time upon waking up, not only did I feel good, but I also realized that death dreams spiritually mean transformation. It doesn't actually mean physical death. It just means that you are being reborn into a new era of your life, usually a more auspicious one. And interestingly enough, after each of those impending death dreams, my life changed for the better.

Dreams are a really good way to experience your "What Ifs." This serves a big function in the co-Creation of prosperity, since these are essentially Internal Experience Meditations (see Chapter 7) of some of your possible lifepaths. Experiencing your "What Ifs" helps to experientially discern which one corresponds to your Ideal Lifepath, and which do not.

Many dreams are astral travels—travels to other realities in which you exist, in order to allow your spirit to experience its freedom and remember some of the important lessons you've achieved in other lifetimes. Many times, astral travels serve to remind you of what's possible, and how powerful your Original Self really is. According to Robert Monroe—a man who was able to have out of body experiences (OOBE) at will and participated in a number of double blind studies on OOBE, most people astral travel during their sleep, and are just not aware of it. In his fascinating books *Journey Out of the Body* and *Far Journeys*, Monroe talks about the difficulty of relating astral experiences as an objective observer. The first difficulty lies in the fact that unlike Monroe, most people do not retain a continuity of consciousness from their wakeful state, through the process of falling asleep, and onto the moment of astral travel. For most of us, the first few stages of sleep are dreamless states. So as we fall asleep, we pass out into a state of unconsciousness from which we do not remember anything, before we actually role out of the physical body and go astral traveling. Then, the astral reality is so bizarre compared to our physical one that it is only "logical" for our here-now mind to later interpret the realities we've visited as simply a strange dream.

The second difficulty in interpreting and relating the astral reality, says Monroe, is that at the human awareness level, our human minds are not capable of relating to us anything that does not have a basis in our human experience. The human mind needs to conform all of our experiences into known moldings. For example, the human mind does not know how to interpret the type of weightlessness and flying that the spirit does during dreamtime. So upon waking up, few people remember the actual spirit-flying that they did, while for most, the "logical" mind converts the experience into images that have more basis in their here-now reality level. Most of us end up remembering that we dreamt of falling, taking an airlines flight, hang-gliding, or the like. Monroe based this idea on his observations, and the people he met in the astral planes, who were astral traveling during dream-state. In the same way, Monroe notes that when you meet people in the astral planes, your perception of them is based on your impression of their "second body's" (the name that Monroe gave what I interpret as the Astral Body). But since you don't always know these people (or Beings) in your wakeful life, your mind has no frame of reference to categorize them—it has no mold to fit them into. So it categorizes them as a familiar person in your life. After I read Monroe's books, many of the symbols my mind uses to interpret dream experiences began to make sense. All of my flying dreams began to make sense. I realized that all those times in which I thought I was dreaming about friends I haven't seen in twenty-five years weren't necessarily about them, but about beings/people whose essences reminded me of them. And all those times when I dreamt about ascending onto an incredibly high snowy mountain with a ski instructor dressed in gleaming white weren't actually about skiing. Interpreting how I was *feelings* after those snowy mountain dreams—like I'd been completely healed and had a new lease on life, I realized that I've probably visited a Heavenly realm of Light, and that my ski guide was gleaming because he was probably the Angelic being who facilitated and guided me through the experience.

In case you are wondering, this is just some of the work we *all* do during our sleep. You don't have to be specially gifted to do this kind of work during your sleep. Your Soul is already gifted, and always leads you through the particular journeys that best serve your growth at each moment of your life. The only thing for you to do is learn to correctly interpret the higher messages from your Soul that are embedded in your dreams. And the first step to interpreting dreams as messages from your Soul is to become aware of them. Important things to notice are: your predominant feelings during the dreams, your feelings about the dream-events upon waking up, and any particular things in the dream which are symbolic to you, personally.

With regards to dream symbolism, it's true that it might be nice to have a good reference book on the spiritual interpretation of dreams, or to lookup online the significance of specific dream symbols. However, dream symbols—the way that your mind interprets your astral planes experiences—are personal. For example, I don't know if you'd find it in any dream book, but I've learnt through *my* experience that when I dream of hovering above looking for my car, that's usually when I'm looking for my physical body just before awakening. But looking for my car is *my* symbol. For you, looking for your car may mean something entirely different. Looking for your physical body just before waking up may appear in your dream as looking for your house, falling, or something else. Another example is: I am morbidly scared of insects, and all crawling things. So for me, dreaming of bees, snakes and green lizards doesn't feel like an auspicious sign. But for my best friend, who is a member of the fairy realm, bees are very auspicious signs, and so are lizards, especially green ones. Therefore, the symbols that your mind uses in interpreting your spiritual dream experiences are personal, and depend on what each symbol means *to you*, and how it makes *you feel*. You can become privy to the decoding information when you record your dreams, and think about them for a few moments upon waking up in light of what you know certain items to mean to you, and how they make you feel about the experience.

So upon first waking up, spend a few extra moments motionless, lying in bed and thinking about the dream, so that you can remember it, which is the first step to learning to interpret its messages. Spending that extra time in bed can also help you make the switch from dream reality, into zesty aliveness and happiness to start your day. I will give you some additional tools for that switch in Chapter 8.

You may achieve a higher level of clarity about the meaning of your dream, and the messages that they encompass for you, if you record them in a journal. Some clarity may come to you simply by doing some automatic writing of your dream-experience. Additional clarity may come over time, when referring back to the dream in light of life-events that followed. Over time, you will learn the unique symbolic language that your mind uses to convey messages from your Soul, Angels, and spirit-guides.

As you discern whether a dream is just a purging of negative themes or a real message from your Soul, remember that the True essence of your Soul is always loving and positive; promotes harmony and happiness; and would always guide you to the fulfillment of your Ideal Lifepath. How does this knowing help you interpret your dream signs? Let me illustrate: Let's say that you're having troubled dreams, in which you're constantly being swindled. How do you know if this is a foretelling sign that someone is going to try to swindle you, or if it's just your low-vibrational fear energy purging out? The first question that you should ask yourself is: what were you *feeling* during the dream? And were you in a very deep sleep state, or just on the verge of wakefulness? If you were just snoozing, and especially if you woke up aggravated, than chances are that this was your fear, worry, and stress energy purging out. Bless that experience; be grateful that now you won't have to experience this theme in your wakeful reality; and let it go—move on, and have a fabulous day. If, on the other hand, this dream came to you in a very deep sleep state, especially if you felt at peace with the experience, it may be a message from your Soul Self, perhaps to watch out. Another way to tell is your perspective during the dream: did you experience yourself from within your physical body, or did you see yourself from above? Experiencing the events of the dream from within your body looking out most likely means that this is a purging out of mundane negativity (stress, worry, fear, etc.). On the other hand, if you witnessed the events of the dream from the perspective of an all-knowing observer—as if you were hovering over the scene and observing your human self participate in the events—this means that your Soul Self was showing you something. But if being swindled was your dream-experience, the message is not necessarily that you are going to be swindled. First of, the whole reason that your Soul is giving you this experience in dream state is to lovingly warn you ahead of time, so that you can peel your eyes open, be aware of what's going on around you, and avoid being swindled in your awakened reality. But secondly, depending on the exact content of your dream, the message may have an entirely different meaning. For example, let's say that in your dream, you observed yourself being constantly afraid that you were going to be swindled; but from the higher perspective (hovering over the scene) that you were afforded during the dream, you knew that there was no danger of that happening, and so you felt very much at peace. Well than, in that case, you need to ask yourself: are you constantly suspicious of people? Are you constantly living in fear of being swindled? The message than may be that you need to work on yourself to shed off that fearful thought-form, because it no longer serves your highest wellbeing as a conscious co-Creator of your life. Throughout your interpretations of dream-signs, just keep in mind that even purging out of negative themes ultimately serves your higher purpose, and that messages from your Soul are always high-vibrational, hopeful, and loving.

Now, while many dreams are indeed specific messages from your Soul, lessons, and sometimes even prophecies from your Angels and Spirit Guides, some dreams are just about experiencing the freedom of your Spirit—giving you a chance to break free, for a while, from the limitations of the physical, feel the lightness and freedom of your Soul, and bask in Its Light. But remember that unless you can retain a continuity of consciousness from wakefulness to dream state and back, the way you cognitively remember the dream upon waking up is almost always distorted by the inability of your human mind to place all of what you've experienced into familiar boxes. And that's OK. For example, I have many dreams in which I fly-hover over a body of water that's gleaming in an unearthly beautiful turquoise Light. The flying I do in these dreams is similar to body surfing on air, except that I glide upward instead of downwards. Over the years, I have come to the conclusion that in those dreams, there isn't really a message or lesson per se, only the experience of pure joy that this upward gliding on the turquoise Light brings me. I don't really know exactly what the gleaming turquoise Light is, only that it is Divine. For when I wake up, I always feel healed and happy, like I've been restored to whom I Truly am, and all possibilities are at hand. And when you have so blissful, who cares what the symbol itself means? It's enough to know that you feel elated and free, and that you've just spent time basking in the Love-Light of the Divine, reminding you that It has always been yours for the having.

Our Multidimensional Senses

Before we can talk about clairaudience, clairvoyance and the like, we need to develop the ability to perceive internally the multidimensional signs that Soul is giving us. Dreams and feelings are things that everyone is gifted at. We all receive dream messages; we all are blessed with the deep inner feelings that Soul is giving us; and we all get guiding synchronistic events, whether we know how to interpret them or not. Other forms of perception are subtler. So in order to give you clearer tools of deciphering internal messages from your Soul, it may be helpful to talk about those internal messages as they relate to your six senses (yes, we all have a sixth sense, even if it is dormant), which correspond to the elements of Creation.

Recall from *Prosperity From Your Soul* that Creation, at least perceptually, happens in stages—from the most ethereal and Divine to the most mundane. Your Soul too starts at the level of the Divine, and steps down Its energy gradually into denser and denser forms until it reaches the forms that your human mind and the senses that you can perceive. Native cultures have found it easier to grasp the layers of Creation in terms of levels of density, expressed as five metaphoric elements: ether, air, fire, water, and earth (or wind, fire, water, earth and metal in Chinese medicine). Kabbalah talks about Creation as occurring in twelve emanations (spheres), through which God is "reducing" (Tsimtsum) Her-Himself into us and our world. Regardless of which tradition you come from, let's now see how this knowledge can benefit our co-Creation endeavors.

In the same way that Creation (including the manifestation of prosperity) happens from subtler to denser, our subtle internal perceptions of the Soul can also come from our multidimensional five senses, as they perceive layers of reality from the most ethereal to the most mundane. You see, besides the obvious physical information that each sense relates to us, each of our senses also relates to a different layer of density, in terms of the dimensions of Creation, which may encompass guiding messages from your Soul.

Light & Music:

While Divine Light is the highest vibration of Creation, it is not perceptible to us-humans with our five senses. As the energy of Creation filters to the element of ether, observable light and sounds are the highest vibrations that we, as humans, can perceive. They retain much of their Divine essence, as evidenced by the fact that they are undifferentiated into form or words. Beyond the external light, observable reality, and the objective sounds that you hear through your everyday perceptions, and even beyond Angelic messages that you may get through music and light flashes, how you resonate with different colors of light and different musical sounds is one key to tuning into your True vibration at any given moment. We will talk about the vibrational meanings different colors in the next chapter. But as it relates to music, say that on a particular day you are very drawn to listen to compositions written in a minor key—sad or emotionally charged melodies. Well, perhaps this is your inner-self telling you that it's in your highest-best interest to take some time to allow yourself to feel things deeply, so you can purge out that sadness and let it go. And say that on another day, you are drawn to very upbeat music. Well, if you are drawn to upbeat music, and it is making you feel good and joyous to the very core, than perhaps this is a foreshadowing clue that good things are coming into your life or already exist underneath the surface of your observable reality. Or it could be your Soul telling you to go out, have some fun, and just enjoy life, so that you may magnetize into your life more blessings. Any way you look at it, your resonance with particular sounds at particular times is a clue about what your inner self needs at that time, to help you blossom.

Truth Hearing:

When you further develop your spiritual attunement with the sounds of your Soul, your musical resonance with the sounds of words being spoken may develop into a discernment of Truth I call Truth Hearing. Truth Hearing is not really referring to one's physical sense of hearing, but to a deep sense of inner knowing. Being able to hear Truth means developing the sensitivity to discern, on a subtle level, whether what's being spoken originates from Divine Truth or from lower-level non-truth. And I believe that to one degree or another, we all have the ability to Truth Hear. Because of society-imposed rules, we may have trained ourselves to ignore and stifle it, so some people's Truth Hearing may have become dormant over the years. But we were all born with it.

What exactly is Truth Hearing? For example, you may find yourself listening to the words of a respected professor and cringing. This doesn't necessarily mean that the information being spoken is untrue. It simply means that the person's consciousness is not what I call God-centered at that moment. It may mean that there is ill intent motivating the person to speak. There may be ulterior motives that may affect you, and if you sense that there are, it's up to your cognitive mind to find out what they are. If you find that the very voice of someone is disturbing or unpleasant to you, just know that there are some non-truths, either in the content of what is spoken, in the motives of the speaker, their intents towards you, their consciousness state, or in their energetic vibration at that moment. When in the presence of non-truth, you should energetically shield yourself with Divine Light (which we will learn how to do later in this chapter).

On the other end of the Truth Hearing spectrum, you may find yourself talking to a person who is supposed to be ignorant (the janitor for example), and his/her very voice sounds like the bells of heaven, or you get a pleasant tingly feeling in the back of your neck when this person speaks. When you find that you just want to listen to someone's voice, it means that his/her motives and heart are pure. It is probably safe to trust him/her. And don't be surprised if you find a reflection of all that you hold dear in the person's eyes, as he/she may be a kindred spirit.

Your ability to Truth Hear indicates that you are evolving spiritually, and have become very sensitive to subtle energies. And that is a gift that has been given to you, to serve as a guiding tool on your new path to co-Creating prosperity.

Truth Hearing refers not only to the human voice, but also by extension, to the energy that the person inputs into an instrument being played. A personal example of this type of Truth Hearing is: my father is a famous violinist who has a magnetic personality; he is usually the life of a dinner party, telling juicy stories and charming the guests. However, when it comes to his inner feelings, he is an introvert who, despite our closeness, has never discussed with me his inner feelings. But ever since I have been on a spiritual path, I find that I can always tell what's in his mind and heart when I listen to him play the violin, or just by the subtle energy underlying his words. This is more than just listening to tone in the traditional way. I can listen to him play the same piece, and on one day I "hear" that he is stressed, or that something is weighing on his mind, while on another day, I'd hear that he is Divinely inspired. In the same way, I can tell his inner feelings just by his "hello" at the beginning of his conversation. And the interesting thing is that most times, the quality of feelings that I "hear" in his music is not describable in words. It could be a certain yearning for the Divine that he as a declared atheist would never admit to in words, a certain openness of the heart, or an expression of the deepest heart-song that could never be expressed in any worldly action. While this type of Truth Hearing takes time to reawaken, it actually is a dormant ability that every human being has, given to us as a basic tool for tuning into Soul Truth in pure form—before it differentiates into the here-now reality.

To begin developing your Truth-hearing, just start being aware of the inner feelings that certain sounds evoke, which may or many not be translatable into cognitive thought. Remember, this is an unspoken and very subtle aspect of the sound. For example, while one person's saying, "have a nice day" can make your stomach crawl, another person's saying "go left after the escalator" may uplift your spirit. Both statements are mundane—there is nothing in their content that is an overt lie or unkindness. But your feelings are legitimate. They stems from the Truth Hearing that you are beginning to develop, which is helping you tune into the speaker's intent and vibrational state at the moment that he/she spoke them.

Scent:

The second element, as Creation gets denser, is the element of air (or wind), which manifests as scent. Modern medicine[1] points out that our sensory organs are hardwired deeply into the primal and emotional parts of the brain, enabling scent to bypass all the logical steps of perception, and be experienced very directly, in order to facilitate survival. But what modern medicine may not tell you is that the immediate nature in which we experience scent is because scent is a more direct way to access the purest parts of ourselves in an untainted way. Ancient Kabbalists intuited that the Hebrew word for spirit—RU-ACH, and the word for scent—RE-ACH stem from the same root, as well as numerologically reduce into the same number, which points to the close interrelationship between scent and spirit. Many healing and New Age practices (including RezoDance) use aromatherapy to help tune our senses into the Divine vibration.

Beyond unexplained flowery scents that your Angels may manifest for you as a sign, being aware of how different scents resonate with you can be a perceptual tool. For example, in relationships, one of the first clues that you no longer love your partner is that his/her scent becomes offensive to you. When you were in love, you could smell his/her sweaty armpits and be intoxicated (turned on) by that smell, and now his/her very scent is offensive to you. This is a clue that your Earthly path together may have come to an end.

Our connection with the air element of Creation is more than just a sense of smell. You know the saying "something just doesn't smell right?" Well, that "something" that doesn't quite "smell" right is alluding to our ethereal sense that something is right or wrong with, say a business deal or a decision. We won't call it clairsentience just yet, but we all have this ethereal sense of how our current action or situation fits in with the bigger scheme of things. Just know that this sense of "smell" is legitimate, and should make you at least investigate the matter further, before you say yay or nay to the particular decision that "doesn't quite smell right."

Abstract Thoughts:

Another type of clue that relate to elements of ether and air is abstract thought. Abstract thoughts are the domains of the Mental Body, which vibrates faster than ether. Of all the earthly life forms that exist, the capacity of abstract thought was given only to humans, specifically for the purpose of perceiving the Soul. Now, the type of abstract thought that could help you tune into your Soul is not necessarily a thought that can be expressed in words. It feels very abstract, like an ethereal energy—a hint of a thought that you haven't quite caught a full glimpse of yet—like something that is just at the tip of your tongue (mind), and you can't quite pinpoint. That's ok. Realize that these very ethereal abstract thoughts are glimpses into your Soul Self that are pure and untainted. They are also the birthplace of future ideas that you will be able to put into words and manifest later. For now, since the first step is becoming aware of clues from your multidimensional expanded Self, the thing to do with these is just to be aware of them, let them be, and perhaps allow yourself some extra time to dwell in these ethereal thoughts without trying to capture them into words or into any specific form yet. One thing you can do is note which activity induced these inspired abstract thoughts—what were you doing or thinking of just before the inspiration occurred? Becoming aware of what induced these abstract inspirations may help you bring them about again, which eventually will help you speed up their crystallization into more formed ideas and manifestations.

Words Have a co-Creative Power:

The next levels of our multidimensional Selves that come into play in co-Creation are words and conscious intents. Words and conscious intents are the first level of differentiating our co-Creations into manifested form, and are thus powerful co-Creative tools. It is true that we tune into the very fine vibration of the Divine and His-Her Creative power with our abstract thought; and that we pull those abstract Creations into physical form using our prosperity-magnetizing vibrational resonance with them, which is driven by our feelings. But we start moving things closer to manifested form by calling it a name. In other words, the Divine abstract and Its vibrational resonance within us are only ripe for full manifestation when we can focus our intents clearly enough to speak them in words.

Now when I say "spoken word," it means a word that has come into form, either in your mind—silently, or spoken out loud. Yogis differentiate words into three categories: silent words are considered the innermost, purest yearning of your Soul; whispered words are the voice of a lover—your consciousness creating a love connection with your Soul and the Divine; and words spoken out loud are considered the voice of the human adult, expressing thoughts into intents that are mature, and ready to take form.

As you may recall from *Prosperity From Your Soul*, feeling deserving, joyful, and grateful for the prosperity you seek shifts your energetic vibration into likeness with it, creating a mutual resonance and a magnetic force pulling that prosperity to you. But while our inner feelings are main driving force that shifts our energetic vibration into likeness and resonance with the object of our desire, words spoken out loud either amplify or dampen the strength of our magnetic pull on the object. That is, if your formed thoughts and words contradict the high vibration of what you seek, than they dampen your attractive mutual resonance with it, which can delay its manifestation in your life. If, on the other hand, both your feelings and your words are in alignment with what you seek, than the vibration of your words strengthen your mutual resonance and amplify your magnetic pull on the object, thus speeding up its manifestation in your life.

To simplify, at the level of your Soul, all ideas are very pure and ethereal. They remain in their pure essence, which to our human-selves seems abstract, when they filter into our Mental Body. They also remain as indefinable deep essence-feelings when they come into the Astral (emotional) Body and into the heart space. But as your vision becomes clear and forms into a cohesive plan in the human level of your mind, as long as the vision has the power of your Soul Self behind it, the first form through which those visions and ideas come out into the universe is through words. You speak your intent to co-Create something; you pronounce yourself one way or another; you express your desire… all in words. Your vision wouldn't come out in words if it wasn't fully formed, or if you aren't ready to co-Create it. So in that sense, words are also the first vehicle that starts broadcasting (vibrationally) into the Universe your fully formed intent to co-Create something. Of course, to co-Create something and pull it into physical manifestation, your mutual resonance with it has to consist of more than words. Your complete vibrational essence has to match that of your desire, creating a mutual resonance with it. But words are the first bridge, which brings that resonance into form, and calls it a name. Thus, words are very powerful.

For this reason, you should indeed be careful what you say, and what you wish for. Because it isn't only that you *may* get it. If your feeling, consciousness, and vibrational essence stand behind your words, you absolutely will get it! So choose your words and your thoughts carefully. When you make a mistake, don't exclaim off handedly "Oh, I'm dumb," because if you keep saying that, you may start to believe it, and then you'd start resonating with being dumb. Instead, say something like, "I'll get it right next time." If money hasn't yet started flowing easily and abundantly into your life, don't say, "I'm poor." Say, "I'm temporarily broke," or better yet say, "I'm becoming wealthier and wealthier every day."

Words that come to you can also help you get a clue of what's going on inside you, and what you need to work on in order to better connect with your Soul Self. For example, if you have a tendency to always put yourself down, that is a sign that you need to bring more on self-love and acceptance into yourself. If for example the words, "I'm going beach" signify in your mind the ultimate happiness, then perhaps your dream business or endeavor should be located close to a beach, or maybe what you need for your personal evolution at that moment is to take time each day to smell the ocean air and relax. We will talk about clairaudience messages later in this chapter. But for now, just listen to the words that are coming to you in your everyday expression (to yourself or to others), and become aware of the significance of those words to your vibrational essence.

Clear Perception

We all have the ability of clear perception, in the forms of clairaudience, clairvoyance, clairsentience, and claircognizance, albeit because of societal norms, it may have become dormant. Also, every person is gifted differently, and is therefore more apt to receptive messages in a different form.

Clairaudience Messages:

Clairaudience messages are actually not that rare—most people get them, and perhaps are not aware of them. In most cases, clairaudience messages are not actual external physical voices that we hear—not quite as dramatic as "If you build it, he will come[2]." Although few gifted people can hear the subtle clairaudient whisper physically, for most of us, clairaudience is nothing more or less than our inner voice—the innermost voice of your heart, which is connecting you to the Universal wisdom of your Soul.

The first issue with clairaudient messages is to allow ourselves to listen to them—to be attentive and truly listen to our internal voice, and give it some credence. This inevitably brings about the second, more serious issue: learning to distinguish True clairaudience messages coming from your Soul (or Angels/Guides), from the everlasting brainfucking noise of the mind. And there are many tools that can help you make that distinction.

The first two tools, given in Chapter 7 of *Prosperity From Your Soul,* are the God Meter, and the Joy Meter. In clairaudience messages as in all other messages, messages that score high on the God Meter are usually real messages from your Soul Self. For example, your Soul would not be calling you a "dumb ass," and It wouldn't be criticizing you unconstructively. Your Soul would also not be telling you to vandalize someone's car in a parking lot just because they took your parking spot. It would, on the other hand, give you constructive advice that promotes life, health, happiness, True abundance, joy, and love, all the way around. Messages from your Soul also need to score high on the Joy Meter: consider how you feel about following the advice given by the message. Do you feel fearful with a knot at the pit of your stomach? Or do you feel joyful? The voice of your Soul can always be distinguished as the inner voice that makes your heart sing with joy.

Clairvoyant Messages:

Few individuals are gifted enough to perceive clairvoyant visions as actual apparitions of Angels or departed spirits. This, I think, is because in our human consciousness, for most of us it would be scary to see apparitions. That is why for most of us, our clairvoyant ability expresses itself internally. And yes, most of us have the ability to internally have visions.

It is true, however, that to receive messages that reveal the unknown ("Sod"—discussed in chapter 5 of *Prosperity From Your Soul*), one needs to be aware of visions, learn to interpret them accurately, as well as keep one's energetic apparatus clear and open to receive Universal wisdom. I'll give you an example: my best friend is such a gifted channeler that she can tell you: "Tomorrow at 8:31am you'll walk around the corner of Church and Main streets, and you'll see a red haired woman wearing a green polka dot dress, with a canary on her left shoulder, and she'll say 'top of the morning to you'." And the next day, even if you have forgotten the prediction, it would happen exactly the way my friend had predicted. But understand that there is no magic involved here! The information of possible future realities is out there in the Universal ethers, available for all of us to tune into. Getting to this level of accuracy simply requires a high degree of attunement with Universal Truth, which takes time to develop (or to re-awaken, really). Even my gifted friend is, after all, only human. She is not always privy to this level of Universal knowledge. In fact, most of the time, she is quite a normal person whose knowledge is limited to normal perceptions. She only tune into this level of accuracy at times in which she sheds off all stress, and meditationally tunes into her Divine connection. And even for her, trusting the Universal guidance, and making life decisions based on It is another challenge altogether.

The first step to developing your clairvoyance, just like in the case of clairaudience, is to simply start being aware of visions coming to mind as possible clairvoyant messages. The visions may come in dreams, in the interspace between dream and wakefulness, in meditation, during daydreams, or even during a fully wakeful state.

Of course, not every vision that comes to your mind is a clairvoyant message from your Soul. For example, if during your morning daydream, you envision yourself being captured by Darth Veda, that's not a clairvoyant message; that's just TV invading your mind as a result of watching way too much of it! If while standing in traffic on your way to a meeting, you envision everything that could go wrong with that meeting, I'm pretty sure that's *not* a message from your Soul either. If, on the other hand, you had an idea or a project you didn't quite know how to execute before, and one day during your morning daydream, you suddenly get a vision in which you "see" an easy way to start and succeed in your project, that certainly sounds more like a clairvoyant message from your Soul, especially if the vision makes you feel joy.

This is another way to say that you should test the validity of any vision that comes to you against the Joy Meter and the God Meter. The God Meter and the Joy Meter will help you distinguish whether the vision is just a manifestation of your subconscious fears, a lower intuitive message related to survival, or a True message from your Soul. At any rate, respect the message. But in order for you to know how to understand the message correctly and what to do with it, you'll need to know which part of your total self the message originates from.

If it is fear based, at least you'll know that you need to do some Dissolving Fear Meditation (Chapter 4) and other meditations to clear that particular self-defeating program. If it is a lower survival-based intuition, it may, for example, be telling you to take a different route to work to avoid traffic, or avoid an accident. And those too are valid and important directives. You can distinguish survival intuitive messages from fear based brainfucking, by evaluating the clarity of your mind and how you feel: in fear-based brainfucking, your mind usually races round-and-round, and you feel troubled; whereas intuitive messages, even if they relate to survival, usually have a clarity about them that makes you feel peaceful and unworried. For example, let's say that while driving, and without any indication of traffic issues in your physical reality, you suddenly get a vision of taking another route. You evaluate, and become aware that the vision was very clear in your mind (your mind wasn't racing or going round-and-round), and you felt pretty peaceful and serene with driving the alternate route. In that case, the message was probably a valid survival intuitive message. It may not be a life altering higher message from your Soul. But it certainly would be a directive worth respecting. And in that case, it doesn't really matter what would have happened had you not followed the message. What matters is that if you don't actually mind driving the alternate route, why not do it? If the vision is indeed a higher message from your Soul, than when dwelling in the vision, you'll feel the supreme peace that comes along with it—a deep knowing that everything is absolutely going to be ok.

Also when it comes to clairvoyant messages, as you'll see in Your Ideal Daily Routine Internal Experience Meditation (Chapter 7), the ease or difficulty of visualizing something is in itself a clairvoyant message. During the meditation, you will envision yourself in a life that most perfectly encompasses your Truest wishes. But what if you've always thought you wanted something, and you suddenly can't even visualize yourself having it? And what if instead, you "see" yourself co-Creating something entirely different, and being happy to the core in that life? In that case, both the difficulty visualizing the originally perceived wish, and the sudden appearance of the new image of in your mind *are* clairvoyant messages. And in that particular meditation, since all that envisioning takes place after you're tuned into your Soul consciousness, the difficulty of envisioning your originally perceived wish probably indicates that you didn't really want what you thought you wanted; and the ease of internally experiencing the new wish with joy probably means that that is what you Truly want.

Clairsentience:

In its pure form, clairsentience is an intuitive, gut feeling, which most of us have, since at a deep level of our consciousness, we are all connected to the unseen levels of reality, and to our individual possible realities (see Chapter 6 of *Prosperity From Your Soul*). We perceive what's going on behind the scenes of observable reality as a deep inner feeling we call intuition or a gut feeling.

An extension of the intuitive gut feeling is the ability to empathically sense the feelings of others—incarnate or not. People who are empaths would feel sad when in the presence of someone who feels sadness, and happy when in the presence of happy people. Essentially, we empathize with what other people are feeling. This is especially common amongst healers. When I perform a reiki healing, I usually get brief feelings of pain in my body, which corresponds to the locations of issues in the receiver's body. The feeling is not quite like a physical pain, and resembles more an energetic density in those areas, and it doesn't last long. Usually, when I start healing those areas in the client, my own feelings also disappear, which leads me to believe that these empathic feelings really are just clairsentient messages to let me know where to lay my hands to heal the client.

Amongst people who are close (family members, Soul brothers and sisters), empathy can be felt across great distances. A number of years ago, my mother was going through carpal tunnel surgery in her left hand. After her surgery, we all called her daily to hear how she was doing and to give her support. But after a few months, we forgot about it, and assumed that her hand has healed. Unrelated (or so I thought), I occasionally started to wake up with wrist pain in my own left hand, and reiking my left wrist only provided temporary relief. On one phone conversation my mother shared with me that she still had pain in her left wrist. That's when I understood that my own left wrist pain was an empathic message about my mother. As soon as I started to regularly send her distant (absentee) reiki healings, my own wrist pain also disappeared.

Empathy aside, clairsentient feelings in general may be messages implanted there by your Angels and Guides, to guide you towards your Ideal Lifepath.

However, some people feel so bound by their traditional upbringing and social norms that they don't feel comfortable accepting gut feelings as real messages from the Divine. Those people would do well paying attention to recurrent emotional and sometimes even physical feelings that they are having, as they too could be intuitive messages from higher aspects of ourselves. For example, a catholic friend of mine was raised to believe *only* in the written word of the Bible, and to discard all visions as unholy witchery. One day while she was visiting me, she told me that she was experiencing physical stomach pain, as well as uneasy emotional feelings. When I asked her what was going on in her life, she described her intricate relationship with her new business partner, and her doubts on the viability of their business. She had a sneaking suspicion that she was being conned, as did I. I told her that she should listen to her feelings—both physical and emotional—and dig deeper into the facts. So following my advice, she started to investigate the validity of the bill of goods that her business partner was selling her. A couple of weeks later, she uncovered the details of the conn perpetrated on her by her partner, which helped her decide to cut her losses, dissolve the partnership, and move on. At that point, both her stomachaches and her uneasy emotional feeling dissolved and healed, and she went back to feeling her happy and healthy self again. Shortly thereafter, she found another business endeavor that suited her more, and started to do well in it. This is an example of a clairsentience message, and how it can help you navigate your way towards prosperity from your Soul.

When something is wrong in your life situation, even though your cognitive mind does not yet know about it, your expanded Self knows. And the first palpable place this imbalance (or lower vibrational energy) registers is your Astral Body, affecting your emotions. Once an issue affects your Astral Body and emotions, the information filters into your Etheric Body, which houses your meridians, chakras, and nadis. From there, the imbalance penetrates one of your chakras, depending on the type of issue at hand, and through your nadis, the energy registers in your physical organs. In my friend's example, the problem was financial and her relationship with her partner, both of which are the domains of the second chakra. So appropriately, the feelings registered in her stomach. If for example, you are having a problem expressing your Truth, the issue may register as either a throat discomfort, or a neck and shoulder issue, since speaking your truth is the domain of the fifth chakra. I have seen this correlation at work in hundreds of massage and reiki clients. Their tight muscles and physical organ issues always correlate to the chakra in charge of their life-issues. Their physical bodies are talking to them. They just don't know how to interpret the signs as a type of clairsentience message. But if you are sensitive enough to your emotions, you may be able to catch and correct the issue before it can degrade your health and affect your co-Created reality. Remember that health and a perfect flow of co-Creative energy are our normal state as human beings.

Claircognizance:

Not every message from your Soul takes the form of visions, worded messages, or even feelings. Sometimes, you just know something with everything that you are, without knowing exactly how you know. This is claircognizance in its pure form. Some people are especially gifted in receiving claircognizant messages. They suddenly just know the answer or solution to something, or the next step to take, without knowing how they know.

There are many other avenues of receiving messages from the Universe. It is important to follow your intuition even on which channel you should use for receiving Universal messages. And it is imperative that in listening to any message, you use the Joy Meter and the God Meter to ascertain that the message is actually coming from your Soul, an Angel, a higher Guide, Source Her-Himself, or an otherwise trusted high source. If it is not, than you should discard it and protect yourself energetically, which we will learn to do later in this chapter. As you will soon find out experientially, becoming proficient at listening to, and deciphering the messages that the Universe is giving you is beyond just preparation for the seven stages of tuning into your Ideal Lifeplan. Since listening to the guidance of your Soul inevitably means basking in Its Light and making high-vibrational choices, it is also a tremendous tool for staying in the synchronistic flow that allows you to co-Create the life that you Truly wish for.

Manifestation Tools

Pure Intent:

When I talk about our multidimensional reality, the first step is indeed learning to tune into the multidimensional signs that the Universe is giving you, as guidance from your Soul towards your most prosperous Lifepath. But it's a two-way street. Your assertion of free will is also a multidimensional process. There are many tools and symbolic acts that can help you assert your free will, in that they help you tune into the power of your Soul to manifest or unmanifest certain things. Harnessing this power is a matter of pureness of intent. The purer your intent, the more powerfully you'll be able to manifest what you want. But the pureness of intent that we're talking about here is not just a singularity of mind. It is also a simultaneous feeling, and internally dwelling in the reality of what you want—having a complete Internal Experience of what you want, which shifts your energetic-vibration into likeness and resonance that attracts it to come to you.

I, for example, achieve much with the power of prayer, the sacred reiki symbols, incense, crystals, and the forces of nature. But despite the profound results that I get from employing these tools in healing and manifestation, I acknowledge that the ceremonies I conduct using these tools are only *symbolic acts*, which help me connect with the Divine spark within, and awaken Its power. The power of all these tools stems from your belief in their power to reconnect you with your Soul, which is where the real power lies.

One issue with using your pure intent to co-Create things is that you have to be careful, and very specific about what it is you Truly want to co-Create. Have you ever seen the movie *Bedazzled?* It is a comedy in which the main character makes a deal with a beautiful lady-devil, and gets seven wishes as part of the deal. But every time he makes a wish, he fails to specify exactly what he wants, and the reality that manifests as a result is always somehow twisted and far removed from what he truly wanted. So for his first wish, he wishes to be rich and powerful, but doesn't specify how. The next morning, he wakes up to find himself a Mexican drug lord. I don't remember the rest of the wishes, but I do remember that the one thing that gets him out of the deal with the lady-devil and gets him to win on all counts is when he "wastes" his last wish wishing good for someone else (the woman he fell in love with, as Hollywood would have it), out of the pure love that's in his heart.

OK. So although Hollywood went to the extreme, and twisted things a bit in order to make it into a romantic comedy, the core idea is actually based on Universal Truth: When praying, intending, or employing any co-Creative tools and symbolic acts, it is important to be crystal clear about what you are trying to achieve. And the more singularly focused you can be on that what you wish to co-Create, the more powerfully it will manifest. For example, one lady told me that after her divorce, and after reading all kinds of books about manifestation, she decided to make her list of the perfect man she wished to magnetize into her life. She listed what she thought was everything: tall, dark, handsome, heterosexual, and loves her, and all the attributes she wished in her "perfect man." But she forgot to mention that it should be someone that *she* would love back—someone she has a Soulmate connection with. Soon after that, she met a man who had all the qualities she envisioned: he was tall, dark, handsome, a nice person, and he fell in love with her. But there was only one problem: she did not love him back, and did not feel a Soulmate connection with him. So I'm not saying that you have to specify each and every small detail of the reality you wish to co-Create, because you do need to leave room for the Universe to meet you halfway. But you need to develop a pure vision of what you want, on which you can focus your mind and heart with a singularity of intent, to have a complete Internal Experience that is *joyful*. And the telltale here is: your Internal Experience of this vision absolutely *needs to be dipped in joy* in order for you to know that it is indorsed by your Soul Self, and in order to empower it to come into manifestation in your physical reality.

Your singularity of intent can be further empowered to come into manifestation if there is a critical mass of people ascribing to the same belief system, tilting the balance of the collective consciousness towards empowering these beliefs. But it doesn't have to be on a global scale. Even on an individual scale, let's say for example that you have a project you believe in and *feel* passionate about. If your friends and family members support you and believe in your success, they increase your odds of success tremendously, because there is now a collective consciousness of co-Creators aiming to manifest the same thing. If, on the other hand, you know your mother-in-law always doubts the validity of any idea you have, it would be best if you delay telling her about your project until it starts being successful. At the same time, it is in your best interest to tell the True members of your Soul-group about this project, so that they can project their consciousness, and by that, energetically help your project come into manifestation, because now you have several people, instead of just one, resonating with your vision and bringing it into manifestation.

Of course, you and I are still going to walk a long path together throughout this book, to help you tune into your Soul's vision of your Ideal Lifepath, and to give you tools for starting to walk that path. The aim in this chapter is to give you some basic tools to communicate with, and tap into the co-Creative powers of your Soul. If you and the members of your Soul-group can keep your consciousness and singularity of intent on co-Creating something, especially if that something is dipped in joy-love, that mutual resonance has a tremendous pull power, and will soon bring your project into successful manifestation.

Symbolic Acts:

As explained in *Prosperity From Your Soul*, anything you deeply believe in is empowered as the paradigm through which you co-Create your life. And if your belief is in conditions that are limiting and self-defeating, than that mental program creates a clogged filter through which your co-Creations must pass, in effect limiting your powers of co-Creation. And in Chapters 3 and 4, we are going to meditationally dissolve all of those conditionings that limit your ability as a successful co-Creator.

But belief systems can cut both ways. A positive belief in the power of a symbolic act can be used as a powerful tool for positive manifestations in your life. Realize that if you have the power to empower non-serving belief systems, than by the same token, you must also be powerful enough to empower the tools and symbolic acts to actually *help* you co-Create a more auspicious, happier, and healthier life for yourself. Science and traditional people alike recognize the power of intent and prayer.

Of course, the tools that you may empower to help you bring about blessed changes are only limited by your imagination. And since we are each unique, we all have different tools and symbolic acts that we like to use to help our co-Creative endeavors. As an example, to help you get the gist of what I mean, here are just some of the tools *I personally* have found very helpful:

- Reiki healing and distant healing
- Reiki symbols
- Prayer—talking to, and communing with God—the Infinite Creator
- RezoDance—a meditative sacred movement that helps free up the body, as well as bring in Divine Light to heal, love, and empower yourself and your Life.
- Meditation—emptying my mind of the brainfucking noise so that I can listen to, and receive messages from my Soul Self
- Saying affirmations—silently or out loud, to shift my consciousness and bless myself and my space (which we will discuss in Chapter 8)
- Prayerfully writing a manifestation goal on parchment paper, praying over it while holding it between my hands, and then burning the parchment paper under the full (or waxing) moon to release my manifestation intent into the Universe for manifestation
- Prayerfully painting pictures that contain symbols (I personally cannot paint realistic figures; but if you can than you should) of what I want to co-Create, and hanging them in my personal space
- Blessing incense—holding incense or candles between my hands, or bringing the incense onto my heart center with prayerful intent, and then lighting them with the prayer that they will help manifest my intent.
- Praying over candles, imbuing them with sacred intent, as guided by my higher being, sometimes even anointing them with aromatic essential oils, and then lighting them, envisioning that through their light, the Light of the Divine will shine in my life
- Imbuing crystals with prayerful intent/visualization, and placing them in particular places in my room, as guided by my intuition
- Placing lucky bamboo or other plants that hold meaning for me in particular corners of my personal space, as inspired by the art of feng shui and my higher guidance
- Visualization and internal experience of auspicious results for prayerful intents that I set (a short version of the meditation given in Chapter 7)
- Envisioning a bubble of Light around myself or the situation (see Chapter 2)
- Meditationally connecting with the spirit of nature, and harnessing the Divine power that it holds to help me heal. For example, at one point, my neighbor was bothering me. I blessed my sacred space, and RezoDanced, envisioning myself as a hawk—a strong prey bird who powerfully defends itself. I know this sounds ridiculous. But the next day, my neighbor stopped bothering me.

These are just some of the symbolic acts that help me tune into the consciousness of my Soul, and bring forth Its Light. Any symbolic act that you do with prayerful intent is empowered by the deep passion of your belief and free will to be an effective tool for influencing your psyche, your emotions, and therefore move your vibrational resonance, which in turn shifts your reality in the direction of your intent. The only rule is: make sure that what you are attempting to do is endorsed by your Soul Self; ensure that it is for the highest good of all (helping all and harming none); and hold a crystal clear intent with a singularity of mind-emotions-Spirit.

Clearing & Protection

No discussion of ethereal realities would be complete without discussing protection from lower vibrational energies that might be out there. As you'll come to understand in Chapters 3 and 4, many low-vibrational themes do not really originate from you, but from the collective unconscious, or from low-vibrational people around you. Protecting yourself and cleansing your space from any low-vibrational energies on a daily basis can go a long way towards keeping your energetic vibration high and in likeness and resonance with your Soul, which of course has pre-designed you to be prosperous.

While it is true that no one can perpetrate on you anything that you haven't at some level agreed to, it is also true that no one is immune to lower-vibrational influences, unless their aura is radiantly strong. The balance between these two seemingly opposite statements is that the universe is run by free will. Let me explain the two sides of this statement:

In order for someone to cause you any harm, or even in order for you to absorb negative energy from your environment, you have to—by Universal law—agree to it at some level of your total Self (either through a past life contract, a karmic agreement made on a Soul level, actions of a parallel universe replica of yourself which share the same Soul and is therefore connected to you, or other deeply unconscious agreement). However, low vibrational themes that lack any growth potential, or which are not for your highest good, are not put there by your Soul Self. Many times we allow low vibrational things to happen to us because of some deeply unconscious self-punishing programing, which obviously needs to be uprooted, dissolved and healed by meditationally asserting your free will (we will do those meditations in Chapter 4). But more often than not, we "agree" to absorb negative energy from our environment not because of any high-level agreement or even any negative programing, but simply because we don't specify our intent to clear that energy and be protected from it, either because we are not aware that we need to specify, or because we forget.

Now, when I talk about negativity that we need to protect ourselves from, I'm not necessarily talking about anything really dark or sinister by any means. Most often, negative vibrations may exist simply because of residual energies of stress, heartache, disappointment, fear, or worry that our fellow human beings leave behind. Some negative vibration may even get created out of completely loving intents, such as when your mother is worried about you because you haven't called her back in a few days, and in her worry, she is imagining all the worst things that could have happened to you. She does that because she loves you. But her worried vibration may create some negative energy that would need to be cleansed. In the majority of cases, people don't dump on you those worried, stressed out energies because they want to harm you, or even because they are selfish. They are simply not aware that their unhappiness causes an energetic ripple effect that echo throughout their environment and adversely affects everyone else in it.

On the other side of the statement, I said that no one is immune to negative influence unless their aura is radiantly strong. And here is how this comes into play: If you share your everyday reality with some low-vibrational people who are grumpy, unhappy, bitchy, or doom-and-gloom-seers, they are co-Creating around them a low vibrational reality that matches their vibration. And their co-Creation starts at the auric level (as we've seen in *Prosperity From Your Soul*). The aura of each healthy person should extend up to nine feet around the physical body. But if you're only sitting three feet away from each other (like in adjacent office cubical), than your auric fields, and therefore the vibrational energies that emit co-Creative vibes into your realities, intertwine, and can affect your co-Created reality if you don't protect yourself.

The good news is that you are the master of your mind and have always been empowered to co-Create your own reality. Living in a universe that is run by free choice simply means that you have to specify your will to rid yourself of low-vibrational energies, either mentally, prayerfully, as a feeling-vibration, or by some symbolic act that more powerfully specifies that that is the way you wish to exercise your free will. It means that by cosmic law, an assertion of your free will is needed to clear and protect you from those low vibrational energies. One way to assert your free will to protect yourself is to invoke the assistance of Angels in protecting, helping, and healing the situation. Once you ask, it is like the magic words "open sesame"—all Universal resources are available to protect, help, heal, and bless you.

The bottom line when it comes to protection is: since no one can perpetrate on you anything that you do not at some level agree to, all you really have to do is assert that you have not, do not, and will not agree to this influence at any time or level of your consciousness (subconscious, lower Nefesh, past lives, etc.). Once you assert your free will, powerful protection and clearing are automatic.

Aura strengthening meditations (visualizations) could be a powerful tool to protect and strengthen yourself. There are, in fact, a limitless number of tools to protect and cleanse you and your environment. But all the tools really do is potently help you tune into the highest aspect of your Soul Light, and harness Its power for protection and clearing. To better understand this concept, let's say that you were going to burn some sacred white sage in your room for protection and clearing. It's true that sacred sage has its own natural life-vibration, which resonates with your own life-vibration in a way that awaken in you the protective power of your Soul's Light. But white sage in and of itself does not really have any power to drive bad spirits away (as is commonly believed). Sage by itself is not really sacred without your prayerful intents. It is your prayerful intent that activates the natural protective vibration of the sage, and through mutual resonance (your interaction with the spirit of the sage), awakens in you the protective Light of your Soul. So it's really your prayerful intent that has the power to protect you and clear away any negative vibration. The sage itself is just another life form whose spirit has a natural protective vibration. And the ceremony of burning it is a symbolic act that helps you tune into the protective powers of your Soul. These tools and symbolic acts will work for you powerfully only if you endorse them with your belief. If, say, you are allergic to sage, or if you have a very traditional belief system, than there are other tools that better resonate with your body physiology and belief system, such as prayer, invocations, visualizations, or sacred art, all of which can awaken your co-Creative powers. And the beauty of it is: the number of tools that are available to help you harness your Soul's protective Light are truly Infinite.

The following are just a few tools I have found useful to eliminate negativity, strengthen the aura, and invoke Angelic help and protection. When you read them, make mental notes of how you feel about each of them, and whether there are ones that resonate with you more than others. You may also get inspired ideas of other tools not mentioned here—tools that are tailored just for you. If you do, this is a perfect time to start listening to these messages from your Soul Self.

Bubble of Light Visualization:

Envisioning yourself and your personal space inside a bubble of the brightest Divine Light automatically summons Angelic protection and help. Which color of Light bubble you "see" yourself in depends on the meaning of the color for you. We will discuss various systems of decoding the meaning of each color of light in the next chapter. But even after that discussion, the most important and valuable color of Light for your healing and protection at each moment is the one that pops into your head first, and feels the most comfortable for you when visualizing Divine Light. No meaning of any system is as important as its meaning *to you*.

The Power of the Spoken Word:

As we discussed, words have a tremendous power to co-Create, or as is the case with protection, to dissolve disturbing influences from your space. As you speak your intent to protect and heal yourself, your space, and your life, you use the power of your free will, spoken out loud, to affirm something strongly, such as cleansing of all lower vibrational energies, and demanding that all entities that are not of the Light leave right now. You can whisper softly intents that relate to the love relationship either between you and the Divine (inviting Love and Divine favor into your life for example), or between you and another person. And you can meditate silently on intents that are the earnest most desires of your heart.

Again, your words have co-Creative power. So use them wisely, and even though we are talking about protection, dwell on the positive. This means that when commanding negativity to leave you, your life, and your personal space, you do not have to list each and every possible negativity you'd like to eradicate, with all due respect to specificity of intent. Don't dwell on it. It's enough to just say something like, "I command all lower vibrational energy to leave now" or, "I now let go and dissolve all that does not serve my Soul Self." I have had tremendously powerful results from saying: "I am perfectly grounded and protected by Divine Light and wisdom! I am perfectly grounded and protected by Divine Light and Love! I am perfectly grounded and protected by Divine Light and power!

At the same time, you should absolutely feel free to elaborate and dwell on all the positive things that you do wish to bring into your life. Remember to thank your Soul, the Angels, or whichever deity you invoked, and to have a complete Internal Experience, even if only for a brief moment, of seeing the situation healed, and feeling light, free, and hopeful.

Fresh Air & Natural Light:

I know that many of the environments that you find yourself in are out of your immediate control as far as redesigning them, like public places, or your workplace in most cases. However, when it comes to your home—your personal space, you have the choice of designing it in a way that will invite plenty of fresh energy, as the old feng shui masters have theorized. On a here-now level, arranging the space you're in with plenty of fresh air and natural light can help dissolve any heavy feelings and lighten up the moods, which in itself is a good co-Creative tool. On a more spiritual level, the first elements that have the potential to direct more fresh life-force and Creative energy into your space, and by extension, align your consciousness and life with the Infinite Funnel of Abundance, are fresh air and natural light.

Music & Wind Chimes:

Since sound is a very pure carrier of Divine energy, it can be used as a tool to hold your intent for manifestation, or for protection. For example, I have a set of large wind chimes right at the entrance to my healing space, which I've imbued with the intent that it will fend off any and all negative energies, and bring in only blessings from the Divine. Music can do the same, as long as you imbue it with your purest intents, by holding the CD or iPod between your hand, and dwelling for a moment in the Internal Reality of your intent.

Candles:

Just like for many people the sun represents an instrument that delivers the Divine's light to us, so can a candle represent a bearer of Divine Light, purity, spirituality or anything else you wish. Natural bee-wax candles are best, as they help spread negative ions into the air, which brings antioxidants into the body through breath coming into our lungs, and through our skin pours. They also smell subtly sweet, and have a naturally high vibration. Before you light your candle, put it between the palms of your hands, or on your heart space, and speak your prayerful intent to purify your space and facilitate all of your co-Creations endeavors.

Plants:

Plants are devoid of the primal instinctual lower emotions that us humans as well as animals can feel. They have a Ruach (spirit) that is very pure but not a Nefesh (animal-instinct). Therefore, they cannot feel the primal fear that drives many of the imperfections of our human condition.

On a physical level, plants convert carbon dioxide (CO_2) to oxygen (O_2) in the process of photosynthesis. They can also help neutralize and clean up some environmental toxins. In the same way, on a spiritual level, plants convert negative energy into positive energy.

Thus, keeping plants in your environment can help keep the vibration of your home/space pure and protected. As it relates to co-Creation of prosperity, plants also give your space a cheerful appearance that inspires feelings of joy and beauty, which helps bring you into vibrational resonance with all the positive things you would wish to co-Create into your life.

Artwork:

There are many artworks that may hold particular meaning to you, depending on your belief system. Some people find it helpful to keep a small statute of an Angel, the Virgin Mary, a cross, a Star of David, a dream catcher, Kokopelli (medicine man), a figurine of their animal totem, of Buddha, Lakshmi, Ganesh, Shiva (Hindu gods), paintings representing Divine Light, or any other item. Use any object that holds meaning for you to help focus your consciousness on what represent the sacred and Divine to you.

Aroma:

Since the sense of smell is so directly hardwired into our emotions, they present wonderful tools that you can use to evoke any specific feelings, bringing your consciousness into these high vibrations, and thus getting rid of all negative vibrations. Which scent you use for which purpose depends on the inner guidance that you receive from your Soul. Of course, it goes without saying that before burning any incense or herb, you should first hold it between your hands, and speak (silently or out loud) your intent. The following is a list of substances that can be used for specific purposes:

Sage & Cedar –

Sage and cedar are used in Native American cleansing rituals. It is the most basic and powerful cleansing method. Burn in a saucer or seashell, or as smudge sticks. Use the smoke as a blessing or for clearing rooms and auric fields. The use of sage or cedar is very powerful when used in conjunction with the spoken word.

Frankincense & Myrrh –

You can burn frankincense and myrrh as incense sticks, in crystal form (throwing little crystals into a fire, if you have a fireplace), or use the essential oil to transmute negative vibrations and to protect yourself or your environment.

Frankincense has the quality of helping you connect with a very deep and ancient part of you. Myrrh is known for its power to connect Heavens to earth, and to help the manifestation of the highest spiritual aspect of oneself. Therefore the combination of frankincense and myrrh could be used to enlist the Light of your Soul to cleanse out any themes that are deep rooted or negative conditionings that originate from past lives, and to instill spiritual Light energy in its stead.

Sandalwood ~

Sandalwood is of a higher vibration and has a gentler smell than sage or cedar. Use in incense or powdered form and burn to cleanse your environment and aura in a more gentle way. Sandalwood is also very grounding and centering, making the protection more powerful.

Vanilla ~

According to some beliefs, vanilla calls the Angels. Vanilla is of a much gentler vibration than even sandalwood. It can be used to purge or cleanse out even the subtlest theme, and tune you into a feeling of gentleness and kindness to yourself. Use vanilla essential oil burned in an aroma lamp, wear as perfume, or mix with distilled water and use as a spray in your home, office, or car. Vanilla candles are equally effective, provided they are not the chemically produced ones.

Peppermint ~

Peppermint essential oil can be used in lieu of vanilla oil. Peppermint scented candles may also be used. Peppermint brings a vibration of life and freshness into the air—more chi.

Lemons ~

Lemons are good for absorbing negative vibrations or energy. Lemon scent is also considered by some New Age thinkers to bring a vibration of prosperity. Lemons can be used in the traditional way as lemon-scented candles or incents. But they can also be made use of with simple household lemon spray (not store-bought aerosol sprays). The best sprays are the ones you make yourself by mixing twenty drops of lemon essential oil with four ounces of spring water in a spray bottle. Don't forget to bless the bottle with your intent before you use it.

Roses ~

Roses represent Divine Love, and God Realization. And there is nothing that can dispel any and all negative vibration better than Divine Love. In fact, there is no force in existence more powerful than Divine Love. Fresh roses in the house, dried petals in your tea and in your hot bath, and burning rose essential oil in a dispenser, are all spiritually very powerful.

Crystals:

Shamans consider Crystals to be living stones—they call them the crystal beings. Crystals are of the earth, but they also hold and reflect Divine Light. Thus they have a very important function of bringing the Divine vibration to the earth. There are many protective stones that help cleanse the vibration of a person or the room.

Stones most known[4] for cleansing are: atacamite, calcite, chalcedony, charolite, **citrine**, dioptase, fluorite, **opal**, **peridot**, **quartz**, sodalite. Amber is particularly known for cleansing the environment.

Stones most known for protection are: blue lace agate, fire agate, amber, **amethyst**, angelite, chrysoberyl, bloodstone, boji stone, carnelian, chiastolite, iron pyrite, jade, jasper, jet, kunzite, labradorite, malachite, **obsidian**, petalite, prehnite, **smoky quartz**, sardonyx, staurolite, tiger's eye, tourmaline, and turquoise.

Stones appear here in bold print are the ones that I have personally had great luck working with, as they are the main stones known for cleansing and protection.

One thing to be aware of is that many of the crystals protect you by absorbing the negative energies from your environment, so that those energies do not harm you. For that reason, crystals need to be energetically cleansed periodically (every week or two). It is especially important to cleanse opal and malachite after each use of the stone. I have a couple of beautiful Australian opal necklaces, and I cleanse them with fresh water, reiki, and my prayerful intent after each use, and program them for the next use. Opal can be energetically tricky to work with if you are not careful about cleansing it. The only stone that does not need to be cleansed periodically is citrine. You need to cleanse and set your intent for a citrine only once, when you first get it, and it will keep cleansing itself while fending off any negativity for as long as you have the stone. Incidentally, citrine is also a very powerful stone for prosperity.

Salt Water:

Salt symbolizes the element of the earth. Sea salt is best to use. Sea salt bathing have been thought of as the ultimate means to purify yourself by many cultures throughout the ages. On a physical level, Epson salt bath also draws impurities out of the body and relaxes the muscles. You can use salt water to purify many objects you wish to make pure, like your crystals for example.

To cleanse your crystals, place them in a bowl, add sea salt, flood them with water, and place outside under the moon and sunlight for at least twenty-four hours. I've been told that it is best to do this in the waning phases of the moon, since the waning moon is a good time to concentrate your intention on removal of what no longer serves. You may then wish to keep them in the moon and sunlight for an additional day when the moon is waxing, since the waxing phase of the moon is a good time to concentrate your intent on bringing things into your life, such as light, health, prosperity, happiness, etc. However, my intuition has always led me to cleanse my stones during the waxing phase of the moon. That is what feels right to me. You should listen to your own intuition as to when and how to cleanse your crystals. The most important thing, again, is the intent that you put into this process.

Column of Light:

The most potently powerful protection tool that I have ever found for cleansing, as well as for many other purposes, is to envision a column of pure Divine Light that extends from you into the heart of God. Into this Light, you can send all negative or heavy energy to be neutralized by

Divine Light, harming no one. As you get apt at doing this visualization, you'll start seeing all the negativity that you send up that column of Light getting completely dissolved—annihilated. It is also a very healing practice, as you will find that using this visualization gives you supreme feeling of safety and peace.

I use this method during every reiki and massage session that I give. I envision the column of Divine Light surrounding both myself and my client, so that whatever aches, pains, health issues, and stresses I help lift out of the client will not be hanging around my treatment room, but will actually go up into the column of Divine Light, and be dissolved by it. I usually also envision that the column of Divine Light will help bring health, happiness, and blessings into my client and myself.

These are just some of the tools that have been traditionally used for clearing and protection. You will find that using these tools with a prayerful intent will uplift your moods, brighten your personal energy, and as a result, reroute your day into a more favorable chain of events. Being able to interrupt an unfortunate chain of events and turn it into a fortunate one is a first step towards becoming a more conscious co-Creator of your life. Just remember that all of these ceremonies are just tools to tune your consciousness into the highest vibration of reality—the domain of your Soul, and to bring Its Light, to dispel darkness and instill health, happiness, radiance, freedom, and prosperity into your everyday reality.

In this chapter, we have taken some great first strides towards opening your lines of communications with your Soul Self. And for the most part, the everyday communications that we've talked about in this chapter are effortless—the only thing that it requires of you is awareness and openness to this type of communications.

But to truly walk the path of a conscious co-Creator, and to become privy to the finest details of *your specific* Ideal Lifeplan of prosperity, you'll need to deepen your communications with your Soul to the point that you can not only receive hints from your Soul, but also dwell in Its consciousness and vibration, receive detailed messages, and have complete conversations with the higher, all-knowing aspects of your Soul. And the way to do that is through meditation.

The next chapter will give you more specific tools for tuning into the different levels of your consciousness through an exploration of meditation. The most profound meditation—Zohar Breath Meditation—is given at the end of next chapter. It is a simple yet profound method of communicating with your Soul Self, which provides the basics of many of the higher meditations we will use in later chapters, when we tune into the details of your Ideal Lifeplan of prosperity.

Chapter 2

Meditational Communications with Your Soul

As you've come to understand, the process of consciously co-Creating your life revolves around bringing your vibrational essence into likeness and resonance with the object of your desire, thereby magnetizing it to manifest in your life. In physics they say that like attracts like. In the same way, if you were a sports lover for example, you would naturally tend to magnetize into your life friends who are also into sports. If you are vibrant, happy, and easy going, you would not attract into your life friends who are completely neurotic, because there would be no glue to keep you together for the long term. Attracting wealth, and anything else you wish to attract into your life, is the same: you have to bring your energetic vibration to be so similar to the energetic vibration of what you want, and co-Create a mutual resonance with it, which is what attracts it into manifestation in your life.

Despite the fact that you have been co-Creating your life according to this principle since the beginning of your existence, I realize that at this point, this all sounds like nothing more than a beautiful theory, which leaves you asking: "How do I actually shift my energetic vibration into likeness and resonance with what I want?" One great tool is meditation, which can help you bring your energetic vibration into likeness and resonance with your desire in several ways, at least internally. As you already know, your request/intent, if it is anchored in Truth, is co-Created ethereally as soon as you Truly desire it, automatically and every time! But to create a real mutual resonance that can attract it into physical manifestation in your life, you first and foremost have to know what you want—you have to have a clear vision of it in your mind. Therefore the first gift of meditation is to facilitate the True vision that would align your mind with your True desires, for only a meditatively clear mind can allow you to see your Ideal Lifeplan with crystal-clarity that is untainted by any human conditioning or limitations.

But in order to really change the your energetic vibration of your here-now self to match that of what you want, you must change the way you *feel*, and you must internally dwell and act according to the reality of those new feelings. It is feelings that really move your energetic vibration into mutual resonance with what you want, more than any cognitive process of even the most powerful mind. And it is necessary to feel love and joy in order to co-Create anything. At the same time, the mind is a powerful tool that can drive your feelings a certain way. The mind may not complete the process, but it starts the ball rolling in the right direction. By facilitating meditative visions and beefing them up with feelings and sensation, the mind can help you achieve complete Internal Experiences, which powerfully shift your energetic vibration that eventually sips out into your external reality and create a resonance with what it is that you are internally experiencing.

But to understand the real gift of meditation in the process of co-Creation and manifestation, let's talk about this mutual resonance that you establish with the object of your desire in terms of a two-part process—transmitting and receiving. Recall from *Prosperity From Your Soul* the multitude of dimensions in which your expanded Self exists, which includes all of your energetic bodies. Normally you transmit your intent into the Universe, and receive Its manifestation quite automatically, and have done so since the dawn of your existence. Breaking it into a two-part process is just in order to facilitate understanding, so that through your meditations, you'd be better able to consciously drive your vibrational resonance the way you want, and thus consciously create an attractive mutual resonance with only that which you Truly want. Let's see how:

When consciously transmitting your request/intent (for manifestation or information) into the Universe, you first harness your physiological brain (the hardware) and breath functions to facilitate clearing and focusing of your mind (the software). On the next level, you use your now clear cognitive abilities to get into a meditative state in which you can envision your request clearly. Your clear vision, if guided properly by your internal observer, can drive your feelings to give you a complete Internal Experience of receiving your request and dwelling in the reality of its manifestation, including all the senses that are associated with it. This in turn shifts your energetic vibration into likeness with your desire, and creates a mutual resonance that attracts it. Your request is then sent up into the Creative core of the Universe, through your Etheric Body, then Astral Body, Mental Body, Casual Body… and all the way to Source, from Whom all manifestations come. Then, as your mutual resonance with the object continues and filters into your everyday awareness, it gets strong enough to gradually pull the object into your everyday reality. It first manifests ethereally in your Casual Body—it'll become an integral part of your True essence, but in a subtly aware way. Then the object manifests in your Mental Body, and you'll begin to clearly perceive the many details and aspects of the plan/object, perhaps even things you can do in the physical reality to help bring it about. The different between the send and receive resonance, as it passes through the Mental Body, is that on the receive wave you'll be able to "see" all the details of the object very clearly, as if you've already seen it, felt it, received it, kind of like at the moment of this writing, I see the details of Soul Path Retreat. I see every detail as if I've already been there, from the reception to the plants and waterfalls, to the juice bar, to the RezoDance studio, to the massage and treatment rooms, to the garden and meditation coves. That is how you experience it when the object of your desire is already on its way to you. Next, the already co-Created object of your desire comes through your Astral Body. When it manifests in your Astral Body, you'll start really feeling excited, and perhaps even edgy to already receive its manifestation in your life. The edginess comes from the fact that on a subtle level, you already feel its closeness, kind of like a kid in a fair, who smells the cotton candy somewhere around. He doesn't see yet exactly where the cart is. But he knows it's there, and so he's getting impatient and starts nagging his parents to buy him that cotton candy that he's smelling. The final stage, before the object manifests physically in your everyday reality, is its appearance as an apparition within your Etheric Body. When you've gotten to this point, kept your mutual resonance with the object of your desire joyous, and allowed all of your actions to be dipped in the joy and peace of knowing it's coming, then the object of your desire is Truly coming into manifestation in your physical reality. While this resonance happens automatically when as you co-Create your life, with meditation, you can consciously drive the co-Creations in your life towards what you Truly want.

Even if you are a complete atheist, from a here-now perspective too, meditation is a great tool for communicating with the various parts of you. It can lead to better self-awareness, which can lead you to be better adjusted, happier, more sure of yourself and your life decisions—all the hallmarks of magnetizing prosperity into your life. Of course, at its height, meditation can lead you to communicate with your wise and abundant Soul, which will, in turn help ground Its wisdom and resources into your life.

So, if meditation is that important to the process of co-Creating prosperity, than we need to lay a strong foundation for it. And at this point of our path together, perhaps we need to respect the fact that not everyone is experienced in, or even knows what meditation really is. I know that to some people, meditation sounds like a scary Eastern beast. But I can't tell you the number of people who have approached me over the years and asked me: "My doctor told me that I need to learn to meditate. Can you teach me how to meditate?" Indeed, a growing number of people from all walks of life are starting to be aware of (or are being told) how important meditation for their health.

In this chapter, I will teach you some of the basics of meditation, and give you some very simple meditational tools to experiment with it. At the end of the chapter, we will do Zohar Breath Meditation—a great tool for clearly communicating with your Soul, which lay the foundation for the meditations in this book that will lead you to become privy to your Ideal Lifeplan of prosperity.

What Is Meditation

It is said that prayer is when we talk to God, whereas meditation is when God talks to us. To truly be able to listen to God (or your Soul as an aspect of God), you first need to reach a point of stillness and peace, discarding all troubling, human-level thoughts, and tuning only into the inner chamber of your heart. For it is within the innermost heart chamber that we are able to feel and perceive God. And since meditation is a way you listen to God, naturally, in order to be able to listen to the Divine, you need to cleanse your mind from what I call "the brainfucking noise," otherwise what's going on inside your mind may be a replay of yesterday's movie, obsessive thoughts about dinner, or a combination of all that has been troubling you throughout your day, swirling round and round in there. That's not listening to God, that's the epitome of the brainfucking noise.

At its simplest form, meditation is an important way to cleanse the subconscious and reduce the noise level of the mind. From a simple psychological standpoint: Our brains process thousands of thoughts, actions, and processes per second. The brain is aware of so many more stimuli than we realize. For example, did you know that while you are leisurely standing in traffic listening to your favorite music, your brain is also taking an impression of every move of every leaf around you, every other car on the road and its license plate, every signal change, and thousands of other details? Every consciousness researcher will tell you that your mind is constantly busy reducing clutter, picking out the important details to be aware of, and ordering all this jumble into a logical flow that you can understand as your reality. On a slightly deeper level, your mind is also busy thinking about all the things that are subconsciously troubling you. It could be an argument with your mother-in-law, a frustrating situation at work… On a much deeper level, your mind is busy suppressing from your cognitive awareness thoughts that do not serve your highest wellbeing, such as the childhood trauma and negative conditioning, all of which form the basis for programs and patterns that have, until now, prevented you from living as you Original Self. We will spend quite a bit of time letting go of everyday stress and removing all of those non-serving conditionings in Chapters 3 and 4. But for now, the first step is becoming aware of all of those activities that are going on in your mind at any given moment, creating what I call "the brainfucking noise," which prevents you from clear thought. Ancient yogis say that unless you clear out all this unnecessary noise while it is still in the subconscious, it will be shoved into the deep unconscious, from where it will become exponentially harder to remove. So even on a purely psychological level, you can look at meditation as a simple way to air out all that clutter from your subconscious, and reduce the noise level in your mind. And as you will soon find out experientially, one of the advantages of meditation is that it makes your mind clearer, better able to focus, and more capable of crystal-clear thought, thus maximizing the potential of your mind. Yet at the same time, meditation makes you calmer, more peaceful and more centered.

To better understand of this elusive cleansing of the mind, let's spiritually understand the nature of mind and thought: Every thought originates from Universal mind at the level of the Soul. At that point, all thoughts are pure, Angelic, and untainted. And some meditations, such as Zohar Breath Meditation, once you become apt at them, can help you tune into pure thought at the level of your Soul. However, by virtue of the fact that we are all human right now, as thoughts filter into the human level of consciousness, most of them—whether conscious or not—are fogged by the biases of our personalities and perhaps by some of the letdowns and scars of life. But there is still plenty for free choice here. The first choice, when having a difficult experience in life, is your ability to choose to let it slide by—not to allow a disappointment to scar you or to form into any self-defeating program. But even after your human programs are already formed and are fogging your thoughts and obscuring their original clarity, it is still your choice whether to attach and dwell on them, or to let them go and not worry about it.

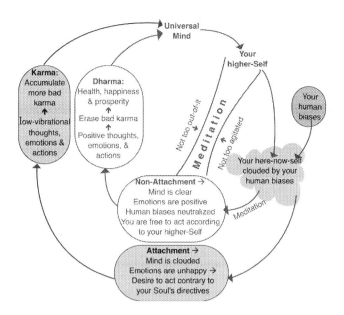

Now, when you discard a thought, it doesn't mean that you push it into your unconscious and stew on it, as that would achieve the opposite of what we are trying to achieve. It means that you acknowledge that worrying about something won't fix anything, and that you have a better chance of fixing any problem when your mind is clear, peaceful, and connected with the Universal mind. For example, if you are troubled by thoughts about how to pay your bills, you may decide to attach to this thought, in which case you attach troublesome feelings to it, which then gather around them the actions of your glands, nervous system, and several other body system, to get the power of your physical body teamed up with your emotions. This may be felt as desperation, or as desire to act out of desperation. At this level, your emotional feelings, coupled with the actions of your body systems, are very potent. If you've let your disharmonious feelings become that potent, than you are transmitting into the Universe a vibe that has a power to attract all that you do not want to manifest into your life. Besides just your vibrational resonance with disharmony, once its gets to the point of potency, you'll usually be driven to action. And if the action low vibrational, you'll accumulate more karma and get further away from liberation, and further away from your Ideal Lifepath of prosperity. But you have free choice at each step of the way. And this applies here too.

To continue out example of worrying about paying the bill, if, on the other hand, you decide not worry about that bill for the time being, you have decided not to assume ownership of this troubling thought—to let it go, and clear your mind from it. In this case, the fogged thought would not beef up with feelings (of fear), it won't gather vibrational potency, and accordingly, it would neither transmit negative vibes into the Universe nor drive you to act disharmoniously. It'll just come up as a thought, and then be released into the ethers (hopefully neutralized by Divine Light so that it doesn't then harm anyone else). This doesn't mean that you won't actually pay your bill. It just means that you've decided not to obsess over it, and to trust that the Universe will provide you with the means to pay this bill and much more. Once your mind is clear and your energies centered, you are always in better alignment with Universal Abundance, from which unexpected resources and ideas will undoubtedly flow into your life, making the paying of this bill a non-issue, since the resources that will then flow into your life will be exponentially more abundant than just the funds needed to pay this bill. It is this meditational alignment and trust, in the Universal Abundance that's in store for you, that shifts your vibrational essence into resonance with the things you desire, as well as makes room in your mind and life to receive the most Divinely inspired ideas and the resources to make them happen.

Another point about meditationally discarding unwanted thoughts is that many thoughts, even if you don't consider yourself psychic, actually originate as a psychic debris from the collective unconscious, either globally, or from the people around you. As we have discussed, we are all vibrationally influenced by the people around us, especially those we care about, and the people in close geographical proximity to us. So it is actually true to say that many of your thoughts have literally not originated from you. For example, you may have a nonchalant thought at the back of your mind that you need to remember to pay a certain bill. At that level, the thought is not a worry, but just a mental note to remember to do it. It therefore is not anything disharmonious that would lower your energetic vibration. If, however, your mother constantly worries about your finances, if you allow her obsessive worry to effect you (mentally and vibrationally), than without even knowing it, the thought that was previously just in back of your mind now beefs up into a full blown worry. The same is true if in the next office cubicle there is a co-worker that's constantly worried about his/her bills. You pick up their obsessive-worrisome vibration (subtly and subconsciously), and somehow it shifts your own nonchalant thought into a worry about your bill. This type of thing happens to us all the time. We just need to be aware of it, so that we can fend off those low vibrations and discard all negative thoughts that do not serve our highest paths as conscious co-Creators.

So far, we have discussed three stages in which your meditative mind can intervene on your behalf: the first being at the level which you may choose not to let any discordant experience form into defeating mind-program; the second is using the stillness of your meditation to tune into thoughts and ideas at their pure essence—at the level of your Soul; and the third being the stage at which you decide not to attach to a low-vibrational thought, not to gather any feelings or vibrational potency around it, and not to act in a disharmonious way. And the one realization that can help you with this non-attachment is the knowledge that your Soul does not and cannot ever perceive of low vibrational thoughts, since it is simply not in alignment with Its True nature. Therefore low vibrational thoughts are simply not parts of who you Truly are.

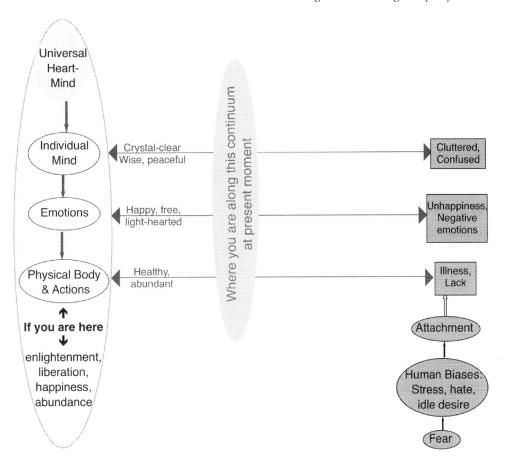

Beyond just the cleansing of the mind, from a metaphysical standpoint, once you have cleared your mind of troubling thoughts and have dissolved the seeds of noise, your mind and your heart become one, and you become naturally centered into the core of who you Truly are. For behind the walls of all worldly thoughts, deep within the core of your heart exists the oasis of your True Light. And once you train your meditative mind, you can tap into Infinite dimensions, and also become better able to project your thoughts into manifested reality—the domain of your third-dye chakra. Meditation can help your mind be strong, thus helping you project your highest thought into manifestation more potently.

How to Meditate

To start zeroing in on how to meditate, let's first understand that meditation is not a focusless daydream, but a particular state of mind. It has some focus, but it is a peaceful focus. Tibetan "Shamatha" teaches us that meditative stillness is achieved by balancing agitation and dullness. According to that discipline, our hectic modern lives make our minds apt at thinking too rapidly, which puts them in an almost constant state of edginess or agitation. I understand this as the over-sharpness associated with juggling all the round-and-round thoughts of the brainfucking noise. On the other hand, when we do find a quiet moment in which to switch off, our minds are so tired from the race, that they almost cannot help but go into a hazy daydream—an endless nondescript jumble of thought that lacks focus and vividness, from which we usually "awaken" not having any idea where out minds just went. Stillness of mind and meditation occur in the perfect balance between agitation (brainfucking) and dullness (hazy daydream)—a state of mind that is neither agitated nor dull, which produces the peaceful clarity that is the hallmark of meditation.

Physical Posture During Meditation:

The perfect posture for meditation, I believe, is an individual thing, which should be based on your inner guidance regarding the best meditational posture for you at each moment. That being said, many ancient traditions do teach a very specific meditational posture that they profess is the perfect pose for meditation: sitting cross-legged (or better yet, in full lotus position), with the spine erect but not tense, the arms straight yet elbow not locked, and the hands resting on the knees in Gyan Mudra (thumb and index finger touching and making a loop). While I do not advocate adhering to any specific tradition other than the one that deeply resonates with you, these ancient traditions do have some valid reasons for advocating this posture. I'll detail here some of effects of each postural component on the meditative mind, so that you can employ your own inner wisdom and choose from them the ones that best serve you.

It is true that you could meditate in any posture. In fact, some of the practices that we'll talk about in *A Lifestyle of Prosperity From Your Soul* are moving and walking meditations, and RezoDance in its entirety (taught in Level-1 Prosperity From Your Soul Course) is also a meditational *movement*. However, just as there is a biorhythmic attunement between the breath and the body's state of alertness (discussed later in this chapter), there is also a direct biorhythmic correlation between our activity level and the activity level of the mind. Yoga tradition have proved for thousands of years that when the body is in movement, the mind tends to be more active; and when the body is still, it is easier for the mind to be still. Modern psychology has actually capitalized on this biorhythmic attunement in their branch of hypnotic therapies. From this you might jump to the conclusion that lying down would be the best meditational posture, since the body is the most still at that point. And if mindless deep relaxation is your only goal, than lying down would be the perfect posture.

However, in meditation, what we are trying to achieve is the perfectly balanced state in which the mind is not overly active, yet not switched off into a focusless daydream. So if we lie down during meditation, we are likely to fall asleep, or otherwise switch off into a focusless daydream. And again, if all you are trying to do is relax and switch off, than you should absolutely lie down, and feel validated in that practice. But that is not meditation. If you are trying to meditate and maintain some sort of focus in order to achieve specific results, such as tuning into your Soul Self and your Ideal Lifeplan, sitting up is more recommended, since it is a posture that is still enough to foster mental stillness, yet active enough to prevent you from losing your meditative focus.

Keeping the spine erect, yet not tense, during meditation facilitates the "rising of the kundalini"—the free flow of Ki energy up your shushmana channel, and the opening of all chakras. Tucking your chin slightly in and your chest slightly forward (with the shoulders relaxed down) ensures that the spine is straight in the areas of the thoracic and cervical spine. A curved or a tense spine would have some restricting effect on the flow of life-force energy along your appropriate channels.

Yogis claim that sitting in lotus pose or cross-legged gives the body and back a strong base that supports the erect spine. I don't know about that one. I have found many other sitting positions, such as sitting with the legs comfortably spread out in front, or even sitting upright in a comfortable chair, to be even more comfortable than sitting cross-legged, and provide just as strong (if not stronger) support for the back. I've seen some fellow meditators fold their legs to one side, and that seems to work for them. The only reason that folding both legs to one side is not ideal is because the spine is then crooked to one side, therefore restricting the flow of Ki up the Shushmana.

With regards to hand positions, yogic philosophy explains that different hand positions promote different effects on the mind, because they stimulate different energetic points in the fingers: Touching the thumb to the little finger (Buddhi Mudra) strengthens communications and mental powers; touching the ring finger to the thumb (Surya Mudra) energizes and strengthens intuition; touching the middle finger to the thumb (Shuni Mudra) increases patience, responsibility and self-discipline; and touching the index finger to the thumb (Gyan Mudra) increases wisdom, knowledge, and an expansion of the mind into Universal Mind. However, I have found that the hand positions during meditations should agree with your state of mind and what you are trying to achieve during the meditation. For example, during Zohar Breath Meditation (end of this chapter), the hand position is with the hands resting on your lap, and the palms facing up, because the target of the meditation is to *receive* knowledge and healing energy from your Soul. Another example is Self-Nurturing Meditation (Chapter 5), in which the hands are placed one on top of the other on the heart chakra, to give you a feeling of nurturing of the heart. You should use whatever hand position you feel guided to use during your meditation. Forget five-thousand-year-old traditions. You can take from them whatever suits you. Feel free to add and modify any tradition in accordance with your inner guidance. You may feel guided to put your hands up to convey a crown on top of your head and signify the opening of your seventh chakra… or make some other movements and gesture that conveys a specific intent for your meditation. And if you are so guided, go with it, even if it seems odd.

The same goes for internal focal point. Yogic tradition teaches that underneath closed eyelids, one should focus one's gaze (carry an intent, or envision that you are looking) at different points to promote different mind focuses: focusing one's internal gaze at the crown elevates into higher consciousness and activates the pineal gland; internally focusing at the third-eye activates the pituitary gland and promotes the intuitive ability to know the unknown; focusing one's gaze at the tip of the nose with the eyes one tenth open (nine-tenths closed) locks the mind into the meditation and forges new pathways in the brain; and focusing the gaze at the chin with the eyes one tenth open (nine-tenths closed) allows one to see oneself clearly. Now, since there is a mass consciousness of people who believe that these techniques produce these specific effects, it's possible that their belief has already co-Created a level of reality in which this is true. It's also entirely possible that those hand positions and internal gazes do produce the energetic effect that the yogis profess them to, but I just have not received any guidance to that effect. I have summarized these techniques here so that you can sound them against your internal Truth-meter. I personally find internally focusing my gaze to be exhausting. It gives me a headache, especially if I focus my internal gaze at the crown or third-eye. The only internal gaze that I have found comfortable is at the heart chakra. So while my eyes are closed for the meditation, I envision myself looking and projecting Light into the heart chakra, and that feels very comfortable. You should go with whichever internal gaze feels right for you.

When meditating, you should wear comfortable loose clothing. First, loose clothing will facilitate fuller breaths, since they would not be restricting the movement of your diaphragm or ribcage. But the main reason for wearing loose clothing is so as not to detract from the focus of your meditation. Just the other day, I had twenty minutes to kill before I needed to leave home for an appointment—not enough time to do any real channeling or writing work, but just perfect time for a meditation. I was already dressed in jeans and ready to leave the house, so I decided to meditate in jeans. I couldn't! I couldn't think of my breath, of Divine Light, or of anything relating to meditation. The only thing I could think about was just how uncomfortable I was trying to sit cross-legged in my jeans.

Being comfortable in your body during a meditation extends beyond just loose clothing. Get yourself some pillows and whatever other props you need to get as comfy as possible during your meditations. Many people have a pillow designated specifically for meditation. This helps them create an association of meditative stillness of the mind with that pillow, which helps trigger that state whenever they sit on the pillow. I have a whole series of pillows and props, starting with a soft furry sheepskin that I sit on while meditating, some cushy pillows I actually set my sensitive toosh on, and a sofa-cushion-size pillow made of tightly packed dawn to support my lower back, so that I can sit straight, but at the same time relax, without falling backwards.

The bottom line is: the mind is sometimes like an impatient overactive child. So don't give it an excuse to divert its attention from the meditation process. Be comfortable in your body first, before attempting to bring comforting stillness to your mind.

Meditational Focal Point:

With all this high praise for meditation, for many people, quieting the mind is not easy. It is said that in biblical time, every man, woman and child knew how to meditate. In many indigenous cultures, this is still true today. But in modern times in Western society, our lives have become so overly cluttered with stimuli and issues that require our attention, that finding mental stillness and inner peace has become a somewhat elusive skill. The good news is: since the ability to meditate is innate (yet dormant) in all human beings, it can be relearnt. However this relearning does take some practice, so don't be discouraged if you initially start meditating, and you find yourself inadvertently meditating on a conversation you've had with someone about the stock market. That occasionally happens even to the most experienced meditators. You're in good company!

Since the mind cannot truly be devoid of any thought at any time, stilling it into a meditational peaceful clarity without a meditational focal point may prove difficult. It helps to have an object on which to re-center your attention every time your mind wonders off. An object or focal point can remind you to discard all low-vibrational thoughts that come up, and help you find a balance in which you aren't carried away by troubling round-and-round thoughts, but on the other hand you haven't switched off into a focusless daydream.

You can choose an object as simple as a candle, an inspiring thought, a short prayerful sentence that you recite over an over, your breath, or anything positive that can help you let go of all thoughts and re-center your mind into a peaceful receptiveness for your Divine essence.

Candle Simple Meditation:

As a meditation beginner, you might find it useful to light a candle and hazily look at its flame. As you gaze at the candle's flame, thoughts will still come up. Don't stifle those thoughts. Allow them to come up, and then release them and bring your attention back into the candle. You can even envision that you are throwing every unwanted negative thought into the candle's flame to be burnt and dissolved, and that every positive thought and expectation is resting peacefully in the halo of the candle, as if empowered by its light awaiting auspicious manifestation soon. You can certainly create your own visualization.

Of course, even the visualizations and the focal point of the candle are still thoughts. Therefore by using this method, you are not completely emptying your mind of all thought. But it is a very basic meditation that's easy to achieve, since it uses the candle to give you a focal point—something to come back to after you discard each thought. The point is to let go of all thoughts as they come up, trust them into the loving hands of the Divine, and come back into your inner oasis of peace.

True meditative stillness may take some practice, or you may be Graced into it in your first meditation. But at some point in your meditation practice, you will come to a point in which your mind is still and clear, and you feel peaceful. It will feel like a very comforting nurturing place to be. And that is a wonderful place to start your journey into awareness of your True Self.

The God Bubble:

One reason that focusing your thoughts may be difficult is the overload of round-and-round thoughts about issues and problems in our lives that need dealing with. One visualization that has helped me tremendously is envisioning a big bubble of Divine white Light floating above and to the right (or left) of my head, and visualizing that I'm sending all of my issues into that bubble, to be handled and resolved in the most harmonious way by the Divine and Her-His Angels.

So let's say that you're starting to meditate on your breath, a mantra, or by holding some vision as a focal point, and suddenly things start to come up from within your troubled subconscious. You may be troubled by how your mother-in-law insulted you; having to spend two more days doing home-office work paying some bills and arguing with your health insurance company; annoyed that your son has not yet made anything of his life… and a million other thoughts that come up and distract you from your meditation. First of all, if those thoughts only come up during meditation and seemingly weren't there before you started meditating, than that's a good sign! It's a sign that you really are cleansing your subconscious, as evidenced by the fact that things that were previously buried inside you are coming up to the surface. And when those disharmonious thoughts and issues are brought up to the surface, the last thing you want to do is pack them back into your subconscious and re-stifle them. You want to let them go, but in a way that would allow Divine Light-Love-Intelligence to assist you and bring into the issue the most harmonious resolution that would be auspicious for everyone. So sending all those issues into a bubble of Divine Light is the best way to do that. After you've entrusted each troubled thought into the Divine bubble of white Light, you can go back to whatever the focal point of the meditation, be it a physical object, a mantra, your breath, or another visualization, until the next issue comes up to be sent into the bubble of Light. Eventually, you'll run out of issues, and will come to a state of peaceful stillness.

This God Bubble visualization is a multidimensional tool that works whether you believe in a higher power or not. Even if you are an atheist, on a purely psychological level, this visualization will help you let the jumble of those unorganized thoughts go, and arrive into a more peaceful state of mind, in which your mind is crystal-clear—a state that makes it easier for you to deal with those issues. Of course, from a spiritual perspective, this placing of all of your issues in a Divine bubble of Light introduces Divine Light and harmony into those issues, and merges them with the most Ideal solutions the Universe has to offer. It also constitutes an active call on your Angels to come and assist you in resolving these issues. So any way you look at it, this visualization is a very potent meditational tool to help cleanse your mind, and bring you into peace and blissful stillness.

One thing I'd like to say right now, which holds true for all the meditations that we are going to do in the remainder of this book: Many of the meditations employ different visualizations as a way to exercise your free will to let go of unwanted energies, or call upon certain Divine Light-rays and harness them to bring about certain healing and manifestation results in your life. However, not everyone is a good visualizer, and even if you normally are a good visualizer, when you're stressed and are too immersed in the grind of your here-now life, you don't always have it in you to visualize a bubble of Light, or anything else for that matter. This has happened to me many times. I am generally an excellent visualizer. But when I let myself slack on doing the daily practices that help me feel balanced, happy, and connected to my Soul Self, I become stressed, and then I can't even visualize this God Bubble. The solution is setting a verbal intent in those cases, which works at least as well for asserting your free will as visualization. So if you find that on a particular time you can't visualize this God Bubble, just affirm your free will verbally: "I am now putting this issue (whatever it may be) in a God Bubble of Light. I ask that all negativity, hardship, and stress that this issue is causing me be neutralized by Divine Light. I ask for the highest-vibrational resolution of this issue, and the most auspicious solutions to come to me easily. I ask for the help of my Angels (or Jesus, Buddha, HaShem, Ganesh, Shiva, Great Spirit… or whomever you believe in) in bringing about a resolution of this situation that serves my highest wellbeing. Thank you."

Meditation on Breath:

If you wish to meditate at a time in which circumstances do not allow lighting of a candle, another basic form of meditation is to focus on your breath. But breath can go much beyond a focal point in your meditations. As I'll explain later in this chapter, certain breath patterns can be soothing, increase your alertness state, balance your moods, and much more. And in that, breath can be an important tool for putting yourself back into a state of alignment with your Soul Self on a daily basis. Using any one of the breath patterns given later in this chapter, and focusing your attention on the breath, constitutes a meditation, since it gives you a focus point to help you discard the noisy thoughts of your mind. And you can do that any place and at any time. Just find a place you can be alone in for at least 3-5 minutes, even a bathroom stall. Then gradually start deepening your breath, so that each inhalation is deeper than the previous one… add focus on the breath… and presto – you are already meditating. To enhance breath as a meditation tool, you can envision inhaling Divine Love-Light, and exhaling—letting go of all stress and negativity. This very basic meditation will surprise you in its profound ability to calm and center you.

Mantra Meditation:

Mantra is also not the scary Eastern beast that many people perceive it to be. And actually, a mantra does not necessarily have to be in any particular language. The word Mantra literally means, "to tune the mind." It originates from two Sanskrit words: MAN=mind, TRA=tune. To tune the mind, ancient yogis used recitation of certain words and syllable they believed to be sacred. Historical records also show that ancient Kabbalists (until 100 A.D.) also used breath patterns, movements/postures, and a recitation of the many names of God (in the original Bible language) to evoke heightened states of consciousness and connection with the Divine. In fact, the use of chanting in higher meditations is used by many different traditions around the world. The yogic explanation of why recitation of mantra helps meditation is that when uttering certain syllables, the tongue touches and activates certain meridians points in the pallet of the mouth and in the throat, which produce the meditative effects. Having studied shiatsu and the meridian system, I personally know of no meridian points at the upper pallet of the mouth or in the throat. Perhaps they exist, and are simply unknown in Traditional Chinese Medicine, or to the shiatsu practitioner who was teaching me. What is true is that every word and sound has a certain vibration to it. But as we've seen in the *Prosperity From Your Soul*, the chief power of all these vibrations to affect you and your life really is your belief and conviction.

So the main thing that publicly known mantras and sacred prayers have going for them is the existence of mass consciousness of belief in them, which quite literally co-Creates a level of reality in which those mantras do have the said effects. For example, I was born and raised Israel, where Halloween is not celebrated. Further, I do not believe in the ability of scary plastic dolls to scare away ghosts. Nor do I personally believe October 31ˢᵗ to be a date in which the veil between the living and the dead is thinner. However, I fully respect the fact that I am surrounded by people who do believe in those things. Beyond my deep respect for other people's beliefs, I acknowledge the fact if there are enough people believing in them, than the energy of those beliefs may create a mass consciousness, which energetically empowers them on some level of reality. It's not that I too put scary plastic dolls to decorate the outside of my house. I don't. But I do light some candles, use some of the procedures discussed in the last chapter, and set the intent to be protected.

That being said, your personal beliefs and convictions are always much more powerful than any mass consciousness to influence your co-Creations and make changes in your life. So since there are no real sacred languages, and since the only sacred language is the pureness of your True vibrational essence, everyone should make their own mantra, in accordance with their beliefs and convictions. If you are Catholic, this mantra could be a "Hail Mary" or any other prayer from your scripture; if you Jewish this can be the Shma; if you are an atheist, it could be "Sunshine, beautiful day," or "don't worry, be happy."

To give you an example, late one evening a while ago, I was playing Solitaire while organizing my thoughts. I must have had some special laughing Angels visiting me that evening, because I suddenly started giggling silly for no reason. As I was laughing, I started to make up gibberish words and singing them to amuse myself. That night, I made up the word "Ma-fua," which means absolutely nothing in any language that I know of. Ever since then, every time I say the word "ma-fua," it makes me laugh, gives me the personal power to rise above challenges, and fills me with pure joy and trust in the Divine plan for my life! So whenever I need to feel lighter about things, I meditate by reciting the word "ma-fua." And since it makes me feel joyous, alive, empowered, hopeful, and absolutely connected to my Soul Self, no yogi or guru in the world would negate its effectiveness as a mantra *for me*! So I invite you to make up your own chant to help you meditate, and use whatever word or combination of syllables that elate your spirit.

Higher Meditations:

All effective meditations cleanse your mind. If the whole concept of meditation is new or difficult for you, just concentrate on doing a basic meditation incorporating the appropriate Mood Fixer Breath you'll learn in the next section, until you become more apt at stilling your mind. With practice, your ability to still your mind and achieve peaceful clarity will improve, and you will require less time to get to that state.

Once you are apt at basic meditation, and you are able to still your mind, you'll be able to use that stillness to tune into many different aspects of your expanded Self. From this stillness, it is possible to experience a higher state of awareness leading to a True state of sublime peace so blissful, that you will just want to keep basking in its Light. This sublime peace, if you are blessed enough to experience it at least once in your life, is the True essence of who you are—a vast being that transcend all human existence and is in oneness with the Divine. This state is beyond meditations. It's an experience.

In *Prosperity From Your Soul*, I told you about my first real transcendental experience during Kundalini Yoga teacher training. But even before that, I was already a reiki master and a spiritual teacher. So I had many blissful meditations and psychic insights during my many years of practicing and teaching reiki. The experience during yoga teacher training, though, was the first time I had a complete experience that transcends here-now existence. I distinguish that experience from all previous meditational experiences by how profound it was, how long it took me to get back into individual consciousness, and how long-lasting its the effect were. That day, even after I was fully back into here-now consciousness, I was in complete peace and stillness. It was a peace that cannot be described in words, but must be experienced. I had opened up to my True Self, and knew beyond the shadow of doubt that I am an integral part of the Divine, and that everything was going to be more than ok.

However, even having had this experience, I am still an ordinary person. I still get stressed out and angry sometimes, just like everyone else. And I don't have meditations like that every day. I do have many wonderful and profound meditations during RezoDance, while doing reiki healing, and while channeling and teaching others, but not as profound an experience as that one. However, even if I never have another experience like this in this lifetime, having Truly experienced my True Self— having been in this realm of total Oneness with All-There-Is—gives me the strength, even in my ordinary reality, to carry on. It reminds me of what's possible. It is like a treasure box within me that I can always peak at when I need extra peace and serenity, or extra reassurance.

A meditation-experience like that is not obtained by skill or earned by right. It is given by Divine Grace only. The point is, once you start meditating, you are opening yourself up to the possibility of having an experience like that. Your experience may have a different flavor than mine, as each of us has our own unique Divine essence. But even if you've never meditated before, because this type of experience is given to us by Divine Grace, you never know; it is entirely possible that at some point of your budding meditative practice, you too would have an experience that transcends the mundane and gives you the True experience of Divine Oneness—a treasure that you will keep in the internal treasure-box of your heart all the days of your life. It may happen during any of the meditations given in this part; it may happen during the Level 1 Prosperity From Your Soul Course; or it may happen in another way. Your gifted Soul can shine your way to deep peace, if you let It.

Mood Fixer Breaths

Breath is more than just one of many possible focal points in meditation. It is a major component of life and of every meditation. Breath is also closely related to our moods and states of alertness, which play an important role in co-Creating your most prosperous Lifepath.

Most people would agree that constantly staying in a peaceful yet positive, vibrant and upbeat high vibration—the kind that resonates with and magnetizes health, happiness, and prosperity—is not always easy to do, especially when you first start your new path of prosperity. But we all know how important this high vibration is to co-Creating prosperity: we don't want your new path to be an emotional rollercoaster ride; we want it to be a consistent easy walk along your most auspicious Lifepath. So having a tool that can help balance your energies and regulate your mood in a short time can be extremely helpful in keeping your vibrational resonance on a high note—aligned with the prosperity that you seek. And mood fixer breaths are exactly such effective tools.

On a physical level, of course breath is essential to life. Without breath, there is no physical life. Physiologically, breathing (along with some one-way valves in our circulatory vessels) also serves as the pump for the lymphatic system, which works synergistically with the circulatory system to supply oxygen and sustaining nutrients to each cell in the body, as well as provides your body with its normal defense system as the lymphatic fluid goes through the lymph nodes. So far, this is all common knowledge. But what is not so commonly known is how important good quality breath is to providing your body with enough energy, and in regulating moods. Even doctors[1,2] acknowledge that yogic deep breathing is very effective in healing depression, anxiety, stress, and other related disorders. And as many doctors point out, most people do not get deep enough breath, which can result in lethargy, depression, or stress. They also tell us that lack of adequate breath is also responsible for a number of sleep disorders.

Science also acknowledges that breath gives signals to the brain on what your mood and readiness state should be. A simple understanding of how breath biorhythmically affects our moods and sympathetic/parasympathetic nervous system is: most people know that when they run, or are otherwise in a state of high physical alertness or activity, their breathing becomes rapid and shallow, the heart rate goes up, and the body is generating heat/energy and is ready for (more) action. Conversely, when we are in a state of rest, our breathing is deeper and slower, our heart rate is slower, and our body temperature and preparedness for action are lower. So the rate at which we breathe goes hand in hand with the body's overall preparedness for action. The effects of this heightened preparedness are also tied to our moods. We know that our heart rate goes up and our breathing becomes shallower not only when we run a marathon, but also when we are mentally stressed. Conversely, the heart rate goes down and breathing becomes deeper and slower not only when we are resting, but also when we are mentally relaxed. In other words, your breath is closely tied in with your heart rate, your body's preparedness for action, and also with your moods. What most people do not realize is the influence works both ways. It isn't just that when you relax your breath and heart rate slow down. Breathing deeper-fuller breaths also reduces the heart rate, and induces a state of relaxation; while breathing more rapidly also increase the heart rate and induces a state of alertness. The science of biorhythm teaches us that different breath techniques can induce various states of readiness, relaxation and centeredness.

Metaphysically speaking, as it relates to the co-Creation of prosperity, if you want to get your body-temple ready to be the vehicle for bringing forth all the blessings you are about to co-Create into your life, one of the first steps is to breathe better. There is more to it than just taking one deep breath every once in a while, when somebody reminds you to do so. From a spiritual perspective, breath is an important conductor of Divine the life-force energy, which is the Creative energy from which all manifestations come.

Before we talk about specific breaths that bring about specific mind states, in order to learn how to deep-breathe, let's briefly discuss some of the basics of breathing.

Deep Breathing:

Our lungs are like two air balloons contained within your rib cage area. These air balloons have semi-permeable walls that allow the blood of the capillaries (tiny blood vessels) in the lining of these walls to dump CO_2 back into the lungs, and pick up fresh oxygen from the lungs, to take to all the cells of the body. In order to keep providing the body with fresh oxygen, the lung's air balloons are in constant flux—shrinking to expel out the CO_2 out of the body, and expanding to suck in new O_2. All this is intuitively understood by most people. However, what is not so intuitive is that the air balloons of our lungs are capable of expanding both laterally *and vertically*.

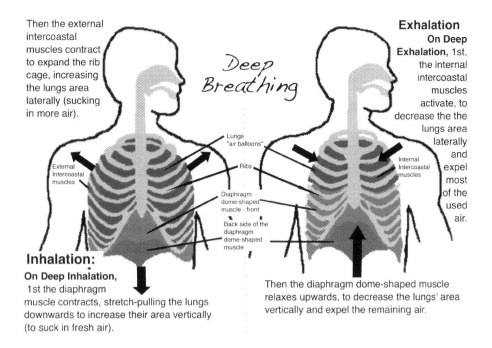

Then the external intercoastal muscles contract to expand the rib cage, increasing the lungs area laterally (sucking in more air).

Deep Breathing

Exhalation
On Deep Exhalation, 1st, the internal intercoastal muscles activate, to decrease the the lungs area laterally and expel most of the used air.

Lungs "air balloons"

External Intercoastal muscles

Ribs

Internal Intercoastal muscles

Diaphragm dome-shaped muscle - front

Back side of the diaphragm dome-shaped muscle

Inhalation:
On Deep Inhalation, 1st the diaphragm muscle contracts, stretch-pulling the lungs downwards to increase their area vertically (to suck in fresh air).

Then the diaphragm dome-shaped muscle relaxes upwards, to decrease the lungs' area vertically and expel the remaining air.

Lateral expansion of the lungs is supported by the muscles between our ribs (inter-coastal muscles), while vertical expansion of the lungs is afforded by the diaphragm. The diaphragm in the side of the schematics is in a relaxed position. When the diaphragm muscle contract (left drawing), it pushes down, and expands the physical displacement of your lungs vertically, thereby allowing them to fill up with more air. As the diaphragm pushes down, it push out the internal organs, and it looks like your belly is inflating. This back and forth pushing actually massages your internal organs, and is very healthy for you. So on a full deep breath, the belly is supposed to "inflate" on the inhalation, along with the lateral inflation of the rib cage. Through misuse and stress, many people have unknowingly adopted a counterproductive breath pattern in which their belly goes in during inhalation and pushes out on the exhalation. And if you are one of these people, this simple understanding of the lungs' anatomy, along with some practice, may help you correct this situation and make your breath more efficient again—expanding your belly on inhalation and collapsing it during exhalation.

The most efficient way to inhale deeply is to expand the belly (vertical expansion) first, and then expand the lungs laterally using your intercostal muscles. The most efficient way to deeply exhale is by allowing the lungs to deflate laterally first (using your intercostal muscles), and then bring the belly towards your back, using your abdominal muscles to help the diaphragm's action. This is a complete and efficient way to empty the lung-balloons more completely of CO_2, so that on the next inhalation they can bring in more fresh oxygen, thus keeping your lungs better oxygenated.

While experienced yogis can make each breath (inhalation + exhalation) last a full minute, the best way to reach deep breathing is actually to just allow yourself to gradually deepen your breath. Don't expect yourself to instantly go from stressed-out breathing to long, deep and relaxed breathing. Allow the breath to normalize first. Then kindly prompt yourself to make each breath just a little deeper than the one before. Be conscious of inhaling "into your belly" first before

55

you expand your lungs; be conscious of emptying your lungs more completely by pulling your abdominal muscles towards your back a bit more at the end of each breath. But do everything gently and kindly. Start your being kind to yourself through this practice of just deep breathing for a couple of minutes each day, perhaps at times in which you need relaxation. Before long, you'll find that you really like doing relaxing deep breaths.

This breath by itself is a wonderful tool of relaxing yourself at will. But as a meditational exercise, once you're starting to get the breath part of it down, you can introduce a visualization of your choice. You can envision all kinds of Divine Light and Love coming into you with each inhalation; and as you exhale, you might envision all stress leaving you, or you can envision that the Divine Light that's within you is expanding and brightening your entire aura. You can certainly find the visualization that comes to you most naturally, and feels the most nurturing. You may put on some relaxing music to get you in a more meditative mood as you practice your deep breathing. You can even light incense that gives you a certain feeling. It doesn't have to be any of the incense I've mentioned last chapter. It could be just jasmine—to connect you with the purity of Divine vibration, or cedar—to induce feelings of freshness and a fresh dawn in your life. Choose the incense or essential oils (burnt on an anointed candle or with a dispenser) that makes you feel most fabulous at that moment. Let this be an enjoyable self-nurturing time.

Moon Breath:

Use this breath pattern when you are going on over-speed or are otherwise stressed out, to relax you, lower your heart rate to ideal, and calm the nervous system.

Start gradually deepening your breath into longer breath… Try and be conscious of inhaling to the count of four, and exhaling to the count of eight, such that your exhalation longer than the inhalation… This may require you to inhale more powerfully, since your inhalation time is shorter, and you should be taking in and out the same volume of air during inhalation and exhalation.

While keeping the exhalation longer than the inhalation, breathe more by expanding your belly, and less by expanding the rib cage…

Once you've found your rhythm with this, use one finger to close off the right nostril and deeply breathe only through your left nostril… Continue this left-nostril long-exhalation belly breathing, and find your own rhythm with it…

Now let your mind go to a calming visualization that feels right for you. You can envision that you are floating on a deep blue ocean of goodness and love, or go in your mind into your private piece of heaven, whatever that may be. For me, I always visualize myself floating on the turquoise warm ocean water around Tortola—my favorite Caribbean island where I've spent considerable time diving. For you it may be a different place, or even a place that exists only in your imagination. Just find the most beautiful and peaceful place you can imagine and go there in your mind as you practice this breathing. Pretty soon, you'll start feeling extremely peaceful.

To help this breath pattern's meditational calming effect, you may put on a background of soothing relaxing music, or burn incense that promotes peace and meditation, such as lavender, lemon verbena, roman chamomile, neroli, frankincense, myrrh, patchouli, vetiver, or sandalwood.

Sun Breath:

Use this breath to help you focus when you are in a brain-fog, a little out of it. It can also energize you when you need to perk up and be ready for a task.

Gradually deepen your breath some… and start being conscious of inhaling to the count of eight, and exhaling to the count of about four, such that the inhalation is now longer than your exhalation. This may require you to exhale more powerfully, so that you can extract all the air you took in during the long inhalation, in a shorter period of time.

This time, let the expansion of your lungs come more from the middle of your rib cage, and less from your belly. Do not force-breathe through your uppermost ribs, as that would stress you out. Just stay within a natural long breath, and be aware of breathing primarily by expanding your mid-ribs, and inhaling longer than exhaling.

Now while still maintaining this breath pattern, use a finger to close off the left nostril and breathe now only through the right nostril…

Again, you may burn incense or essential oils to promote peaceful alertness, such as rose, pine, cedar, cypress, eucalyptus, peppermint, rosemary, basil, lemon, or juniper. You may put on music that is soothing and uplifting, and yet have an energizing effect on you. After a short while, you'll start feeling much more focused, perked up, and ready for the task at hand with peaceful alertness.

U-Breath:

Curling your tongue into a U-shape while breathing deeply through it brings about a tremendous cooling relaxation on the body, while maintaining mental alertness. This breath also helps digestion, and lowers fever.

Grounding Breath:

This breath has a tremendous grounding and centering effect. It is also very helpful in balancing the left and right brain hemispheres. When you need to be calm, yet logical and ready for action, say for an important meeting, just three minutes of this breath will get you completely balanced, peaceful, yet clear-minded and ready for action. And it is very simple to do once you get the rhythm of it.

I've done this breath pattern many times while driving to teach yoga and other events. On those occasions, I was stressed by the LA traffic to get there on time. Yet I knew that once I got there, I needed to exemplify the yogi, the reiki master, and the spiritual guide that would hold space and uplift everyone else. So my solution was engaging in this Grounding Breath while driving, along with some visualizations in the back of my mind.

To do Grounding Breath, start by gradually deepening your breath into a deep, long, yet natural breaths…

Now use one finger and your thumb to close off the inactive nostril each time:

Inhale deeply through the left nostril…

Exhale deeply through the right nostril…
Inhale deeply through the right nostril…
Exhale deeply through the left nostril…
Repeat - Inhale left… exhale right… inhale right… exhale left…
Basically, you switch nostrils every time when you are at the top of the breath.

As trivial as the idea of simply deep breathing may seem to the overall process of co-Creating the life that you want, the more fresh air you bring into your total being, the more Ki energy you bring into your body-vessel and life, which is the same type of energy as the co-Creative energy that pours into your life through your Infinite funnel of Abundance. And as explained above, these breathing techniques can also help you maintain a balance between upbeat vivaciousness and peaceful calm, which naturally enhance your vibrational resonance with the abundance you seek. So when you look at these simple breaths in this light, it becomes easier to understand how profound a tool they really are in the process of co-Creating prosperity. We will also build on these breathing techniques in all the meditations of this book.

As you practice all these deep breaths, it may further your co-Creative endeavors if you also envision Divine Light coming into your body and being as you inbreathe. You'll find that it puts you in an extremely good mood. After you try these different breaths to regulate your moods, you'll be in awe of how profound a tool they really are. As with everything else, I encourage you to make these techniques your own. You should choose only the techniques that are best suited for you and serve your needs. For example, if you are normally stressed, you may find that your most natural affinity is to Moon Breaths. If you are normally too out-of-it or in la-la-land, you'll probably feel very good doing Sun Breaths. If you normally are stressed, but ungrounded at the same time, you will be very magnetized to doing Grounding Breath. You may even receive guidance from your Soul on how to modify these techniques to answer a particular need in your life. And it goes without saying that as you start tapping into these basic meditational tools, your Soul Self will probably guide you on different visualizations, to heal specific things in your life. But you won't know how profound a tool these simple breathing techniques really are until you experiment with them and make them your own.

Colored Light Invocation

Colored light rays are ethereal vibrations, representing the different aspects of the Divine, as they filter into a physical level that can be perceived in the here-now reality. Music is another type of ethereal vibration that can be perceived on a here-now level. And aroma is another one, although aroma is more physical, since it manifests as the element of air. In the physical universe, scientists say that music and color (or light) are all energy waves, but are on two different areas of the wave spectrum. But the Truth is that all light, all color rays, all music, and all aromas are but aspects of the Divine Her-Himself.

When you choose to listen to different music at different times, it isn't just the mood you're in, but the specific aspect of yourself you wish to give rise to that makes you choose that music.

And as each type of music brings with it a particular flavor of Divine Whole, when choosing a particular type of music, it is really the resonance with that particular vibration that you seek. You may choose certain music that helps you externalize some of your rough edges, bringing certain deep feelings into completion; you may choose music that connects you with joy and the zest of life; or you may choose music that puts you in complete peace. And when it comes to music, most people intuitively know which music induces what mood for them, kind of like I know that Vivaldi concerti induce in me an upbeat morning mood, and Beethoven and Chopin induce in me an afternoon relaxation mood, and Mozart's music helps me balance and sharpen my mind. For you it will, not doubt, be a different selection of musical pieces, since we are all different. What is the same is the fact that the music you choose to listen to evokes certain feelings and moods, and the need to be conscious of that effect of music in order to regulate your moods and alertness/peace level.

Aroma is very similar to music in that it brings the particular vibration of the herb/flower, as an aspect of the total Divine vibration, to awaken certain feelings and ethereal vibrations in us. There is a whole science of aromatherapy that can cognitively teach you which flower/herb evokes which feeling. But for the most part, most people know that certain aromas awaken certain memories and feelings in them.

In much the same way as in music and in aroma, envisioning certain colors of light can be used to evoke certain feelings in us, and to resonate and call upon particular aspects of the Divine for our healing, well-being, and co-Creation.

However, there are many schools of thought on color therapy, and what each color means. The bottom line is: as you may remember from our discussion on "The Sacred Language of Creation" (*Prosperity From Your Soul*), color therapy is also in the eyes (and belief) of the beholder. Like any other belief system, you and the wisdom within you should always be the ultimate authority on what they mean *to you*, and how to best use that meaning to assist in your healing, protection, or co-Creative endeavors.

That being said, to give you a place to start, I have listed here a few belief systems relating to the invocation of each colored-light and its meaning. Each of those is complete system. So as you read through these different systems, regard them as suggestions only. The intent here is to give you a wide range of possibilities, so that you may then employ your internal wisdom to find the one that best resonates most with you. Keep tuned into the highest observer in you, so that you may detect which meanings you should adopt for your own meditative color invocation.

Doreen Virtue's Bubble of Light Protection:

Doreen Virtue is a psychic and a channeler of information relating to Angels, whom I have come to trust over the years. She has written many wonderful books and inspired oracle cards to assist people in connecting with Angels and other Divine deities. In her oracle card deck called *Angel Therapy,* she lists a simple method of calling upon Angelic help by envisioning oneself inside a bubble of colored Light, each color of Light producing specific healing results. I have used some of these visualizations many times, and felt like I was helped. Was I really receiving Angelic help, or did I simply feel better because of the autosuggestion effect of the visualization? I don't know. But does it matter? The point is that this method makes people feel better.

Here are the specific healing effects calls forth according to Virtue:

"Blue: Increased communications and clarity
Green: Healing and protection of health
Pink: Lightheartedness and romance
Purple: Spiritual protection (shielding from psychic attacks)
White: General protection"

Corinne D. Heline:

In her book *Healing And Regeneration Through Color* (written in 1943), Corinne D Heline details several different systems of color therapy, and meanings of different colors, which she had obtained through her meditations.

Heline's ideas may sound strange to you, or they may resonate with something you believe in. The purpose here is to give you some choices of visualization tools, so that you can choose to empower the ones that best resonate with you. After you start meditating regularly and using color visualizations, you'll probably develop an affinity to certain colors in your visualizations. At that point, you will probably give each color a meaning of your own—a meaning that is special to you. All these lists are just to give you an idea of some possible meanings that certain colors *may* have, in order to help you tune into the True vibration of each color, and how it can serve you personally.

Corinne D Heline's Zodiac Chart –

The first serious system of color symbology that Heline details relates to the zodiac signs and their influence on certain minerals, imbuing them with rhythms and forces that are characteristics to that sign. By extension, the colors of these gems then correlate to the influence of a particular zodiac constellation.

Sign	Color	Metal	Jewels	Flowers/Aroma
Aries	Red	Iron	Ruby, bloodstone, red jasper	Red carnations & red rose
Taurus	Yellow	Copper	Golden topaz, coral, emerald	Roses
Gemini	Violet	Mercury, carbuncle	Crystal, aquamarine	Lilacs, old lavender
Cancer	Green	Silver	Emerald, Moonstone	Lily, jasmine
Leo	Orange	Gold	Ruby, amber, sardonyx	Orange blossom
Virgo	Violet	Mercury	Pink jasper, turquoise, zircon	White rose, Heliotrope
Libra	Yellow	Copper	Opal, Diamond	Rosemary, Sandalwood
Scorpio	Red	Iron	Agate, Garnet, Topaz	Chrysanthemum

Sagittarius	Blue	Tin	Amethyst	Violet
Capricorn	Indigo	Lead	Black & white onyx, Beryl	Black narcissus & tulip
Aquarius	Indigo	Lead	Blue sapphire	Gardenia
Pisces	Blue	Tin	Diamond, jade	White narcissus

Notice that this chart is totally different from today's chart of gemstones and their correlating birth months. Also, in this chart there are some colors that correlate to more than one zodiac sign. So are you beginning to get the impression here that the meaning of each color, like everything else, is very much in the eyes (and belief system) of its beholder? Good.

Heline's Weekdays Gems Chart –

One system that Heline intuited was that each day of the week is influenced by a different planet or star, which also exerts its influence on particular semi-precious stones. According to this system, wearing these stones, having them in one's sphere, or visualizing the color of the stone, helps one resonate with the healing influence of the planet/star whose influence is strong that day.

Day	**Star/Planet**	**Gem & Color**
Sunday	Sun	Gold & Yellow gems
Monday	Moon	Pearls & all white stones
Tuesday	Mars	Rubies & all red stones
Wednesday	Mercury	Turquoise (air element protection), Sapphire & blue stones
Thursday	Jupiter	Amethyst & purple stones
Friday	Venus	Emerald & green stones
Saturday	Saturn	Diamond & also black stones

Heline's Glandular Colors –

Corinne D. Heline gives two more color healing systems, which may be of more specific healing value, the first of which relates to the glands.

She notes, "Each ductless gland, for example, possesses what we may call a 'color power', which is the energy radiation visible to the extended etheric vision. This color power when properly focused will overcome and eradicate certain diseases caused by a lack of stimulus native to that color.

Pineal – blue-lavender   Solar plexus – orange
Pituitary – blue-yellow   Thymus – golden-pink
Thyroid – green-gold   Adrenals – bright purplish red

Concentration on each color stimulates the associated gland to secret more ideally to heal the body."

<u>Heline's Planetary Healing Colors</u>

The last system that I'll summarize from Corinne D. Heline's book is the one where she explains that different colored rays emit from different planets, and affect healing of specific aspects of our personalities and bodies:

<u>Red</u>: The rays of Aries and Mars, brings dynamic life energy. It stimulates the physical and mental bodies; improves circulation; helps anemia sluggishness

<u>Orange</u>: Acts on the solar plexus and charges the body with the harmony of new rhythmic impulses; heals functional disorders; helps weakened lungs

<u>Yellow</u>: The Chi healing energy that surrounds the Earth. Contains cleansing purifying Uranus and Venus rays; Stimulates nerves; Heals and benefits all functions in the body and mind.

<u>Green</u>: Earth forces. Helps head colds, hay fever, malaria, jaundice and all liver disorders; also helps sooth overstimulation & over excitability.

<u>Blue</u>: Neptune ray. Cooling, soothing; helps inflammatory illnesses, headaches, neuralgia, rheumatism, sciatica, and all organic disabilities

<u>Indigo</u>: Saturn ray. Alleviates fever, counters all skin diseases and irritations

<u>Violet</u>: Combines Mercury and Neptune's rays. Along with yellow, it helps conditions particular to men or women.

As you are beginning to see, with so many systems of color therapy, coming through one individual no less, the way you use each color in your meditation and healing endeavors is totally up to you.

Colors of The Chakras:

Then again, colors could very traditionally be the Light-color of a particular chakra that needs an enhancement of energy. I use this system of colored light invocation more often than any other system. We'll also employ this system in Nature Meditation (Chapter 5) and in Nature Walk (*A Lifestyle of Prosperity From Your Soul*). Here is a review of the chakras and their colors:

1st "root" Chakra – Red
2nd Sex organ chakra – Orange
3rd solar plexus chakra, also referred to as navel center – yellow
4th heart chakra – green, or pink for Divine love
5th throat chakra – cobalt blue
6th third eye chakra – indigo
7th crown chakra – purple – violet

When envisioning the color of each chakra, it is important to start by envisioning the most Divine white light coming from the heart of the Divine, entering you through the crown of your head, and then as the Light settles in the area of the chakra that needs its feed, it shifts its color and becomes red (root)... orange (second)... yellow (third)... green (heart)... cobalt (throat)... indigo (third-eye)... and finally magenta (crown).

White light is always safe to meditate on, since it includes all colors of the spectrum, therefore your Etheric Body can absorb from it any color that it needs. Most healers also agree that violet is a Light ray that can cut through all negativity, transmute all that needs to be changed from negative to positive, and therefore uplift the spirit.

Effect of Color According to Modern Psychology:

Mainstream psychologists[3] believe that the physical vision of color passes impulses not only to our brains, but also directly to our pituitary and pineal glands via the hypothalamus, thereby affecting our body systems. They also believe that it has been shown that envisioning a color affects the body systems in much the same way as colors that you actually see. But of course, mainstream psychologists also have their own decoding system of what each color means, and how they believe it affects our psyche.

Red:
: Physiologically stimulate the adrenal glands and raise blood pressure. Psychologically, it has been shown to associate with anger. But can also be the color of vitality and ambition. Red can also be associated with sexuality. (Da! The root chakra!)

Pink:
: Has the opposite effect of red. It helps relax the muscles and calm, protection, warmth and nature. Associated with unselfish love.

Orange:
: Stimulate the sexual organs, and can be beneficial to digestion and strengthen the immune system. Psychologically, orange has the affect of an antidepressant, and can relieve feelings of lack of self worth, and self pity. All in all orange affects our emotional state positively.

Yellow:
: Stimulate the brain thus inducing a better state of alertness, activates the lymph system, and make the muscles more active. Psychologically, it is an uplifting color associated with clear thinking, good judgment, that can aid organization and understanding, and encourages self-confidence and optimism.

Green:
: Relaxes the muscles and helps breathe deeper and slower. It thus relaxes physical and emotional balance. Psychologically it is associated with comfort, calmness, and soothed emotions.

Blue:
: Lowers blood pressure, and has a cooling effect on the thyroid gland. Deeper blue stimulates the pituitary to better regulate sleep patterns to eliminate insomnia, and help the skeletal structure in keeping the bone marrow healthy. Psychologically blue affects calm relaxation, control, creativity, and clarity.

Indigo:
: Has been used by doctors as a mild sedative. Known to stimulate intuition.

Purple:
: Purifying, antiseptic, can alleviate sunburn, suppresses hunger, and balance metabolism. Psychologically it has been shown to balance the mind and transform obsessions and fears. Violate is known to cleanse fear, shock, and emotional disturbances and bring peace.

Brown: Brings feeling of stability, security, and is associated with home feeling and emotional retreat.

Black: Comforting, protective, and often associated mysticism and silence.

White: The ultimate color of purity, bringing peace, freedom, openness and softness.

Gray: Can be associated with independence.

As much as I personally do not put any stock in modern psychology, there are some similarities between their interpretations and actual spiritual truths. If you look at some of modern psychology's interpretations, it almost looks like the influence of each color correlates with the influence of the chakra associated with it. This fills me with hope that perhaps one day, modern medicine will catch up with what Light workers have known for thousands of years.

Personal Association & Meaning:

In any meditational process, whether you are invoking colored Light rays or not, the most important meaning of any symbol is the meaning it has *for you*. It is the meaning that you imbue any color, light, image, candle, mantra, or any other tool with, that awakens in you the power of your Soul Self, and the vibrational likeness and resonance with that which you wish to co-Create. Therefore it is important that you meditate only on what resonates deeply within you as True, without regard to whether or not it makes sense.

For example, I use a few personal systems of color visualizations that help my personal healing very effectively: In one system, I envision a gage of red energy to represent my level of head pressure building up to a migraine. So after I get myself into a meditative stillness, I ask my Higher Self to show me, through this gauge visualization, what percentage of pressure has built up, in other words – how certain are we that a migraine is coming, and how imminent it is. This helps me plan when to get home and take medication. Another system of color visualization that I employ, also in relation to my migraines, is envisioning a flow of healing-cooling green-blue light washing over me from head to toe, cooling down the red energy and replacing it with green-blue energy. This system works so well for me, that I don't have to justify it by any research or belief system. I mention this example, because you too may use a similar method of indication for almost any medical condition you may have. In this type of visualization, the colored gauge is just a method for your subconscious to communicate to you the severity of the condition. You may also devise your own unique visualization of healing Light, which works ideally for you. And in it, you should use whichever color you feel is most healing for you.

Another is a system of colors that I use in my everyday life is I wear and surround myself with colors that remind me of the colored Light ray that I wish to invite into my life on a particular day. For example, for me, very light lime-green represents inviting a new spring and lightness into my life; yellow helps me tune into my Zohar—my Divine radiance; white helps me tune into Divine purity; very light turquoise-whitish-blue, for me, is the color of Angels, and reminds me of the color emanating as the Soul is carved from Oneness and as makes It travels through the ethers to Earth. It therefore reminds me of HOME. But these are just examples of my own personal meanings. For you the meanings will no doubt be different. Maybe a color of red reminds you of grandma's tomato soup. Maybe green reminds you of your garden. The point is, in your visualizations, use the colors that have a good, nurturing, and healing meaning to you.

Remember also that all the systems I introduced in this chapter have came from somebody else's channeled information, filtered through their subjective perspective. As much as I respect some of the individuals who channeled the above systems, they too are only human, affected by the same biases that you and I are. No healer can be in your shoes. No one can channel Divine information, which more accurately pertains to you, than you yourself. So I invite you to experiment in your meditations. Envision wonderful colors that make you feel radiant. Remember that if you can't visualize, either because you're not a good visualizer or because you're too stressed on a particular day, speak your visualization and the results you intend for it to bring you. For example, "I am now surrounding myself with healing green Light," or- "I now bring the Divine purple Light-ray to dissolve all negativity from my life, and to strengthen my connection with the Divine at my crown chakra." Invent your own silly little mantra (like my "ma-fua"); and go nuts with imbuing objects such as candles and crystals with your intent. As long as it passes your Joy Meter and God Meter (*Prosperity From Your Soul*), it is getting you closer to who you Truly are. When you employ the right meditational tools, you will really feel more peaceful, more focused, and more ready (on all levels) to co-Create your most Ideal Lifepath.

Angels & Archangels Color Invocation

As I mentioned earlier, Angels and Archangels are not really separate from God or from us. In fact, the fifteen known Archangels are merely the different aspects, or emanations, of the Creator. This comes into better focus when you consider the fact that the numerology of one of the Biblical names of God (YaH) equates to fifteen, and incidentally (or not), fifteen is also the number of Archangels that exist. So calling on Archangels just means that you call upon a particular aspect or emanation of God. And for the most part, there seems to be a consensus amongst Light-workers on the type of issues that each Archangel can help with.

However, as far as summoning a particular Archangel, many Light-workers believe in this system summarized below, which professes that envisioning a particular color, or working with a particular crystal, automatically call upon the Archangel associated with that color or crystal. I myself question this method of invocation, since I feel that each colored Light may bring a magnitude of messages from the Divine. Similarly, each crystal can be programed (by you) for many healing purposes, and used as a tool to invoke specific co-Creative effects. Therefore, making a hard link between each color or crystal and a particular Archangel may limit all the other messages that your Soul may be communicating with you through your affinity to a particular color or a particular crystal. So I suggest that you employ your own inner wisdom to decide for yourself if you wish to use this system of invocation.

The meanings of the names of the Archangels are my own translation from their original Hebrew (Biblical) name. The names of thirteen of the Archangels end with "El," which in Hebrew is short for "Elohim"—one of the biblical words for God. The only two Archangels whose name

is far removed from their Hebrew names are Metatron and Sandalphon—the two Archangels who were at one point human, and walked the earth plane.

Archangel	Meaning/ Origin	Color	Crystal	Helps With…
Ariel	=lion of God	Light pink	Rose quartz	Manifestation, environmentalism & protecting animals, messages to/from the deceased
Chamuel	=like God	Light green	Green fluorite	Relationships, soulmates, life purpose & world peace
Ezrael	=help of god	Vanilla cream	Yellow calcite	Confidence, courage, dying, grieving
Gabriel	=masculine power of God	Copper	Copper & citrine	Artistic expression & writing, conceiving or adopting children
(h)Aniel	=I am God	Bluish-white light	Moonstone	Grace, balance, healing abilities clairvoyance & moon energy
Jeremiel	=height of God	Deep purple	Amethyst	Clairvoyance & psychic visions life reviews & life changes
Jophiel	=beauty of God	Deep pink	Pink rubellite	Anything relating to beauty – internal or in your surrounding
Metatron	The prophet Enoch	Violate & light green	Red tourmaline	Recordkeeping, children, ADHD, spiritual understanding
Michael	=he who is like God	Deep blue & magenta	Sugalite	Clearing, protection, freeing from bondage, protecting, life's purpose, self esteem
Ra(g)uel	= God's friendship	Pale blue		relationship harmony, resolving arguments, compassion, forgiveness
Raphael	=healing of God	Deep green	Emeralds	Healing on all levels
Raziel	=secret/wisdom of God	Rainbow light	Clear crystal	Clairvoyance, psychic abilities, Divine alchemy, esoteric information
Sandalphone	the prophet Elijah	Turquoise	Turquoise	Music, answering prayers, miracles, determining sex of an unborn baby, and is also believed (in Jewish tradition) to be the foreteller of the coming of the messiah
Uriel	=light of God	Pale gold	Amber	Illumination of any situation, earth changes, spiritual understanding

Zadkiel	=justice of God	indigo blue	Lapis Lazuli	Divine order & justice, healing, enhance memory
General angel invocation		White Light		Protection, healing, help

Zohar Breath Meditation

There is an infinite number of ways to tune into the many aspects of your Soul Self. The most profound tool that I can give you is Zohar Breath Meditation. I have named this meditation Zohar Breath not because Zohar is my spiritual name, but because the Hebrew word "zohar" means: Divine splendor or Divine radiance. And it is my prayer that this meditation will help you tune into *your own Divine radiance*—the True nature of your own Soul.

This simple yet profound meditation is the basis for many, more complex, meditational processes that we will do in the coming next chapters, which will lead you to tune into the details of your Ideal Lifeplan. So the importance of this meditation cannot be overemphasized, since it lays the foundation for all the processes that will lead you to co-Create your Ideal Lifepath of happiness, health, and prosperity.

The main purpose of this meditation is to facilitate free communication between your here-now self and your higher Soul Self—the part of you that is always connected to your all-knowing Creator. You may employ this technique in any life situation in which you really need answers from a higher Source. It can help put a harmonious stop to the endless internal dialogue of: "Should I, or should I not do such and such?" by giving you a method of getting answers from the wisest aspect of You. This meditation is designed to bring your here-now self and your Soul Self into a harmonious unity that fosters a state of grace, peace, and clarity. Some may say that this is an Akashic reading. Indeed, the information coming through this meditation come from the heart of your Akashic Records—the ethereal records of all of your Soul's history since Its inception, which encompasses wisdom the core of your Soul. That is why the answers and solutions that you get when you truly delve into this meditation usually resonate so deeply as the best answers/solutions to any dilemma or situation you may be facing in your here-now reality.

When you become proficient at Zohar Breath Meditation, it is a very pure meditation, which has the ability to send you soaring to the bliss of oneness with the Divine, Her-His Angels, and your high-level Spirit Guide.

Prepare for the Meditation:

Before you start this or any other meditation, it is important to adopt a habit of energetically cleansing and blessing your space. Regularly cleansing your living space helps dissolve any lower vibrational energies that no longer serve, instills the peace of knowing that everything is going to be OK, and imbues your space and life with fresh inflow of Divine energy that facilitates your highest Lifepath. But cleansing and blessing your meditational space is especially important for this meditation, to insure that the information you will receive would come from the highest-purest Source possible, and in a crystal clear way.

There are many ways to cleanse a space, many of which are explained in the last chapter. And as always, I recommend that you use the methods that most resonates with you. But for this meditation specifically, there is a unique and specific way for preparing your space and focusing your intent for this meditation. This preparation will help ensure that you would indeed be tuned into information from the highest Divine wisdom of your Soul—taking into account all of your Soul's history since Its inception, as well as your Soul's goals that It has set for you for this lifetime.

If You Are a Reiki Practitioner –

Use your fingers to draw-trace the sacred reiki symbols in the air as instructed:

Draw the #1 (Divine Light-Power) symbol on each of the four walls of your space. Intend the utmost Divine Light to flood over your entire space—within you, each aspect of your life, and throughout your space. Pray/intend for the Divine Light to eliminate all lower vibrational energies, all entanglement cords, all negative karma, all mental or energetic blockages that might be delaying the full manifestation of Divine favor in your life. See and feel these symbols bringing you lightness, and freedom from any and all bondage.

You may say silently or out loud: "Through Divine Light-Power, I ask my Angels and Archangels to stand guard and protect me from any energetic disturbances during your meditation. I now bring the utmost Divine Light to illumine and heal the situations/questions I ask about. I now empower my Soul Self to guide me according to my highest Lifeplan, and to bring into my life Light, love, prosperity, lightness of heart, health, happiness, joy, radiance, and Grace, and the manifestation of all of my highest wishes."

Draw the #2 (Divine Heart-Mind) symbol in each of the four corners of your room. Pray/intend for the utmost Divine wisdom, clarity and harmony to inspire your meditation. You may say silently or out loud: "I ask my Spirit Guides and the Guardians of the Akashic Records (A special group of Angelic beings that guard each person's Akashic Records) to relate to me the highest level of information from my Akashic Records, in a crystal-clear form that I can easily understand."

Draw the #3 (Space-Time) symbol on the ceiling of your space. Use the symbol to first and foremost invite your Angels, Archangels, Spirit Guides, ascended Masters, and the Guardians of your Akashic Records to facilitate your tuning into the highest level of wisdom during the meditation. Ask and intend for healing on all levels to occur during this meditation. Affirm that you wish to tune into the highest level of information from your Soul, taking into account all of your Soul's history since Its inception, goals that It has set for you for this lifetime, and your Soul's behind-the-scenes knowledge of your possible futures.

If You Are Not a Reiki Practitioner –

Use the same exact prayers and intents as described above, just without drawing the reiki symbols. To help strengthen your prayerful intent, you may choose to invoke a particular Angel or deity that has been helping you in your life. You may also wish to hold a candle or incense between your hands, and prayerfully bless them with your intent, before lighting them. Or you may decide to place certain crystals or other blessed objects in a sacred circle around the spot of your meditation. Use whichever object or medium "speaks" to you, to make your prayer and intent most potent. I find it useful to wrap the crown of my head with a shawl made of very thin white silk. This helps me feel and vibrationally connect with the highest vibration of Divine Light and purity. The important part is that the prayerful invocation for this particular meditation be exactly as I had described it above, for it to be the most effective. When I say "exactly as," I mean in essence, not necessarily in my words. You do not have to work hard to memorize my verbiage. The idea is that you ask for protection, clarity, and Divine wisdom; invoke/bring lots of the purest Divine Light to facilitate protection, shedding of light on the situation(s), and for your healing; affirm that you wish to tune into the highest level of wisdom available at the time of the meditation. And once you become proficient at doing this meditation, you'll be able to do all this preparation and invocation in just a minute or two.

Whether you are a reiki practitioner or not, as you start the meditation, trust that you are now in the purest space, and that the highest level of information is now going to be delivered to you.

As in any meditation, this meditation too will be greatly aided if you put on some music that highly inspires you. Some music track that I have found very good in facilitating this meditation is Snatam Kaur's *Ray Man* from her album *Release & Overcome* (my #1 choice); the second movement of Beethoven piano concerto number five ("The Emperor"); or Singh Kaur & Kim Robertson's Crimson Collection 1 & 2. But that is just my taste, since I like yogic and classical music. For you, the music selection may be totally different. Just make sure that the music is relaxing, preferably non-verbal; does not take your attention away from the meditation; and that it connects you with the most inspired part of you.

The Meditation:

Next, sit comfortably cross-legged (or in your preferred meditational pose) on your meditation pillow or on your bed, with your spine straight but not tense, and your palms open and facing up on your lap. Close your eyes, concentrating your internal view (envisioning that you are looking) down towards your heart chakra. Become aware of your breath as a source of life and Divine Light, gradually deepening your breath with each inhalation and exhalation, until you reach a breath that is deep yet feels natural and comfortable. That is meditational breath.

Now, as you are situated to start your meditation, it is very important that you state out-loud to affirm: "I am now privy to my Akashic Records!" or "<u>My Akashic Records are now open to me</u>!"

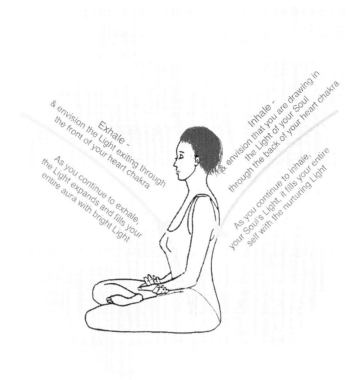

As you inhale, visualize a pure white Light, flowing from the center of the Universe—the heart of God, entering your body through the back of your heart chakra, and flooding-pouring over your heart, spreading throughout your entire body, and filling your whole being with Divine Light. It's as if you allow in more of that pure Divine white Light with each full inhalation.

As you exhale, envision the Divine Love-Light exiting through the front of your heart chakra and filling your whole aura, so that the incoming and outgoing breath form sort of a V-shape or funnel, which anchors your Soul at your heart center.

Envision that your entire body and being is engulfed in the most magnificent Divine white Light, the feed of which is the back of your heart chakra (the back side of the V), and the exit of which is the front of your heart chakra (the front of the V), such that as you exhale, the Light seeps into your aura and feeds all of your Light-bodies. You are one with the Divine funnel of Light and Love. As you continue to breathe deeply, your entire being and aura will be flooded with an ever more radiant and expanding white Light and Divine radiance.

If you can't visualize, speak your intents: "As I inhale deeply, Divine white Light will be coming into the back of my heart chakra, flooding over my entire being; and as I exhale deeply, the Divine white Light will be exiting through the front of my heart chakra, and filling my entire aura." And once you've spoken your intent, if you still can't visualize, than just keep your consciousness on the breath and on the thought of the Divine Light coming in and out of your heart space.

In the beginning, your thoughts may wonder. This is normal, since stilling your mind is a skill that requires some practice. Just allow all thoughts to surface, but don't hold on to any thoughts, especially not to troubling ones. Let them all surface, and then release them into the Light. Keep bringing your mind back to the breath of Divine white Light coming in and out of your heart space. If you have a lot to release, you may visualize that as you exhale, all stress, all negativity, and all lower vibrational energies, are leaving you and being instantly dissolved (harming none) by the scintillating white Light that you are now bathing in.

After a few minutes, the process will become just a pure heart to Heart exchange of Divine Light. As you continue breathing, envision that you are completely basking in Divine white Light that is nourishing each cell and organ, and brightening your entire being and aura. Your heart and God's heart are a continuous beam of Light pulsating as One with each breath.

It is at that point that your mind will start being very calm and very still—no more brainfucking noise. It is within this stillness of mind that you'll experience a supreme peace, and the feeling that all is right in your world in the deepest sense; you are validated by just being you; you want for nothing; and all you want to do is continue to dwell in that blissful nurturing peace that you are experiencing. This blissful stillness is your sign that you have transcended the consciousness of the here-now self, and are tuned into your Soul Self. Another sign is that within this blissful stillness, everything that you do "see" or "hear" (internally) is crystal clear, extremely high vibrational, and in many cases profound.

This is the time when your here-now self can have a conversation with your Soul, and with the Guardians of your Akashic Records through your Spirit Guides and Angels. However, before you have this conversation with your Soul, it is absolutely essential for you to make sure you have reached the peaceful stillness, so that you can ensure that who you're actually talking to is indeed the higher aspect of your Soul, and not some lower aspect of your subconscious. The peaceful stillness, the clarity of messages, and the blissful feelings described above are your telltales at all times that you are tuned into your higher Soul consciousness.

When you ask each question, make sure that you are not collapsing your consciousness completely into the vibration of the here-now self. Just become loosely aware of the questions that your here-now self wants to ask, speak (silently, whisper, or out loud) those questions briefly as they surface, and then go back to your focus on the Divine white Light going in and out of your heart space. After each question, it is important to then breathe yourself back into the point of basking in the white Light… to bring yourself back into that blissful stillness that you were experiencing before asking the question, to make sure you go back into Soul consciousness. Then just be receptive to the visions, words, feelings, knowings, and healing energy that come to you from your Soul.

You may use this meditation to tune into your Soul consciousness to ask anything, even if you think it's trivial. Or you may, instead, direct this process to heal and receive nurturing energies. And that's the beauty of it is: the meditation is simple to do, and can offer you so much!

Of course, once you're in the blissful stage of the meditation, you'll usually just want to stay in it, since it is so nurturing, peaceful, and pleasant. Try doing this meditation daily, and you'll find it a useful tool to help you flow with your life more harmoniously, and in a way that is more closely guided by your Ideal Lifeplan.

Grounding

At the end of each meditation, you'll need to ground yourself. What is grounding? Grounding is really just another word for bringing your consciousness back into your here-now reality, and anchoring your energies into Earthly physical life. Along with this shifting of consciousness and energy, grounding also helps anchor the positive changes of your meditation into the here-now level of consciousness and reality, whether those changes are just peace of mind, clarity, or healing and co-Creative energy.

Many positive changes may happen in meditation: You may tap into important realizations and powerful Divine resources. But during the meditation, you usually are just blissed-out. It is the grounding of all these Divine energies that makes you feel awake, alert, balanced, sharp-minded, yet at the same time peaceful and in a state of Grace. And if through grounding you're bringing not only the bliss of your meditation into this reality, but also healing and Creative energy for your manifestations, than as you might be starting to realize, grounding is important.

There are many ways to ground: The simplest is by shifting your consciousness from your internal reality to your external one, and from meditatively dwelling in Universal Consciousness to your everyday wakeful state of mind. However, when doing this consciousness shift, make sure that you are concentrating on beautiful pleasant things in your external here-now reality. There'll be plenty of time to think about the grind of life later. Right now for the first few minutes after meditation, especially after a deep and blissful meditation, you want to bring the high vibration of the meditation into the here-now level of your reality, not crush your vibration into the gutter of life. So for the first few minutes after meditation, concentrate on happy beautiful things.

An effective and simple way to ground is through gentle body movements. Your ability to gently move your body in a healing and grounding way will increase when you learn Kindness Movement (taught in *A Lifestyle of Prosperity From Your Soul* and in the *Level 1 Prosperity From Your Soul* retreat course). But in general, let say that you were sitting for this meditation cross legged, with your spine erect, and your palms up on your laps for twenty minutes, breathing deep-yet-natural and comfortable Zohar Breaths. The first movement that will start your grounding process is to start deepening your breaths again into full deep long breathing. Then, start wiggling your fingers and toes; gently move your wrists and ankles in small circles; make gentle circles with your neck, and gently shake your shoulders feeling the fabulousness of your body. Then, start moving your upper body in a bigger, yet still gentle wave that feels very indulgent. It could be a forward and backwards snaking of your spine, or a side-to-side swing, a figure eight of some sort, or another type of movement; just make sure the movement is indulgent, gentle, and absolutely conveys kindness-to-self. Finally, open you physical eyes.

Another way to ground is to envision roots of orange Light connecting your root chakra and the soles of your feet with the center of the Earth. You can use your breath to exchange the orange Light with the center of the earth. Your crown and higher chakras will already be anchored into Divine white Light. So to ground, just envision that with each inhalation, you draw orange Light from the center of the Earth through your feet, legs, and perineum; and with every exhalation, are sending Light energy from your root chakra and through the soles of your feet to the center of the earth. After a few breaths, you'll feel peaceful yet very alive—grounded.

If you are a reiki practitioner, grounding is very easy: You just draw the #1 (Light-Power) symbol on the soles of your feet, reiki your feet, and intend to ground.

Sitting or lying close to the ground, especially close to nature, is grounding in a most natural way. If you want to more actively ground, stand up and envision yourself as a tree that has life-giving roots extending from your feet to the center of the Earth.

If in the middle of a hectic day, you find yourself losing your balance, prone to accidents (things falling out of your hands, you keep bumping into things, etc.), or just plain old feeling out-of-it, than you are definitely in need of grounding. If there are trees in your vicinity, touching or even hugging a tree will very actively ground you and make you feel more balanced. If not, than eat something, as food is very grounding too. A most wonderful way to ground, if you have access to it when you really need to ground, is go to the beach, bury your feet in the sand, deep breathe the fresh ocean air, and contemplate beauty for a few minutes. You can do something similar if you have access to mountains or any other place of nature. Just stand or walk barefoot for a few minutes, take in the fragrance of fresh air, and contemplate beauty.

If you are doing the meditation just before going to sleep, don't worry about grounding. You will ground yourself when you wake up, the way you normally do. You will probably wake up feeling very refreshed, and in a particularly good mood, like a new dawn of wonderful things has just started. This is the result of the healing that you receive during the night, as a result of your meditational invocation.

In this chapter, we have laid a strong foundation to the art of meditation, and I have given you the simple yet profound Zohar Breath Meditation, which lay the foundations for the more advanced meditational processes of the coming chapters, leading up to your tuning into the full detail of your Ideal Lifeplan.

Through this chapter, I hope you've realized that meditation is not some scary Eastern beast with horns; that it is really nothing more than just tuning your mind to… anything you want. It is a process of clearing your mind from junk, which allows you to use it more sharply, yet from a place of peace, to serve you in any way that you choose, from tuning deeper into your physical body functions; to achieving relaxation and peace at the end of a day; to tapping into the highest guidance of your Soul. If you think of your mind as a powerful beast that tends to get wild if not properly husbanded, than meditation is a way to ensure that you are in control of the beast, and not allow the beast to control you. When you become master of your mind, you become better able to use it to shift your emotions and energetic vibration into likeness and resonance with your True desires, and thus more powerfully co-Create your reality.

What's interesting is that sometimes you don't realize your need for meditation until you have experienced how much better you feel after it. Imagine that you were constantly (24/7) carrying on your shoulders a heavy toolbox full of unnecessary junk. You wouldn't notice the burden because you'd be used to carrying it all the time. But once you open the box and start throwing out the heavy junk that is no longer useful, you'd suddenly notice how light the box is, and only then you'd realize just how much junk you'd been carrying all this time. Well, meditation is a way to cleanse out the heavy junk you're carrying around in the "black box" of your mind. And you will find that once you lighten the load, all kinds of ideas and solutions will just come to you effortlessly.

In the next chapter, we'll start walking together through Stage 1 of the seven-stage process of becoming a more successful co-Creator of your most prosperous Lifepath.

Chapter 3

From Stress to Self-Validation

In this chapter, we actually begin our seven-stage process of becoming a conscious co-Creator of your reality—the process that would help you bring into focus the specific ways through which you are meant to bring about the all-inclusive prosperity for you and for your family.

As we have talked about, the first step in this seven-stage process is to dissolve all blocks and restore your free and unobstructed connection with the Infinite Funnel of Abundance. You see: you already are beloved, beautiful, radiant, worthy of every blessing, and Infinitely endowed. That is: your Soul Self is made of God's Love-Light, and is therefore endowed with every possible resource there is, including the financial prosperity you seek. We simply need to lift off all that might have, until now, been obstructing your connection with your Soul Self, so that you can tap into the Infinite resources that your Soul has been given mandate to manifest for you.

Now don't get too alarmed about the word "blocks" here. Carrying some energetic debris and subconscious programing does not reflect badly upon who you are, because who you Truly are is a radiant a child of God. It is only the human aspect of you that dwells in the illusion of this "physical" reality, and can therefore accumulate stress, anger, and all kinds of mental "I can't" blocks. What's more, you are in very good company, since everyone, including the holiest of religions leaders, accumulates some form of negativity, by virtue of the fact that we all human right now. And part of this human existence—by prior agreement—is that we dwell in this physical reality and buy into its perceived limitations, in order to gain the experience and growth it affords. With this reality's perceived limitations comes stress, sometimes anger and fear, sometimes disappointment and frustrations, and some mental and personality blocks that you've taken on as "challengers of the game" (remember our discussion on that in Chapter 2 of *Prosperity From Your Soul*). But again, you were never meant to carry all of those burdens throughout this lifetime. They were only meant to challenge you to grow from the experience, and be discarded once you have achieved the potential growth they afforded. So by virtue of your God-given free will, you have the power to order those negativities out of your life!

Once you remove all stuck energy from yourself and your life, your natural connection to the Infinite Funnel of Abundance will be restored, and the prosperity that was always meant to be yours will start flowing easily and abundantly into your life. Also, once you are free of all those burdens, you will naturally flow into stage two, as it will become easier to feel the joy, love, kindness and gratitude that would magnetize even more prosperity into your life. And of course, once you are living in a vibration of joy-love-kindness-gratitude, you are ripe to tune into your Ideal Lifeplan in all of its details, and to devise an active plan of action to make it all happen. But this flow of wisdom, bliss, and the resultant prosperity starts with cleansing out energetic, mental and emotional blocks. In fact, this cleansing is so important for the manifestation of your Ideal Lifepath that I have devoted two chapters to it.

This chapter is mostly about halting any additional stress from accumulating, by giving you some conceptual tools to fend off, discard, and rise above stressors in your everyday life. As trivial as it may seem, this is a monumental first step, since *choosing* to live every moment in life from a perspective of your Higher Self—taking the highroad, so to speak—is a moment-by-moment choice of directing your life towards your Ideal Lifepath.

Although most people tend to think of removing negativity as an uncomfortable process, you will find the discussions in this chapter logical and uplifting. Using the thought process included in this chapter will simply allow you to stop feeling stress, fear, self-judgment, frustration and the like, at the moment that you catch yourself starting to feel them. By halting any future negativity from "sticking to you," you are in effect retraining yourself to think more positively, rise above challenges, and therefore sharpening your ability to tap into your Infinite Funnel of Abundance at every moment in life. In the next chapter, I will give you specific meditational tools to cleanse and uproot any deep-seated negativity, so you can restore the flow of Abundance from the Divine in a more proactive way.

But the first layer of negativity is stress. Everyone gets stressed at one point or another, because in today's everyday reality, we all face circumstances that put us in a tight spot and stress the heck out of us. We all get agitated and angry sometimes. It could be because your boss pissed you off; you had an argument with your spouse; you are between careers and you have no idea how to make ends meet; you have PMS (men have them too); or the classic – there are too many things on your daily To Do list, and you are stressed for time. And when you get stressed, you know that you are not operating according to your Soul's guidance. In fact, stress is detrimental to your positive co-Creative efforts. So as a first step, understanding the nature of stress may help you blow its cover right out of the water. Because rationalizing away the causes for stress in your life will help you let go of your feelings of stress, at which point you would be able to use meditational practices to help you establish a new way of life that is more peaceful and better focused on your Ideal Lifepath.

So the first step to blowing stress out of the water is to mentally step outside your life circumstances for a moment, and see yourself from above the situation, with the view of an objective observer. We all have an objective observer inside us, one that is constantly in touch with Divine Truth. All you need do is remind yourself to tune into that observer, and once you do, it becomes very apparent that most stress (other than physiological stress) is self-imposed, and stems from the perspective that you adopt on each situation. Once you realize that, it becomes easier to either adjust your attitude and instantly dissolve the stress, or change the situation that's causing the stress. To help understand the roots of the stress in your life and how to "blow its cover," let's discuss some of the main categories of stress.

Three Minutes to Dissolving Stress

Because the very discussion about stress may bring up some stressful thoughts, before we start analyzing stress, where it comes from, and how to rationalize it away, I'd like to give you this magical tool that can alleviate stress energetically, in just three minutes! As you read this chapter, and in any stressful situation in life, remember that just three minutes of this visualization and deep breathing can reduce stress dramatically.

Find a quiet place in which you could be private for a few minutes (in a pinch, this could even be a bathroom stall on a short break during work). Briefly envision a bubble of white Light around you and your space to quickly cleanse that space of any low-vibrational energy. Sit down as comfortably as the situation allows, with your spine loosely erect, and your chin slightly tucked in. Close your eyes, and start gradually deepening your breath…

Start with Moon Breath (See Chapter 2)—breathe deeply in and out through your left nostril. Be very conscious of drawing the breath into your belly (working the diaphragm), and of making the exhalation a bit longer than the inhalation.

Once you get comfortable in Moon Breath pattern, start visualizing a scintillating column of slightly bluish-white Divine Light all around you. This Light is a very pure and distilled protective Cosmic Light-ray that has the ability to dissolve-neutralize any negativity (including stress). Envision the column of bluish white Light as coming from the center of the Universe, engulfing you completely, and continuing down to the center of the Earth… washing away all of your stress, worries, and issues in that moment. If you can't visualize, speak your intent to be engulfed in this column of Divine bluish-white Light, and keep that thought in your mind as you continue breathing deeply.

As you continue to breathe deeply, envision that with each inhalation, you are drawing the bluish white Light into you to nurture and protect you… and with each exhalation, you are actively sending all negativity up into the column of Light, to be completely dissolved and neutralized by the Light, harming no one. If you can't visualize, speak that intent. If your mind is really wondering, than every time that you take a deep inhalation, you can affirm to yourself silently: "I am now drawing the Divine bluish-white light to nurture and protect me," and with each deep exhalation, affirm to yourself: "I am now sending all negativity to be dissolved by the column of Divine bluish-white Light that's now surrounding me.

If you are experiencing extreme stress and fear, you can envision that as you inhale, you are taking the bluish white Light into your solar plexus area, and as you exhale, the Light is spreading out from that hub into a million spokes to spread all over your body and outwards. As you exhale the bluish white Light, envision that you are sending all stress, all worry, all fear, and all that doesn't serve your highest wellbeing, up the Light column. Again, if you cannot visualize, speak that intent as you deeply breathe. This bluish-white Light, since it is a distilled aspect of the Divine, along with your intent (free will), has absolute power to instantly dissolve all of what you do not want. It also calls upon Infinite resources to nurture you with kindness, peace, and abundance, to replace the energy that you let go of. So do not worry about polluting the Light or depleting it. Just keep inhaling the bluish white Light of the column and letting it nurture all of you… and keep exhaling and letting go, sending all negativity up the column to be dissolved. Allow yourself to feel the protection and safety that this Light column enwraps you with.

After a short while, you will begin to feel peace. Finish the meditation by envisioning yourself in a white-purple bubble of Light. Envision roots of Light extending from your perineum and feet into the center of the earth to ground yourself back into ordinary reality.

Now that you have this tool to energetically help you let go of stress, you should be ready to talk about the nature of stress, assess the stressors in your life, and decide what to do about not letting them get the best of you.

The Nature of Stress

Modern psychology's definition of stress[1] includes excitement as a form of "positive stress" (eustress) designed to activate your sympathetic nervous system in preparation for an enjoyable activity. However, when I talk about stress here, I am not referring to excitement, or to any type of "positive stress." If you are feeling positively excited and joyful about an activity, that is an indication that the activity is in alignment with your Ideal Lifeplan, and is therefore not a "negativity" that needs to be eliminated or even worried about, but simply constructive positive excitement and readiness.

Another type of stress that we will not discuss here is physiological. Physiological stress is legitimate and real. Lack of sleep, downtime, proper nutrition, adequate breathing, exercise, or sex can throw your body off balance to the point that it would not be able to perform at its best. The only way to alleviate physiological stress is to make sure you are being kind to your body-temple—the temple that your Soul inhabits in this lifetime—and giving it what it needs. Further, I can almost promise you that once you take better care of your body-temple and minimize physiological stress, about 70%-80% of your day-to-day stress and foul moods will disappear. You and I will still walk a long path in *A Lifestyle of Prosperity From Your Soul* to learn to be kinder to your body-temple, and prep it for the reception of the enhanced Creative energy that is to come through, as you start actually walking the path of a conscious co-Creator of your life. For that reason, I will exclude further discussion of physiological stress from this chapter.

The American Psychology Association[1] talks about three categories of stress. They describe Acute Stress as short-term pressure triggered by the demands of a particular event, such as a car accident, or having to meet a deadline at work. They further explain that certain types of personalities, such as type-A personality and perpetual worriers, tend to experience acute stress frequently, which then shifts their category of stress to Episodic Acute Stress. According to the APA, Chronic Stress "comes when a person never sees a way out of a miserable situation. It's the stress of unrelenting demands and pressures for seemingly interminable periods of time. With no hope, the individual gives up searching for solutions."

With all due respect, we are going to ignore the APA's definitions, firstly because when it comes to "Chronic Stress," you and I both know that no situation is ever really hopeless. This is what this book series is about: reminding you how empowered you Truly are to bring blessed changes into your life. And when it comes to the difference between "acute stress" and "episodic acute stress," I do not respect the way that they categorize people. Who are they to judge you, or me, or anybody else?! Who is to say that someone is a perpetual worrier? Perhaps a person used to frequently worry because that was how they were brought up. But at the core of each person is an angelic Soul who absolutely knows how to be peaceful and happy. So everyone, even if the circumstances of their lives have taught them to stress, can absolutely learn (maybe with the help of this book) to meditate, relax, enjoy life, and to always see the upside of things. And who is to say that someone is a type-A personality? Many people get trained from very early on in childhood to be competitive overachievers, but later learn that this way does not serve their highest Lifepath, doesn't make them happy, and doesn't necessarily lead to success. For example, I was trained by my father from a very early age to be a perfectionist. He used to say that when he plays a concert, he has to be 300% ready, because during the concert, 100% falls away due to nervousness, another 100% could go out the window if anything goes wrong, which still leaves 100% readiness. I was also trained by my mother (probably inadvertently) to worry and be suspicious about everything, since that was how she saw reality. But as I grew up and got to know my True Self, I discovered that I am a spiritual person first and foremost; that I naturally love and trust people; and that actually do enjoy flowing in harmony with life and letting Universal guidance carry me through life effortlessly. I leant to be kind to myself, to meditate, and I adopted a healthy, relaxed, and centered attitude about life, which is hopefully taking me towards my Ideal Lifepath. The bottom line is: People can and do change. It's not so much that they change at the core of who they are. It's that they restore themselves, or at least get closer to, whom they Truly are. Even at the core of our Souls, we are all constantly evolving (each at his/her own pace), growing, and making our Oneness more glorious with each life-lesson that we achieve.

So in this section, we look at stress from the perspective of knowing that you have the power to change anything you wish to change about yourself and your reality. Thus, I have divided stress into three new categories, based on what you can actually do about them:

Childhood Conditioning:

Childhood conditioning is related to any programing, abuse or trauma we have unknowingly been subjected to during our childhood, and unbeknownst to our conscious logical mind, is still affecting our decision-making, and clouding our view of reality. For example, my father was a very old-school educator. So growing up, in order to motivate me to excel, he used to often tell me: "You're not smart, and you're not the type of girl that a guy would turn his head to look at. You're going to have to work hard for everything you get in life." This caused me to grow up with a low image of myself. I understand now that my father's negative motivation was simply the only way he knew how to motivate his children to strive hard, which was the only way he knew to succeed. But as a young adult—throughout my twenties and thirties, I developed an overachieving "type-A" personality, as if to prove him wrong. His statements also made me develop a belief that everything in life must come hard, which became a self-fulfilling prophecy until I was in my mid thirties. Indeed, until that point, everything was hard to come by and required hard work. I began to work on myself to better my life. I was 21 years old when I first discovered (through testing) that my IQ was actually measured at 145, which blew my dad's statement right out of the water. But the cognitive knowledge still did not filter into real self-love and inner peace. My beloved grandmother told me that as a child, I was exactly the type of girl that strangers would stop and gosh over in the middle of the street. Of course, now as an adult, I look at my own childhood and teenage pictures, and I see that my grandma was right: I was a cute baby and a very pretty girl growing up. But it wasn't until I gained some spiritual wisdom that I gained the self-love and kindness to accept who I am, and the compassion to forgive. As I continued to meditate and heal myself with Reiki, my outlook on life gradually changed. As I opened myself to the radiant power of my Soul Self, everything started to flow into my life much more easily and abundantly. And I know now that the best treasures in life are the ones that flow easily and abundantly by Divine Grace. This is one example of childhood conditioning that was counterproductive to the manifestation of prosperity, and how to overcome it.

A more extreme example comes from the movie *The Three Faces Of Eve* (1957), which details the true story of a young woman with a three-way split personality, and the long process her psychologist went through to help her. One thing I found interesting in the movie was that at the end of the long process, they learn that the woman's complex condition was actually triggered by a one-time childhood event, which seemed pretty trivial to me: as a child, she was asked to say goodbye to her dead grandmother in an open casket funeral. And that seemingly trivial moment was the moment that split her personality into three. Although *The Three Faces Of Eve* was an extreme example, seemingly minor incidences affect major conditionings in all our psyches. Therefore stress relating to childhood trauma affects everyone to a lesser or greater extent, and it doesn't have to be a major incident that implants those stressful thought patterns in our minds. A simple incident of your older brother telling you that you can't do something because you are too little could have formed a major "I can't" program in your subconscious mind, of which you might be completely or partially unaware. One afternoon incident of following your mom around as a toddler, and her accidentally slamming the door on your face when she went to the bathroom could have formed within your psyche a pattern of feeling left out, unloved, or alone.

We all have these types of negative conditionings. And if you think about it, many of your everyday stresses are also rooted in deep-seated childhood programing like, "I'm stressed out from this test because deep down I think of myself as incapable" or, "I'm worried about what will happen because whenever things could go wrong, they will" or all kinds of other negative attitudes and expectations that you have internalized from somewhere during your development, but which do not originate from Truth.

The good news is that you have the power to change all those conditionings, and replace them with healthy attitude. And it does not take nine years of psychotherapy to do it either. It can be done in a few simple meditations, performed over a period of few weeks. The next chapter offers a meditation called Meditation To Remove Childhood Trauma, which I'm sure you'll find instrumental in eradicating and harmoniously dissolving childhood traumas and negative conditionings. It is the only meditation that will lead you through a process of recalling specific events in order to deprogram the limitations they have formed in your mind. The rest of Chapter 4 is devoted to meditations that will help you dissolve the energies of deep-seated conditionings and blocks without having to re-experience the traumas or recall the events associated with their forming. And if you live in a city where RezoDance is offered, attending regular RezoDance sessions will often affect a more powerful removal of all negativity, including unconscious childhood traumas. An even more powerful removal of deeply seated internal blocks is offered in the processes taught in the *Level 1 Prosperity From Your Soul* course. But even without RezoDance or the course, you are a powerful being. You have the power to discard any traumas, heal any scars, deprogram any limitations they may have imprinted in your mind, and reprogram your mind to help you live a life that is inspired by your Soul, so that you can manifest your most prosperous Lifepath. And the meditations in the next chapter will help you do all that deep deprograming in a comfortably nurturing way.

Self Expectation:

Everyone has self-expectations both on an everyday basis, and at the level of asking yourself periodically where your life is compared to where you think it should be at that point. We will talk more extensively about adjusting your daily expectations of yourself to incorporate more kindness-to-self later in this chapter, in Chapter 8, and in *A Lifestyle of Prosperity From Your Soul*. But when it comes to where your life is right now in relation to where you ultimately want it to be, that is a huge question, especially in light of the fact that we are in the process of removing any self-imposed glass ceilings.

Every adolescent boy and girl has grand dreams they expect themselves to fulfill in order to feel worthy and successful. Some of them were imposed by our parents who love us, and want us to be and have all that they never had. It's not just Jewish mamas or Italian mamas. It's everyone's mama who wants her boy or girl to grow up to be a successful lawyer, doctor, engineer… the next Napoleon Bonaparte or the next superman/superwoman. However, what your mama wanted you to become when you grew up—which you may have unknowingly internalized as your own will—and what You Truly want for yourself may be two entirely different things. A doctor friend of my dad's once told me the true life story of one of his colleagues. The colleague's dream was to become a violinist, while his father *for him* was that he be a doctor. The man ended up following his father's passion, not his own, until he became one of the most successful plastic surgeons in Europe. Although this man's medical career spanned over thirty years, his true passion remained playing music. So in his leisure time, he secretly learnt to play the violin, and began to give concerts with amateur chamber music ensembles. Though his achievements in the classical music arena were not extravagant, they made his heart sing. At the death of his father, after thirty years as a successful surgeon, he left his medical career, and devoted the rest of his life to music. The point is: most of us spend our twenties striving hard to establish a career path that we think would fulfill everyone's expectations. Then we spend our thirties and forties advancing that career, digging ourselves deeper into the niche that we've dug for ourselves. And then come our mid-forties and fifties, when we take a deep hard look at our lives, and realize that all this striving didn't quite get us to where we thought we wanted to be in life. We didn't exactly pin down that rainbow; and we didn't quite build that ladder to the moon. So we judge ourselves harshly for our past mistakes, and for all of those stars we haven't quite managed to capture.

But it doesn't have to be that way. For deep down, you must know that all of this self-judgment is unfair, unkind, and puts a tremendous pressure on you. No one is meant to capture the moon or become superman. You too aren't meant to be a super-mom, super-employee, super-brother/sister, or super-spouse to anyone. Rome wasn't built in one day either. And the funny thing is that the achievements that would give us each that deeply satisfied feeling that we seek (like we have indeed climbed Mount Everest) are much humbler, yet exponentially more profound. You see, the meaning of life isn't to become CEO of a Top-500 company; and it's not to have an investment portfolio worth over a million dollars. The meaning of life is to fulfill our life-missions—to learn the lessons and gain the experiences that Soul needs of Its growth—while experiencing love and joy. It is true that once you merge with your Ideal Lifepath, financial prosperity *is designed* to flow into your life easily and abundantly. But to avoid the pressure of "what the heck have I done with my life," and to actually feel fulfilled, you essentially have to feel love and joy deep within the core of your being. And if you don't feel that Love, joy, and connectedness with the Divine deep within, you will be dissatisfied with your life no matter what your tangible achievements are. For example, most people who know me outside the spiritual circles (including my parents) consider my having been a captain in a major airline my greatest achievement. But having also taught many budding pilots, I know that you can teach a monkey to fly an airplane, and given enough time and determination, the monkey can eventually reach the goal of being an airline pilot if it stays the course. What *I* actually consider my greatest achievement is: having a heart that loves people unendingly, being a reiki master—a safe-keeper of the Divine reiki energy, and being a clear channel for the wisdoms in this book series. I know that being a loving person, teaching reiki, and writing a few books don't seem like much to most people, compared to the achievements of some successful executives. But for me, those humble achievements are what alleviates my self-expectations stress, and gives me the feeling that I've done something worthwhile with my life. And incidentally, it is these small achievements that connect me to whom I Truly am, and thus what brings about real prosperity from my Soul into my life.

To translate all this into a more realistic understanding: The professional arena that each of our True talents translate to may be different for each of us. But if you recall our discussion about your Ideal Lifework (in *Prosperity From Your Soul*), the deep feeling of professional satisfaction and self-actualization that we all seek comes from your Ideal Lifework—the occupation that capitalizes on your Truest gifts and desires, as inspired by your Soul, which lead to and through your Ideal Lifepath, dipped in Love and joy in all the small moments of life. And when you are walking this Ideal Lifepath, you feel so fulfilled that it doesn't matter what other people think. They'll all come around once you start treating yourself with kindness, and reclaiming your True radiance. And as we've discussed, don't worry about the money either. Once you shift yourself to engage in your True Ideal Lifework, financial prosperity *is designed* to flow into your life effortlessly, as an integral part of your Ideal Lifepath.

And the interesting thing is that once you stop judging yourself and start trusting the Universe to provide for you, you'll be surprised just how huge the reduction of stress is.

Once you let go of judgment—when you start looking at your life objectively and honestly in light of what you know now (after having read *Prosperity From Your Soul*), you may as well acknowledge that your best opportunity for the manifestation of prosperity does not necessarily lie in the career path that you and other people have previously expected it to, but in the that path that most closely resonates with the deepest yearnings of your heart— your True bliss. At the same time, your life may not be as far off course as you may think. In fact, it may not be off course at all. If you meditate deeply on the lessons learnt through your life experiences so far, you'll most likely realize that at least some of your life experiences have been perfect as they were, because through those experiences, your Soul has learnt many lessons that It needed for Its growth. You'll also realize that many of the difficult circumstances of your life allowed you to come into your power and rise above them. Of course, when you meditate on where your life Truly is from the perspective of your Soul, you will no doubt find that where you are right now is a perfect jumping board towards your Ideal Lifepath of prosperity, health, and happiness. This is the process that we are going through together: tuning into the Ideal Lifepath that will make you ultimately happy and successful. So the bottom line is: even if it doesn't seem that way, everything is going perfectly according to plan, and nothing can undo God's perfect handiwork, crafting this perfect moment in your life.

All that being said about the perfectness of this moment in your life, there is the matter of knowing which of your life circumstances you should gracefully accept as blessings in disguise, and which circumstances no loner serve on your highest Lifepath of success. And this is an art form that can be learnt through tuning into the wisdom of your Soul, which you have already started to do do in Zohar Breath Meditation.

But just to put your mind at ease about where you are in life: By virtue of the fact that you are reading these lines, I know that you have already started walking the path of a conscious co-Creator of your life. Even if you have done nothing but read until now, just developing the consciousness that you are worthy and capable of reclaiming a more Ideal Lifepath already puts you at an advantage over where most other people are in their lives. Because sadly, most people go through life like a herd, neither knowing nor caring to find out what their potential Ideal Lifepath is. And though seeing manifestation results may take some time (depending on how ripe you are), you have already begun to contemplate your Ideal Lifepath, and therefore have already begun to alter the mundane course of your life, and navigating it towards your Ideal Lifepath. You already passed the hardest part of realizing that you want more and are worthy of it. It took courage to imagine more for yourself, and go for it. And you have already mustered that courage. So trust your process, and know that it will lead you to co-Create for yourself all the blessings that you Truly wish for in the days to come. It is not me that I'm asking you to trust. It is yourSelf—the inner wisdom that made you pick up this book series and read it, your inner wish to co-Create a more prosperous life for yourself, the way that the Truths of these books resonate within you, and the new path that is already starting to formulate deep in your subconscious. Most importantly, trust your Soul's guidance, and keep tuning into the joy and radiance of who you Truly are as a beloved child of God.

Daily Stress:

Daily stress comes in many forms and shapes. But if you meditate on the stressors of your life, and are able to at least momentarily see your life's circumstances from the viewpoint of a conscious observer, you will realize that much of the stress that afflict your life is—no offense—self-imposed. From the vantage point of your Soul, whatever the cause of your stress is, all you can do is your heart-centered best, and then set your deeds free and let the chips fall where they may. The rest is up to the Universe. So you might as well relax, breathe, and think positive, so you can magnetize good things into your life. To fully understand this, here are some examples of daily stresses that typically afflict people (myself included):

Time Stress ~

During our everyday lives, most of us take on ourselves way too many tasks in a short period of time. And if you think objectively about what's on your daily To Do list, you'll conclude that this heaping list would have best been stretched over at least a week. If you really think about this list that you demand of yourself, many of the To Do items were not immediately necessary. In fact, many times (not always), what drives you to procrastinate is that at a higher level, you are tuning into the fact that something is going to happen in the near future that would make achieving some of the tasks easier or non-issues. Think about how many times you have stressed yourself to find time and patience to call the phone company or a doctor's office about an overcharge in your bill, only to find out that an adjustment of this bill in your favor was already in the mail. For example, in the writing of these books, I had some periods in which I simply felt like I was just not able to complete a chapter. And a week or a month later, I meditationally received additional channeled information that made the chapter complete in a way that I (my here-now self) could not have logically completed it before. Many times, the need for some of the items on your To Do list dissolves in the perspective of even a couple of days later.

Another example of time-stress that is illogical is when you're driving somewhere, you're running late, and traffic is horrendous. In this situation, you already have mounted too many things for yourself to do that day; you already have left your point of origin too late; and traffic is already what it is. So logically, from the cool perspective that you are in right now, do you think there any point in worrying about it? Or does it make more sense to call and let someone know that you're running late, put on some relaxing music, engage in some uplifting thoughts, and make the drive into a beautiful moment in life that you can enjoy?

Now I'm not saying that procrastination important tasks, or being careless about showing up for appointments on time are good policies in life. But not showing up for appointments on time is clearly the result of your daily To Do list being too long—you didn't allow enough time for unexpected delays or for the drive, not to mention time for slowing down, smelling the flowers, and just enjoying the day. Procrastination is the other end of the spectrum in terms of time-stress. While it sometimes is anchored in your higher guidance telling you to that a more harmonious solution is already on its way to you, other times procrastination just originates from a self-defeating old programing that does not serve your highest good. But it's not an either-or proposition. It's a matter of finding balance—a balance that only you can find. Yes, I don't doubt that most of the things you've mounted on your daily To Do list were anchored in some level of truth. But the pressure to finish *all* tasks in the short amount of time that you arbitrarily allotted for them stems from *you*. You are the one who is imposing this pressure on yourself, where instead, you could have taken a few deep breaths, and felt validated enough to tell the world to hold off. Stretching the completion of these tasks over a time period that would allow you to really enjoy each one of them would not only eliminate stress, but would also get you into an energetic vibration of joy, pleasure, and a feeling of self-fabulousness, all of which co-Create an attractive resonance with the prosperity you seek.

The Stress of Satisfying Other People –

Many types of circumstances fit under this subject, from satisfying your boss, to satisfying the expectations of your parents, your friends, or your spouse… The stress really originates from *your* perception of the demand of others in your life, *your* spoken agreement with concepts that contradict to your True beliefs, *your* agreement do things which fall outside your True ability or will to do, or another conflict with what *you* Truly want.

Now, others may indeed have expectations from you. But the most important expectation you should worry about fulfilling is that of your Soul: speaking your highest Truth out of a position of peaceful strength; and doing your heart-centered best to fulfill each task that your Soul inspires you to fulfill. Following your Truth and doing your heart-centered best is all that's required of you! And incidentally, these are also the Truths and actions that are ultimately the kindest to everyone involved. So once you speak and act from your core Truth, there is no place for worrying about what other people think. If others are not satisfied with actions that are inspired by the Truth of your Soul, than nothing on Earth could satisfy them. And that is totally their issue. Realize that as much as you love and respect the people in your life, they may have their own issues, biases and karmas. Therefore they may not be acting from their core Truth. Walking your Ideal Lifepath of success, you cannot go wrong by following your heart. Acting on your Truth is the ultimate way to manifest all-inclusive prosperity! So knowing that you did your heart-centered best should give you enough peace of mind to dissolve all stress of satisfying others.

However, this is not about being stubborn and bunkering in your position. Keep in mind that your Soul's Truth may not necessarily be the same as your initial position on a matter. What it is about is *finding out what your highest Truth is first, and then acting on that conviction, doing your heart-centered best joyfully, and then feeling complete with your actions, without feeling the need to argue about it, defend it, or feel guilty about not satisfying others.*

So when you realize you are stressed because of other people's perceived expectation from you, or because of a disagreement with others in your life, the first thing you need to ask yourself is: "How do I (my Soul Self) Truly feel about that? What does my Soul think is the right thing to do in this situation?" Here is your first opportunity to use Zohar Breath Meditation to tune into some answers from your Soul's perspective. But even before the meditation—even at first glance—here is one quick way to know which level of truth you are tuned into with regards to your thinking about the matter: your here-now level of truth can leave you feeling uneasy, not fully satisfied from the solution, and incomplete – like something is missing. And it usually perpetuates the brainfucking noise going on in your mind. On the other hand, your higher-level Truth leads you to a peaceful serene feeling of deeply knowing-feeling that your choice was right. No brainfucking. No excuses. And no need to justify yourself or bend over backwards for others.

<u>Financial Stress</u> –

Financial stress is a big subject. But I hope that by now, you are beginning to internalize the knowing that the Universe will always provide for all of your needs. More than that, the Infinite Divine will fulfill all of your earnest desires. If you open yourself up to prosperity from the Infinite Source, and walk the highest path you were meant to walk in life (which we are learning to do in this book), the amount of financial prosperity that's in store for you is truly Infinite, and will most likely surpass your highest expectations.

What to Do When Stressed, Agitated or Just Pissed Off

At this point, we understand that dissolving stress, agitation, foul moods, and anger is an important step towards shedding off the first layers of unnecessary energetic density, in order to allow the true Light of your Soul to flow more freely into your co-Creative endeavors. And from our previous analysis of stress, we also understand that stress is subjective. But you might be asking is; "What shall we do to eliminate stress?" Of course, the most immediate and basic tool to alleviate stress is to just remind yourself that stress is self-imposed. And in the last section, I've given you some conceptual tools to do that.

But this rationalization may not always be enough to uplift and dissolve moderate or severe stresses that might be weighing heavily on your health, happiness, and co-Creative abilities. So this section will give you some practical tools—a logical step-by-step instruction to deal with stress as it comes, dissolve it, and wind up on a higher road.

Step 1 – Remove Yourself from the Situation & Cool Down:

It is never a good idea to make important decisions fueled by anger! Recall from *Prosperity From Your Soul* the discussion about non-reaction as a way to achieve liberation and a resultant auspicious life. But non-reaction is not just a loftier-than-thou idea. It has very practical implications. Even the most practical thinkers agree that a knee-jerk reaction is not the smartest move when it comes to relationships, business, work environment, health, and just about any important area in life.

So the first step in dealing with a negative situation is to remove yourself from the situation. This is especially true if you are in a situation when you are physically in danger. I mean, you don't want to allow yourself to get mugged in a dark alley in Beijing just because of a self-imposed need to be more polite to your muggers. Removing yourself from danger is not considered a low vibrational reaction or cowardice. You are removing yourself from the situation, in order to reassess and regroup.

However, this non-reaction does not mean internalizing the anger and stewing on it. It doesn't mean letting the other party have the upper hand, not by a long shot. And it definitely does not mean sucking up to your boss, betraying your own inner convictions, or rolling over and playing dead. For example, if you were about to get mugged, once you remove yourself from the situation, you can always call the police. If you got unjustly yelled at by your boss, spouse, mother-in-law… you can always give them a piece of your mind later, after you have given yourself a chance to cool down, re-center yourself, and measure your response. Once centered, you can measure your response based on the wisdom of your True Self. And any Truth obtained from your Soul Self does not need defending or justifying, as it will always be calm, graceful, yet firm, and in line with your True beliefs.

This doesn't necessarily mean that you take the rest of the day off every time you've argued with your boss. You can absolutely take a bathroom break, where you can do a Three Minutes to Dissolving Stress Meditation, or even just a few Moon Breaths in the bathroom, so that you can then carry on your day without stress. Save your real response for the next day after you've had a chance to cool down further, and meditate more deeply. This cool down time is also a time to meditationally tap into the wisdom of your Soul, who has the advantage of all-knowingness, and can therefore afford you an invaluable perspective on how to act most appropriately in this situation.

Step 2 – Burning Off Steam & Letting Go of the Anger:

This may seem pretty elementary, but – why is anger such a bad thing? Because harboring negative feelings and thoughts ultimately eats at the person carrying them. This is a well-known fact, from both a spiritual and a psychological perspective. If you have a neighbor who is trying to make your life miserable, your anger at him/her means that he/she has succeeded in making your life miserable. Your neighbor may have a much thicker skin than you. So just minutes after he/she's yelled at you, your neighbor may be enjoying watching the ball game or laughing out loud watching a movie, while you are left stewing on the anger. Eventually, these negative thoughts and feelings will turn into negative energies that block the free flow of Creative Ki into your life, which can manifest as health ailments, unhappiness, and restrictions in the flow of your Infinite Funnel of Abundance. Your anger may be absolutely justified. But in the end (and in the middle too), the person who is most severely taxed by it is not the object of the anger, but the person who carries it. This is why Mikao Usui, the founder of reiki, lived by five principles: "Today only, do not anger; do not worry; live with gratitude; work diligently; and be kind to every living thing." Notice that letting go of anger and worry are the first two principles.

Indeed, removing the negative energetic imprints of a bad situation is essential to regaining the perspective of your Soul, receiving Its directive on the best course of action, and allowing prosperity to flow in more freely through your Infinite Funnel of Abundance.

There are three levels of purifying yourself from these unwanted energetic imprints:

Physical Level – Blow Off Steam –

Blowing off steam by engaging physical activity is the physical aspect of removal of negativity. For some people going to the gym and blowing off some steam does it. For others, swimming, kneading dough, yoga, or other activities is their way of blowing steam. Most people already know, at least in the back of their mind, what cools them off and brings them back to their center. Just keep in mind that the physical activity you engage in should be enjoyable, even if it's just meant to blow off steam. And I'll explain in *A Lifestyle of Prosperity From Your Soul* the multidimensionality of why it is so important for it to be enjoyable.

As always, I recommend tapping into your considerable inner wisdom to know which activity to choose, in order to cool yourself off and reconnect you to your most peaceful centered Self. Here are some things I have found useful for burning off negativity and instilling peaceful positive feelings on a physical level:

- ☯ Moon Breaths (Chapter 2)
- ☯ Chocolate contains a substance called phenyl ethylamine (PEA), which is mood-elevating, antidepressant, and promotes euphoric feelings of love and happiness. Besides that, chocolate contains large amounts of the important antioxidants flavonoid and phenolic, which help prevent heart disease, stroke and many cancers[2]. But when I say chocolate, I am not talking about your average supermarket Hershey's-style chocolate, which is high in white sugar, saturated fats, and all kinds of unpronounceable ingredients! I am talking about chocolate that contains a high percentage of cocoa beans, and not many other ingredients. I like Scharffen Berger 82%, which has only three natural ingredients in it besides pure cocoa beans, or Green & Black 85%.
- ☯ Herbal tea brewed from chamomile, mint, lavender, passionflower, motherwort, celery, hop, skullcap, or valerian (not all together) can be extremely relaxing. I remember shopping one day and feeling pretty agitated and stressed. I mean, as spiritual as I am normally, on that day I was so agitated, I was ready to punch someone. Then I stumbled across a specialty tea store, which carried all kinds of herbal tea combination that they brewed from loose-leaf herbs. I ordered a tea that contained chamomile, mint and lavender, and sat at the tea-bar where sipped it slowly, taking some deeper breaths of the tea's aroma as I sipped it. By the time I got halfway through the cup, I was so relaxed I was almost ready to sleep. So don't underestimate the healing power of herbal tea to relax you. Be careful, thought, with hop, skullcap and valerian root, as those *will* put you to sleep. Do not drink a tea from those herbs if you intend to drive, operate machinery, or do anything that requires focus and concentration. Next comes the question of whether to drink the tea hot or cold. If you are really rattled, than after you allow the tea to brew and absorb the herbs' taste for at least 10 minutes, pour it over ice and drink it cold. The cold temperature of the tea will cool off your excessive chi. If you want the tea to soothe you into a deep relaxation or sleep, drink it hot. And if you are ready to sleep within an hour or two (and don't intend to drive), than you may as well spike it with some valerian, skullcap and hop. That way, you'll at least sleep very well.

- Food – In many cases, the reason for our agitation is hunger. Not that our opponent is without blame. But on a full stomach, you usually would not react as harshly to the same insult as you would on an empty stomach. So carrying some healthy snacks with you may help tide you over until the next meal, and prevent hunger-induced overreaction. In extreme stress situations, any comfort food can help soothe your moods from a physical standpoint.
- Nature Healing (Chapter 5) and Nature Walk (*A Lifestyle of Prosperity From Your Soul*)
- Beach walk – the negative ions released by the ocean mist saturating the beach air have a very soothing, grounding affects on the body and mind.
- Gym workout, if you know that to be effective for you
- Meditative swimming. Movement through water is slower and more peaceful than movement on the surface, because of the water's resistance. Water also allows us to float and move in three-dimensional space that's reminiscent of our Soul's freedom in Its natural habitat. And because seventy percent of the human body is composed of water, we have a natural affinity to it, which along with water's yin-like energy, makes water very soothing and grounding. I usually spend my lap-swimming time meditatively letting go of stress and worries, visualizing Divine Light engulfing me, and mentally projecting the sacred reiki symbol to heal me and my life-issues. While your meditative process in the pool (or ocean) may be different than mine, this is a practice that always restores my peaceful radiance, and makes me feel more aligned with my Soul Self.
- Attend RezoDance daily (if it is offered in your area)
- If you decide to participate in *Level 1 Prosperity From Your Soul Course*, once you become initiated as a reiki practitioner, doing daily reiki self-healing will do wonders to eliminate all levels of stress and restore your radiance.

As you can see, the suggested activities range from just doing some deep breathing and eating a snack, which only take a few minutes to do, to going for a walk, a swim, or a gym workout, which take at least an hour to do, to participating in RezoDance and *Level 1 Prosperity From Your Soul Course*, which are more time consuming. The effectiveness of the tool depends of course on the cause of the agitation, and on what resonates with you. But generally, I have found Nature Walks, RezoDance, and retreat courses to be the most effective. They are the bulldozers that lift the large boulders out of your path. On the other hand, other activities such as beach walks, Moon Breath, or doing any of the meditations detailed in this book, take less time, and are therefore useful for burning away negative energy and restoring your peaceful center on a more daily basis.

<u>Emotional Level – Exorcising The Agitation & Sadness Within</u> –

Most times, your Soul's wisdom will guide you to rise above negative feelings. In some cases, however, a persistent stressed and agitated emotional state is a cue from your Soul Self that some issue in your here-now reality needs your concentrated attention. In such cases, it may be wise for you to use the sharp energy of your agitation to confront the issue head-on. I've had plenty of times in which I woke up uncontrollably agitated, and decided to use that energy to pay and argue about some bills, only to discover later that the deadline for addressing some of those bill-issues was that same day. What really is happening in those cases is that your Soul Self is giving you an extra oomph to deal with a certain issue with gusto. Not knowing what the issue is, or ignoring it out of fear, causes the extra oomph energy to accumulate as agitation. And in these cases, harnessing the agitation energy and converting it back to gusto and courage will absolutely dissolve the agitation, as well as help you confront the issue. However, knowing when there is an actual underlying issue, and when your agitated moods just stem from the overflowing brainfucking noise is the domain of the Soul.

If you think of agitation, anger or sadness from the perspective of your Soul, you will realize that the current drama in your life is but one episode of the particular theme that is to give your Soul the experiences needed for Its growth. Many difficulties were meant for you to immediately circumvent or rise above them in order to let you experience of your own strength. Other challenges were meant to redirect you into a different path, give you a message, or teach you something. But some situations were set up for you by You in order to help you experience more fully the well-rounded flavor of your many aspects. Remember that the whole of who you are is not just a whitewashed image, but richly colored picture with a full array of color – the most symphonic version of yourself. So some of those seemingly dissonant themes, which are meant to help you experience yourself more fully, must be allowed to run their course and purge out completely, before you can reconnect with your inner cell of Godlikeness.

When a particular (relating to a particular theme) sadness or anger keeps reoccurring in your life, it might be a calling from your Soul to get to the bottom of it and dissolve the core issue that is causing these feelings. It just might be one of those themes meant for you to let run its course. Because if the persistent sadness is an aspect of yourself that you were meant to fully experience in order to learn something that can only be learnt by reaching into your depth, than until you allow yourself to fully immerse in it, the same theme will keep reoccurring in your life over and over in different versions… until you exorcise it. It is like a pimple: if you squeeze some of the pus out, than the pus remaining inside will keep getting re-infected and creating new pimples again and again… until you go to an esthetician who can squeeze all the pus out, disinfect the area, and by that, start the healing process. Essentially, that is what you are doing by allowing yourself to exorcise the sadness: allowing all the pus to drain out and disinfecting the area in order to give it a chance to heal. So for those themes that you feel may have a deeper root, you must allow yourself a quiet evening of music, moonlight, feeling things deeply, and perhaps even letting yourself cry it all out, in order to fully purge that theme out of your life, and feel relieved and lighter the next day. After all, tomorrow is another day.

And here is why it is important to purge out uncomfortable feelings: because if you stifle them inside, those feelings can create energetic blocks that can make you doubt the Divine plan, the righteousness of your path in it, and the hopefulness of your situation. Moreover, it is this internal heaviness with which external negativities (stress, worry) energetically bind. Purging out these feelings dissolves the roots of the negativity, so that it never has to manifest again. Once you have devoted a short time (an evening, a day) to letting yourself fully feel them in a very concentrated way, you have fully gained the benefit of the experience and the growth it affords, and therefore there would be no need for this theme to reappear in your path again.

One thing to do on a quiet alone evening is to play music that you know sends you into those deep spaces within. Lighting candles and incense can help. Allow yourself to go to the core (the reason) of the sadness, feel it deeply, and cry out those tears. As you unload these tears, you purge out the negative feelings. Don't forget to pray and ask your Angels to help heal those issues at the core. When things get too heavy, envision sending that heaviness into a God Bubble of Light, and then take a few Zohar Breaths to tune into your Soul's perspective. Your Soul may have a better perspective on all the issues of your life, so asking It to help you see the lessons that were embedded in difficult themes can help you finish the lesson, and thus dissolve the difficult themes associated with it. As you fully delve into the depth of a particular theme, it may help you to end the evening with Cord Cutting Meditation (see next chapter), followed by a Self Nurturing Meditation (Chapter 5).

Finally at the end of this catharsis, rise above, and write down in your journal any important messages from your Soul. Thank your Soul Self for all that you are, for all that you have, and for this opportunity to deeply experience your own vastness. Set a prayerful intent to wake up in the morning feeling cleansed, refreshed, and positively vibrant, and I can almost promise you that it will be so (especially if you invite Archangel Raphael to help you heal).

All this being said, if the sadness within is *not* a reoccurring "must experience" theme set up by your Soul Self—if it is just a fleeting emotion (PMS, for example), than exorcising it *can* be done just as effectively through laughter or singing. Laughter is a great tool. The new research field of gelotology teaches us that laughter can lower blood pressure, increase the flow of oxygenated blood, reduce the levels of stress hormones in the body, increase the effectively of tumor and disease-fighting cells, and increase your alertness and mental agility. Laughter also gives your face, neck, chest, back, and diaphragm muscles a good workout. Laughter is the opposite of stress. And on an energetic level, laughter breaks through negativity by tuning into joy and grounding its high vibration to help dissolve stress.

Singing is also a great way to exorcise the access energy, while shifting your mood to joy. And True joy is of Divine essence—it is the energy of Her-His Light that can break through any negativity, and burn through any energetic blocks. As always, use your considerable inner wisdom to ascertain which way is best for you to exorcise and purge out negative emotions. The important thing is that you squeeze out all of the pus, so to speak, so you can rise up fresh in the morning – ready to grab life by the balls and say, "here I am life – I'm a winner!"

Spiritual Level – Energetic-Spiritual Removal of Negativity –

As a spiritual practice, it is always important to energetically remove negativity from your life and your space. But it is never more important than at times in which negativity has actually manifesting in the circumstances of your life. Especially in those times, it is particularly important for you to energetically cleanse yourself and your personal space several times a day with your prayerful intent and the tools given for clearing and protection in Chapter 1. Some additional calming tools are: Moon Breath, Grounding Breath (Chapter 2); aromatic essential oils, such as lavender, chamomile, frankincense, orange, mandarin, vetiver, sandalwood, or ylang-ylang, burnt in a dispenser or even rubbed on your chest; and adding a few drops of Bach Rescue Remedy (a flower essence available in health food stores in the forms of tincture or candy) to a glass of water that you drink.

Amazingly, cleansing negative vibrations at the energetic level is the most powerful tool to removing negativities from the physical level, since by doing so you are correcting things at their source—the energetic imbalances that allowed the negativity to manifest in the first place.

I get that at this point, you might be shaking your and saying, "Well, in the heat of a stressful moment, I don't have time to pray, let alone burn sage." You might be thinking that this process is too long, and therefore not handy enough. But consider the following scenario: Your boss pissed you off and you feel you are about to explode—an instinctive reaction that you may regret later. But you happened to read this book, and so you have started carrying with you some healthy snacks, Bach Rescue Remedy, and a tiny bottle of soothing essential oils. So you decide to try this process. You immediately remove yourself from the situation by taking a bathroom break. In the bathroom, you rub on your neck some of the calming essential oil, put three drops of Bach Rescue Remedy under your tongue (or suck on one of those Rescue Remedy candies), and then sit in your bathroom stall to do two minutes of Moon Breath, then a minute of Grounding Breath, and end with envisioning yourself in a bubble of violet Light. Then, feeling much better, you return to your office relaxed and ready to complete the day's work. You cruise through your day more calmly, knowing that later that evening, or during the weekend, you will do a Zohar Breath Meditation to find a solution that draws on the wisdom of your Soul, and hopefully eliminate the problem at the core. And miraculously, somehow it seems that your boss, and everyone in the office, is nicer to you for the rest of the day. The "objective" circumstances that were causing the argument or the stress seem to have subsided. This is just one scenario to emphasize how effective this process can be. There are obviously an endless number of causes that could have brought about this stressful situation, all of which can benefit from this process. This brings us to Step 3.

Step 3 – Determine the Root Cause of the Issue:

After you have removed yourself from the situation, have cooled off some, and have eliminated the first immediate layer of negativity, it is time to get to the core of the issue and solve it. So find an opportune moment in which you can have some alone, quiet time, perhaps in the evening or weekend after the event, and do a Zohar Breath Meditation (Chapter 2). Use the process of the meditation to deeply tune into the highest wisdom of your Soul. Verbally ask for guidance from your Angels and Spirit Guides (or any other deities that you believe in).

This time, in the first few minutes of Zohar Breath Meditation, you'll probably devote the exhalations to visualizing the elimination of negativity. But after a few minutes, hopefully you'll be able to focus on inhaling and exhaling the Divine white Light, after which the now familiar sublime peace of your Soul will set in.

This peace means you are tuned into the wisdom of your Soul and are privy to your Akashic records. From this sublime perspective, let your here-now self ask your Soul Self (and your Spirit Guides) what the root cause for the issue is, and what the highest-vibrational solution to it is.

If no message immediately jumps to mind, that's OK. Keep in mind that your Soul might be conducting some energetic healing on you, which in this case may be more pressing than the cognitive understanding. You might also be receiving wisdom in a higher form that your cognitive mind is not yet capable of deciphering. And that is OK. Bathe for a while in this sublime peace, while you do more Zohar Breaths… until a message appears in the form of an inner vision, voice, feeling, or knowing.

Although it is impossible to forecast and list all possible causes for negative feelings, here are some common issues that often cause people unexplained feelings of stress, agitation, sadness, foul-mood, and the like. Of course, these are only examples. The real issue that you are dealing with may be more complex, and your Soul's wisdom is the only one Truly qualified to advise you exactly how to solve it.

Physical –

Despite the fact that your Soul is always in a state of bliss, the condition of your body-temple can greatly affect the flow of Spirit through your energetic bodies and centers, which consequently affects your mental, emotional and physical states. So the first level of causes that needs to be ruled out is physical. Exactly *because* your Soul is always in a state of bliss, most often it is a physical issue that causes you to feel uneasy, agitated, or pissed off. And the reason that physical things need to be ruled out first, is that they are the easiest to fix in most cases.

So while you are at the beginning stages of your Zohar Breath Meditation, before you tune more deeply into the highest consciousness of your Soul, ask yourSelf:

- Have you gotten enough sleep in the last 24 hours?
- Could your agitation be attributed to accumulated fatigue?
- Are you hungry? (Hypoglycemia causes foul mood in many people)
- Are your sexual needs satisfied? (Don't laugh too hard. You'd be in awe of just how much calmer, more helpful and polite customer service representatives, and indeed everyone in your immediate surroundings would be if they all orgasmed regularly. This is a valid question that directly relates to your overall wellbeing.)
- Are you PMSing? (Men have PMS too, as they too have hormonal cycles. They just don't bleed, and their cycles are about 45 days instead of 28 days.)

Continue asking your Soul questions, as you feel guided to do, until you either get to the reason for your foul mood or rule physical causes out.

Empathy –

The second level of causes that you should check for is empathy. Are you absorbing others people's stressed energy through your empathic connection with them? As previously discussed, empathy is a wonderful thing, but needs to come out of a strong spirit, so that you can actually send positive energy towards the object of your empathy, not absorb their negativity.

So while still in your Zohar Breath Meditation, bring your mental focus back into breathing Divine white Light in and out of your heart-space… go deeper into your Soul's consciousness, until you feel the supreme peace, nurturing, and clarity-of-mind of your Soul's presence. Then ask your Soul if the negativity originated from you, or whether you absorbed if from someone else. Ask your Soul to help you dissolve that negativity and heal yourself. You might have to do some deeper breaths to facilitate the enhanced healing energy.

Also ask your Soul what the best way is for you to avoid absorbing other people's negativities in the future. This is a personal question, since everyone's situation is different. There might be behavioral things or conceptual things that you need to change to stop absorbing negativity from others; it might be some specific aura-strengthening meditation; or any other practice that makes you immune to such influences, and your aura strong and radiant.

Nurturing ~

Are you having a healing crisis? One of the most basic human needs is the need to be loved and nurtured on all levels, which in today's society is a need that is not being met enough, especially in single, divorced, or widowed people living alone.

So again, while still in Zohar Breath Meditation, ask your Soul if your crisis is indeed a healing crisis—if your agitation originated from not having received enough Love. Also ask your Soul what the best avenue is for you to receive loving-nurturing energy. For some people, it is getting together with some good friends, talking things out, and exchanging bear hugs. For others, a professional massage can do the trick. So ask your Soul about the best way that is available to you and would make you feel nurtured.

Bigger Life Issues ~

Most people are aware, at least at some level, of bigger life issues that are weighing on them, such as an existing relationship or work issue. However, even in those times in which you think you know what the problem is, it is wise to still do the meditation to calm yourself down and tune into your Soul Self, as the issue might be effecting you more than you realize; or it might have deeper roots that you have not considered, which may have worsened the potency of the issue. Your Soul Self is also *the most* qualified adviser on what to do with bigger life issues

If you are stressed out because of some bigger life decision that needs to be made, this might actually be a good thing. In many cases, the feeling that your cognitive self interprets as stress actually originates from the inner you, who has realized that you are indeed worthy of having a better life—a realization that is bubbling up inside you, giving you new strength. And this bubbling feeling that a positive life change is imminent is a wonderful thing, because the deep knowing that you are validated, beloved and capable of achieving greatness can really only come from one place: your Soul Self. It's only your here-now mind that is dreads of the coming change and automatically assumes it is a threat that you need to be protected from. But that's natural, since your here-now (ego) self's job is to protect your human form. So out of that fear the coming change, your subconscious here-now self creates a defense mechanism that tells you that you need to stress and be afraid of the coming change. Part of the here-now self's assumption that the change is a threat comes from its ignorance of the bigger Infinite resources that your Soul Self has at its disposal. But your Soul Self never loses sight of Its Heavenly existence, because the majority of It lives in Heaven even during your lifetime. So if your Soul is telling you that you are fed up with your life, than something better is, no doubt, already underway. And the solution that your Soul finds for your present issues may not even be in the same neighborhood of possibilities than your logical mind could perceive. In the same way that you cannot perceive that 2+2=9 because your logical mind tells you that it equals 4, from your Soul's perspective, 2+2 may very well equal 9, the unseen 5 coming from Divine intervention in your favor, because you aren't meant to go it alone.

Even from a here-now perspective, we've all had situations when we have spent long periods of time trying to solve a problem with no luck, getting more frustrated by the minute. But I'm sure that in some of those situations, you had the wisdom to step away from the problem for a while, and go do something enjoyable to get your mind off things. And I'll bet that it was exactly in those cases that you were able to then go back to the issue and tackle it in an effective way that you couldn't think of before. In bigger life issues too, sometimes stepping away from an issue to do some meditation is just the thing to do that would elevate your solution capability to the level of your Soul. And you'll be amazed at how different your outlook could be after a RezoDance session, or even after a short Zohar Breath Meditation. From a more metaphysical perspective, you'd be in awe of how differently people respond to you, as well as how your luck changes for the better, when your energetic vibration is in resonance with your Soul.

At the end of this Zohar Breath Meditation in which you have conversed with your Soul and received It's guidance and healing, don't forget to ground yourself well, so you can go back to your wakeful reality and be calm, peaceful, in a state of Grace, and yet feel upbeat, positive, very alive, and refreshed.

Step 4 – Solve the Issue:

It is always helpful to remember to pray and invoke Divine and Angelic help (in whatever form the Divine is for you), and ask for a most harmonious resolution of the situation that is in alignment with your Ideal Lifeplan. But praying is not instead of doing. Once you ascertain for yourself what needs to be done, you still have to take all the necessary actions in your here-now reality, to ensure your health, happiness, and success. Let's discuss some examples of actions that would be appropriate to serve your highest wellbeing.

Physical –

If your issue stems from any kind of physical deprivation (sleep, food, etc.), the answer is simple: take care of your body-temple first. Your physical body cannot function ideally—as the vessel that facilitates your Soul's experience in this lifetime—if you do not take care of its basic needs. So with this type of issue, there is no magical tool except to tell you that if you're hungry, eat. Have a nutritious meal and don't ingest any guilt along with it. If you're tired, get some good quality sleep. If you're PMSing, take a PMS pill (I don't know what the solution for men PMS is; as Midol and the like are all targeted at female hormones). If you are worn out and confused, schedule some "Me Time" (more on Me Time in *A Lifestyle of Prosperity From Your Soul*). Physiological needs are the easiest ones to take care of. So there is no reason to allow yourself to get so hungry that you feel hypoglycemic and agitated, just because you didn't schedule any time to eat for example. There are many needs, the fulfillment of which compels you to wait for the perfect timing that's in Universal harmony with the mosaic of everyone else's lives, such as the need to find love for example. And those needs are beyond the immediate control of your here-now self (not beyond the control of your Soul Self though). Physiological needs, on the other hand, are one level of needs that you have immediate control over, and the immediate ability to take care of. You have been doing it pretty much since birth.

In *A Lifestyle of Prosperity From Your Soul*, you will acquire a whole array of new tools to take better care of your body-vessel, so as to best facilitate the flow of Creative energy into your life. For now the point is to eliminate physiological and other types of stress, so that the Divine Creative energy *can* flow freely through your Infinite Funnel of Abundance, to manifest blessings in your life.

Empathy ~

As discussed, being empathic is a very good quality to have, particularly if you are a healer or are in a profession of helping others. But you don't want other people's stress and anguish to weigh you down and mess up your energetic vibration. So here are some techniques to help you avoid picking up other people stress or negativity, and keep you centered:

- ☙ Use the tools for clearing and protection given in Chapter 1 on a daily basis.
- ☙ As you take a shower, envision that as the water is washing your physical body, you are also receiving a shower of nurturing-healing energy from the Universe.
- ☙ When you call upon your Angels, call upon them not only to protect you, but also to heal-nurture you, as well as the person you were empathically giving your energy to. This way, you are giving the responsibility of taking care of other people to the Angels, and not carrying it yourself.
- ☙ Cord Cutting meditation (detailed in the next chapter) can help you sever energetic entanglements that are keeping both parties in an unhealthy relationship.
- ☙ Nature Healing Meditation (detailed in chapter 5) can help you recharge your energies from nature, and not depend on other people to give you energy.

Life Decision Issue ~

Zohar Breath Meditation can not only help you tune into the core of an issue, but also help you tune into the highest-best solution for you – from the perspective of your Soul.

<u>Relationship Problems</u> –

We have discussed in detail the process of dealing with the energy takers in your life in *Prosperity From Your Soul*. But here are just a few processes that can help you stay centered, and solve the issue in the most harmonious way:

- ☯ Cutting Cords Meditation (Chapter 4) is most effective in dissolving energetic entanglements with other people, and restoring the harmony and balance in the relationship.

- ☯ Nature Meditation (Chapter 5) can help you nurture yourself from the elements of nature as synthesizers of Divine energy, so you don't have to feed off of each other's energy in an unhealthy way. It can also help you gain some perspective and sense of self in the relationship, which will also contribute to the solution. The idea is that if your Ki energy is recharged, and your personal powers strengthened—by Nature Meditation or any other process—you will be peacefully strong enough to be unaffected by the other person's low-vibrational stunts.

- ☯ Radiating-Sending (mentally and energetically) Universal Love energy to the person with whom you have a relationship issue. Wonderful things happen when you just radiate Love towards someone, even if it's an opponent. You not only become less affected by their low-vibrational stunts and better able to stay heart-centered and happy, but the Love energy that you radiate to the other person also has a very healing, appeasing effects on them, and an actual power to resolve any issues between the two of you.

<u>Money Problems</u> –

Don't worry. By the time you are done with the processes of *A Lifestyle of Prosperity From Your Soul*, you'll be well on your way to co-Creating a new flow of easily flowing prosperity. So trust the process. More than that, trust your Soul's Love and perfect plan to shower you with all the blessings that your heart desires. Trust that the best paths to financial prosperity are not the ones you suffer through, but the ones that are anchored in the truest vision of your Soul, in which you are, of course, joyous.

<u>Bigger Life Issue</u> –

Since we have already established that your Soul is the best guide for bigger life issues, once you've done Zohar Breath Meditation (Chapter 2), and have tuned into the perfect solution that resonates not only with your Soul Self, but also with every level of your here-now self, all you will need to do once you wake up from the meditation is lay out the logical steps to follow the instructions that your Soul gave you.

<u>Incorporate Kindness-To-Self Into Your Solution</u> –

You should always nurture and be kind to yourself. So especially at times in which you are experiencing excessive stress, it is even more important to eat right, get adequate rest and sleep, meditate, and pamper yourself. But remember that kindness-to-self is a three faceted thing:

```
                          ┌─────────────────┐
                          │   Kindness      │
                          └─────────────────┘
```

Respect Legitimate Limitations/Blocks:
Some limitations are legitimately there, like physical body limitations and circumstances that are beyond your control. Don't critique or punish yourself for not surpassing limitations that are legitimately there. Breathe. Relax. You weren't meant to change the unchangeable. This is time to self-nurture!

Push Past the Emotional "I Can't" Factor:
Many limitations are self-imposed. Be kind enough to yourself to push yourself through emotional or mental blocks. It'll help purge out these blocks, so you can live a healthier life, and be the best version of yourself. This will go a long way towards becoming a more conscious co-Creator.

The god/goddess within You:
There is always a kinder softer ways to achieve a task/exercise. This is the way of kindness, grace & joy. Your body and here-now self are the vehicles for your Soul to experience itself in this lifetime. Nurture them during a challenge. There might be some purging happening as energy blockages are lifted. Take precautions to ensure that this process is harmonious and joyous! In the same way, there is always the way of Grace through (or around) most Soul lessons—the way of Prosperity Form Your Soul.

Now is the time to decide which facet of kindness should be incorporated into your perfect solution to this issue. Is it time to push yourself forward? Or is it time to slow down and nurture yourself?

If nurturing is the side of the balance you need, than if you can go get a massage with a good nurturing therapist, do so. Be amongst loving friends and family who will give you plenty of hugs, love and acceptance. And always remember who you are and Whom you represent: You are a beloved child of God. All you need do is be true to your heart, and act from your earnest- most Truth. It is this deepest Truth, which resides in your inner cell of Godlikeness, that makes you worthy in the highest degree. Many times, when our lives are in transitional times, we lose sight of the fact that this is just a transition into a healthier, happier, more prosperous life situation. So don't let yourself sink into despair. Forgive yourself the mistakes of the past. Know that this situation is just a narrow bridge into the next phase of your life, which simply must be more auspicious and happy! And above all, keep reminding yourself that you are a beloved child of God who deserves every good thing.

Step 5 – Trust:

As you implement the steps that this process details, you will experientially know how to address the problem, and how to resolve its core issues to benefit your highest good. And by the time you complete all the steam blowing, meditations, and self-nurturing steps, you'll feel the wonderful peace of knowing that you are indeed on a new promising path. But again, it is not me that I am asking you to trust. It is your own Soul, and the wisdom that It gives you that you should trust. And as you start walking this new path of peace and hope, it is also important to keep listening to the synchronistic signs that the Universe is giving you along your path.

Self Validation

One of the key ingredients to successfully dissolving stress and other negativities is self-validation—knowing that you are worthy and beloved. Because if you think of stress, agitation and foul-moods, the nature of these feelings is rooted in non-acceptance of what *is* in the reality of your life. And let's face it: within your immediate here-now reality, either a circumstance is there or it isn't (can't be half-pregnant). No need to stress about it. Ultimately, every circumstance in life can fall into one of three categories: things that you like, and don't want to change; things that don't really like, but have hidden lessons (blessings) that you need to learn before they will change; and things that you don't like, but have already learnt the lessons of, and therefore, as you are just now learning, you (your here-now self) have the power to change.

Metaphorically speaking, in any given circumstance in your life that you don't like, each boulder is meant to be on your path. It is either meant to drive you to circumvent it, go a different route, gather the strength to remove it from your path, or learn that you are strong enough to surmount it. But know with absolute certainty that if the path with this bolder is indeed your Divinely guided best path through life, then at the perfect timing, the Universe will send you all the help needed to climb it leisurely and joyously, if you allow it (free will). Of course, the sooner you learn the lesson afforded by each boulder (difficulty) along your path, the sooner the need for this boulders to be in your path will dissolve, and your path will magically smooth out and become easy and enjoyable to walk. Once you trust this Truth, there is no point in stress, is there?

The important thing is to know that you did your heart-centered best joyfully, as guided by your Soul Self. When you are in peace with having done your heart-centered best in a situation, and having experienced it with joy, than it is time to start giving yourself some credit. Recall our discussions of kindness-to-self. One of the most profound tools in dealing with stress is self-validation. It is essential for your happiness and success that you give yourself credit for the things you have achieved, even if they only constitute a third of what you had set out to achieve. So take some deep breaths, and remind yourself throughout the day how fabulous you are. You are validated for just who you are as a beloved child of God, not for what you do, or how much you achieve. It is therefore ok to set boundaries, and not to let others push them. It's ok to complete some of the tasks tomorrow, or next week. As long as your path is guided by your Soul Self, everything will turn out better than you expect it to.

It is often said that you are your own toughest critic. From the accounts of people who have had Near Death Experiences, it becomes even more apparent that our harsh critique of ourselves serves no purpose. Virtually all NDE'er who experienced a life review reported that the Light (God) never judged them, but that they were the ones to judge themselves. The Light only projected unconditional Love and acceptance, and lovingly showed them how they could have shown more love in each situation. This proves that harsh judgment serves no purpose. The only thing that serves a purpose is learning how to express more love in every situation, which includes self-love. Incidentally, this focus on experiencing love is also the way to tune into the Divine Creative energy that manifests prosperity.

Even in here-now situations, harsh self-judgment is never productive. Say that you have just messed up one of the biggest projects of your career. If you've already messed it up, there is no point in judging yourself, is there? The best thing you can do is make this a learning lesson—draw conclusions on how specifically you should perform better in future similar projects. That would make you a veteran and an expert on the next project.

However, on a deep level, I believe that people don't really overtask and stress themselves for fear of judgment. They overtask themselves and demand too much of themselves in search for greatness. The internal dialogue is usually something along the lines of, "oh, if I just go through this stressful time, I'll be promoted, earn more money, have a better position… and then maybe I'll feel more worthy and validated." But keep in mind that True greatness is not measured by how much money you have, or how important your position is. And it is not even what you do that counts. Your real greatness comes from whom you Truly are – a beloved child of the infinitely loving Creator. Your True greatness is the vibrational essence of your Soul, which can never be taken away from you. The only measurement of greatness is how much of your Soul's radiance you actually ground (integrate) into your physical 'I am.' When you ground your True essence into this reality, you will stop running around your life like a crazed rabbit in a maze, and start experiencing the peace that comes from just dwelling in the Light of your Soul in each moment. And from that peace comes the true vision of your Soul's highest mission on earth. Acting on this vision does not mean overtasking yourself to the point of stress. It means enjoying every step of the process of bringing your Soul's earthly mission into fruition. The prosperity, health, and happiness that naturally fall into your lap as you walk this path are just byproducts of the walking your most blissful Lifepath—a true Heaven on Earth!

Chakra Clearing & Balancing Meditation

In this chapter, I have related to you many conceptual tools to help you rationalize away, deal with, and reduce some of the stresses in your life. But no rationalization is as good as experiential knowing. So let's finish this chapter with a meditation that will help you clear and balance all of your chakras and energetic bodies. This meditation is a wonderful tool to help you feel True energetic-mental-emotional balance, peace and clarity. Depending on the situation, you can do this meditation in just a couple of minutes, or devote more time to delve into it deeply

To prepare for the meditation, protect, cleanse and bless your meditational space in accordance with the procedures we've discussed in Chapter 1. Set up your cushy meditation pillows and props, or get as comfortable as the situation permits.

Come sitting down cross-legged or in your chosen meditation position (with your legs spread out in front of you, or even sitting up in a chair), with your spine erect but not tense, your chin slightly tucked in, and your hands resting on your lap with your palms facing up. Now gradually start deepening your breath…

First envision yourself in a bubble of protective and nurturing Divine Light for a few moments… (if you can't visualize, speak your intent to be engulfed in the Light). Once you settle in and feel comfortable and locked into a meditative state, envision this bubble expanding… and you are now inside a column of the purest, most powerful Divine white Light—a Light that can dissolve any negativity, heal anything, and implant the most nurturing life-force in its stead. This column of blazing Divine Light originates from the heart of the Divine, engulfs you, and goes into the center of the Earth. Again, if you can't visualize, speak the intents that are detailed in the process of the meditation…

Now, take a particularly deep breath, envisioning a ray of white Light coming through the column into your crown… As the ray comes into your crown, it descends through your third-eye chakra, throat chakra, heart, solar plexus, second chakra, and finally floods your entire root chakra area. As the Light descends down all of your energy centers, it blazes through and dissolves all debris, and replaces it with Divine healing Light. As the Light ray floods your root chakra, it changes its color to red… until your entire root chakra is scintillating with the Divine red Light ray, dissolving any negativity, and healing it completely. As you exhale, see the red Light seep out your root chakra and connect all that is of the same vibration in Nature… You may spend several breaths bringing more and more of the blazing-healing Light into this chakra until you feel that it is totally clear, open, healed, empowered, and its energy is expanded.

Now, take another specially deep breath, envisioning again the Divine blazing Light coming into your crown, descending through your third-eye, throat, heart, third, and finally flooding the entire area of your second chakra. Again, as the Light descends through each of your chakras, it completely dissolves all lower vibrational energies, melts any blocks, and replaces those spaces with Divine healing Light. Once the Light blazes-dissolves all debris from your second chakra, it settles-floods the entire area, and the Light changes to a beautiful glowing orange Light. This orange Light is the Divine spectrum of energy that has the power to nurture, heal and empower the second chakra. As you exhale, see the orange Light expand, and seep out of your second chakra to connect with all that is of the same vibration in Nature. You may take several breaths to draw in more and more of the orange Light… until you can envision a big bright orange Light flooding your entire second chakra area and all around it. You may even feel a physical openness in your second chakra area, if you are sensitive to energy flow.

Next take another significantly deep breath, envisioning the Divine Light coming into your crown, and descending down your third-eye, throat, heart, and finally flooding into your third chakra area. Once the blazing Light finishes dissolving all debris and blocks from your solar-plexus area, it turns to the brightest yellow, and you feel empowered, and you physically feel that it is easier for you to breathe. Exhale and envision the yellow light seeping out to connect with all that is of the same vibration in Nature… Take several of these breaths, until you can envision your third chakra area completely engulfed in that scintillating yellow Light, and feel peaceful, emotionally nurtured, and completely empowered.

Take another deep breath, and envision the Divine Light again coming into your crown, and descending down your third-eye, throat, and finally flooding into your heart chakra. Once it dissolves all debris from your heart chakra, the Light turns into the most beautiful swirl of green and pink—the Light vibration that feeds the heart chakra, and the Light-ray of Divine Love. Exhale, and see the green-pink Light expand, seep out, and connect your heart chakra with all that is of the same vibration… And as you continue to inhale and flood your heart with that beautiful Light, it uplifts you and makes you feel beloved, nurtured, and connected to all that is good.

Take a deep breath again, and envision the Divine Light again coming into your crown, and descending down your third-eye, and finally flooding into your throat chakra. Once it dissolves all debris from the throat chakra area, the Light turns into the brightest cobalt blue Light—the Light-ray that has the power to heal and recharge your throat chakra. As you exhale, envision that the cobalt-blue Light seeps out and connects with all that is of the same vibration in Nature. As you continue to breathe and bring in that beautiful cobalt blue Light, you feel empowered to speak your Truth, and project your pure intents into manifestation in the physical universe.

Take another significantly deep breath, and draw more of the blazing Divine white Light into your crown, and let it descend into your third-eye chakra. Once the Light finishes blazing through any debris, see it turning into the most gorgeous indigo Light—the Divine Light-ray that has the power to heal and recharge the sixth chakra. As you exhale, allow the indigo Light to expand out of your third-eye and into Infinite dimensions… Remember that this is the chakra that gives you insight into Infinite dimensions, as well as the power to project your will into co-Creation. It is also a chakra that most people ignore in their everyday lives, since society has wrongfully told us that it is not ok to have visions, and that we need to listen only to here-now level "logic." So you may take several deep breaths, to let the white Light blaze through <u>all</u> blockages in this chakra, let the Light turn indigo… and allow the indigo Light to empower of this chakra and merge with the Universe. It's ok if you have some visions while you are expanding this chakra. Take note of them.

Now take another significantly deep breath, and draw more of the blazing Divine white Light into your crown chakra. Once the Light finishes blazing through any debris, see it turning into a beautiful violet Light—the Divine Light-ray that has the power to heal the crown chakra and connect you with the Divine… As you exhale, allow the violet Light to expand. Remember: the crown chakra is the first seat of your Soul. It is one of the keys to being able to tune into, and live by the Light of the Soul. So you may draw several healing-expanding breaths into the crown chakra, until you feel that your crown and whole being is pulsating as one with the Universe.

Out of that pulsation, now visualize the magenta and violet coming down and engulfing your whole being, turning into a huge glowing bubble of magenta-violet Light… until your whole aura is filled with magenta-violet Light. This Light ray has the power to dissolve all negative vibration, imbue you with the highest spiritual energy, facilitate communications with your Soul Self, and stabilize-ground your energy at the end of the meditation. So take a few deep breaths, and all yourself to bathe in that magenta-violet Light for a few moments.

Now ground yourself: take a few more deep breaths… visualize that as you inhale, you draw Divine white Light into your core… and as you exhale, you send that Light down your legs and out the soles of your feet to unite with the light at the center of the Earth.

Now gently massage your feet very lovingly… Open your eyes, and feel awake, refreshed, perfectly balanced, and peaceful, and good.

In a pinch, I've done this meditation while standing in the crowds of the Santa Monica Promenade, or in the middle of a spiritual convention. The diverse energy of the crowds was getting to me, and I felt the need to balance, protect, and ground myself. And I had no access to a quiet meditation room in those moments. So I just spread my legs shoulder-width apart and unlocked my knees, so that I'm standing in a grounding loose tai-chi stance, closed my eyes halfway for just a few moments, took one deep breath for envisioning the bubble of Light, and then proceeded to take about one to two deep breaths for each chakra. Then two breaths for grounding… and presto—I did the meditation. The whole thing took less than two minutes to do, and I felt very balanced: calm yet clear and vibrant, connected to my Divine Self yet grounded, and my chakras felt balanced. Of course, the effects of this meditation are more profound if you have time to really delve into it. But you too can use it as just a few visualizing deeper breaths, when you really need to calm, balance, and ground yourself, and don't have the time or the quiet meditational room to do it in.

In this chapter, we have tackled the first layer of negativity that might have, until now, been blocking your connection to your Infinite Funnel of Abundance. I have given you some food for thought in dealing with, and dissolve most common stresses, as well as two meditations to help alleviate stress in a very real way. Except for the two meditations, the specific steps outlined in this chapter are mostly conceptual tools. It is the actions that you take to implement them as habits that will decide how effective they are in aborting crisis, dissolving stress, and avoiding further buildup of negative conditionings and energetic blocks, thus allowing you to actively choose your highest Lifepath of prosperity in each of the small moment of your life.

However, as important as it is to look forward towards your Ideal Lifepath of prosperity, some deep-seated conditionings that do not serve your Ideal Lifepath have already been built within your psyche in various stages of your life, and along with them, some energetic blocks limiting the Infinite Funnel of Abundance from flowing into your life. And in order to completely open up your Infinite Funnel of Abundance to the inflow of Universal prosperity, some deeper 'housecleaning' is in order. So in the next chapter, I will give you some profound tools to uproot any energetic, emotional, and mental blocks that may have been with you for years, so you can restore the free flow of Divine Creative energy into your life and co-Creative endeavors.

Chapter 4

Using Your Soul-Light to Lift Blocks

In the beginning of the last chapter, we have established the importance of unblocking the Infinite Funnel of Abundance and allowing it to flow more freely into your life. I have given you some conceptual tools for avoiding stress and rationally uprooting it from your life, as we went through the detailed process of removing the outer layers of stress, agitation, anger, and frustration from your everyday life. All of those processes were important steps towards being able to approach each moment in life with the serenity of knowing that you are acting as the highest version of yourSelf. But in order to Truly open your communications channels with your Soul Self—to Truly allow the Divine Creative energy to flow freely and easily through your Infinite Funnel of Abundance, a more active cleansing of any deep underlying energetic, emotional, and mental blocks is needed.

This chapter contains meditations and processes that will help you remove deeper negative conditionings that may be blocking the manifestation of your most auspicious Lifepath. But this process is actually not as difficult as one might expect it to be. It's not like sitting on your shrink's couch three times a week for twenty years and being dredged through the mud of recalling your traumatic childhood memories. Not by a long shot. Except for one meditation, you will not be recalling any painful memories in these meditations, so do not be afraid of the process. Besides, you will not be alone doing these meditations. You will be protected and nurtured by the Light of your Soul, and the Angels (or other deities) that you invoke prior to each meditation. As we have seen in Chapter 2, by virtue of your God given free will, envisioning Divine Light around you during meditation actively calls upon Divine Light to be there for you, for whatever purpose you intend it. So during the meditations in this chapter, you will be surrounded and nurtured by Divine Light, and therefore the purging process will not feel heavy or uncomfortable. And of course at the end of this stage, you will feel much lighter and freer, and ready to manifest your Ideal Life.

As light and free as you will feel at the end of this stage, and as nurturing and good as these meditations feel, you will still be doing some heavy-duty purging of all the "stuff" that no longer serves your highest Lifepath of prosperity. So some issues may come up into your aware consciousness in order to be resolved and let go of. So above all else, remember to be kind to yourself! Give yourself enough time to process the changes that are occurring within you as a result of the meditations, as well as lots of self-nurturing to go along with it. Always listen to your inner wisdom when choosing which of these meditations are best suited for you at each moment, and throughout the process. It would be good if you try all the meditations given, so you can experientially know how they make you feel (empowered? peaceful? cleansed? lighter?) and not reject them based on old notions or fear. But feel validated to adopt into your daily meditational routine only the practices that you feel are "calling" you. For the meditations that are calling you, or that you feel the happiest doing, are probably the ones that are most indicated for you personally. The feel-good fuzzy feelings that you get during and after these meditations are the barometers of your inner guidance. Listen to them.

Dissolving Fear Meditation

Fear is a terrible master. On a here-now level, fear narrows your perceptual field and can drive you toward knee-jerk reactions and solutions that bring with them negative consequences. Contrary to common belief, fear doesn't really drive you to a healthy alertness. For the alertness that fear drives you to rejects everything non-discriminately, and thus may cause you to reject blessings from coming into your life too. From a metaphysical perspective, fear lowers your energetic vibration, and brings you into likeness and resonance with all that you *do not* want to magnetize into your life, which by virtue of your God-given co-Creative powers, keeps perpetuating that lower reality, or even shifts your reality for the worse. Feeling fear is the opposite of feeling safe, peaceful, beloved, and joyous. Therefore fear keeps you segregated from the Infinite Funnel of Abundance. Think of fear as a strong dark barrier blocking Divine Creative energy from flowing into your co-Creative endeavors, thereby blocking prosperity from flowing into your life. So dissolving fear is of paramount importance, if you are to become a more conscious co-Creator of your life.

Now that's not to say anything bad about being cautious, and planning the steps of your life carefully. According to yogic concepts, manifestation of prosperity comes only when the three aspects of the mind balanced. Remember that ancient yogic wisdom defines our Light Bodies differently than our New Age system of Etheric, Astral, Mental, and Casual Bodies. In the yogic system, three of our Light Bodies are actually devoted to the mind. According to that system, if the Negative Mind is too strong, it tries too hard to protect you, which would cause you to live in fear, and prevent you from moving forward with any Lifeplan you might have made. On the other hand, if the Positive Mind—the Yi-Ha factor—is too strong, you would be too apt to splurge and take unnecessary ill-advised risks. True prosperity is a gift of the Neutral Mind—the meditative mind, leading you to take steps inspired by your Soul Self, not too risky or temperamental, but not driven by fear. Although somewhat simplistic, this yogic concept gets the point across.

But how do we reach and maintain that balance? I mean everyone gets scared from time to time. Fear is not logical. Almost everyone has an irrational fear of something sublimated into their deep subconscious. So it becomes clear that fear is not something you can dissolve just by rationalizing it away. Dissolving fear requires a more multidimensional process.

So in this meditation, you will be using your higher consciousness to call upon a certain aspect of Divine Light, which has the power to remove deep-seated fears, as well as nurture you and enwrap you in a protective Light. But in this meditation, you will not be dredged through the mud of recalling any of the deep subconscious roots of your fear, as it works energetically—multidimensionally to uproot the fear. Your aura is your protective energetic and electromagnetic field whose job it is to fend off all negativity. A strong and radiant aura gives you a fearless spirit. Therefore, this meditation works by increasing the radiance of your aura, invoking the protection of your Angels, and embodying personal strength that comes from the Divine.

This meditation will dissolve all negativity and fear within you, evaporate disturbances, powerfully protect you, and give you a feeling of complete peace—like all is right with your world.

Preparing Your Space for the Meditation:

Clear and protect your space using the techniques detailed in Chapter 1 (Clearing & Protection). Use the power of your intent and prayer, and call upon your guardian Angels to help you with this meditation. It is especially helpful to call upon Archangel Michael—the Universal protector. His presence (in my meditations and dreams) always makes me feel incredibly safe and protected.

Put on some non-verbal meditative music that usually relaxes you and propels you into a higher vibration. You may want to hold the CD (or MP3 player) between your hands, and imbue it with your prayerful intents for the meditation before you play it. You may light a candle or incense that you imbue with similar intent.

Prepare a space for yourself to sit on that is as nurturing and comfortable as possible. This may be on a cushy meditation pillow on the floor, preferably with another pillow supporting your back, or it may even be on a bed or sofa. The important thing is that there isn't any physical discomfort that could detract your attention from the meditation.

The Meditation:

Sit comfortably cross-legged (or with your legs spread out wide apart), with your spine erect yet relaxed, your shoulders relaxed down, and your chin slightly tucked in. Close your eyes, and begin gradually deepening your breath…

As you deeply inhale, envision whitish-blue Light coming from the heart of God, entering your crown, then washing over your third eye and throat chakras, and indulgently pouring over your heart center like honey over an apple… As the Light nourishes your heart center, it is amplified and becomes wonderfully radiant by the eternal Divine resonant within you. As the inhalation gets deeper, and envision that this whitish-blue Light now descending to empower your solar-plexus (third) chakra—your center of your personal power—lighting it up with the radiant Divine whitish-blue Light. If you can't visualize, than during inhalation, silently speak your intent: "I am now bringing Divine whitish-blue Light to empower my solar plexus." The main focus of this meditation is increasing the radiant whitish-blue Light in your solar plexus… until it becomes glowing, strong, and huge.

Dissolving Fear Meditation:
In the actual meditation, envison the lines of energy coming out of
your solar-plexus chakra and out through your arms, hands, legs, feet,
shoulders, head, and all the orafices of the body.

The energy radiating out of the Solar Plexus chakra as a result of your
visualisations is actually coming out of the nadis, meridians, and all the
natural energy flow channels of the body. I drew the lines straight for
simplicity's sake, just to emphasize the point that the energy is shooting
outwards in all directions from the enhanced energy that you have
drawn into your solar plexus chakra.

Envision that as you exhale, some of the radiant whitish-blue Light from your solar plexus
spreads out throughout your body, and exits through thousands of energy channels, like spokes
from a hub, along its way clearing and dissolving all fear, all lower thought forms, all lower
vibrational energy, and all energetic blockages... If you can't visualize, than as you exhale, silently
affirm your intent: "I am not sending the Divine whitish-blue Light that's illumining my solar
plexus out in all directions, to dissolve all negativity, stress, fear, and lower vibrational energies."

Continue inhaling whitish-blue Light through the crown... allowing the long and deep
inhalation to pull that Light fully into your solar plexus... and exhaling the whitish-blue Light
through every pore and orifice of the body... until a gently glowing whitish-blue Light surrounds
your whole body and aura with Divine peace, nurturing, and protection...

To seal the cleansing and protection effects of this meditation, envision yourself in a clear bubble of Light that is impenetrable to anything but the highest Divine blessings and manifestations… Envision this crystal-clear blazing Divine Light enwrapping you in a diamond shape. This is the Light and sacred geometry of ultimate protection. And any time that you are this well protected, there is never any room for fear. Only Light, bliss, happiness, and Divine abundance.

Cords Cutting Meditation

We all go through life attempting to experience it joyously according to our Ideal Lifeplans. But free will is still king at every level of our existence, including the level of our here-now selves. So as we grow up, and throughout our lives, we each cross paths with other people, who are also exercising their free will. And despite the fact that each person's highest free will is always loving, at the level of their here-now selves, some people's free will may be somewhat distorted from the original will of their Soul, like the all-loving will of their Souls somehow got lost in translation into their here-now consciousness.

This forgetfulness of the angelic nature of Soul-communications results in the formation of unhealthy energetic cords, with which most of us become entangled. It is these underlying entanglement cords that cause many relationships to be less than harmonious. But don't get too alarmed here… we all have energetic entanglement cords with at least some of the people in our lives, consciously or unconsciously. Even when the entanglement cords are not formed by us, in order for them to form at all—since the Universe operates on free will—we must have, at some level allowed others to attach those entanglement cords to us, out of fear, neediness, or even empathy. Since everything in the Universe is composed of Love energy, even fear can sometimes be a misdirected form of love: for example, fear that the other person won't love you, fear that the other person will leave you, fear of not being needed… Neediness is also a misdirected form of love: It is a forgetfulness of the Infinite Source all of Its resources that makes people seek for the fulfillment of those needs by other people, which gets them entangled in unhealthy energetic patterns with each other—entanglement cords.

The unhealthy thing about entanglement cords is that through those cords, you are allowing your energies to be drained, most times unconsciously, by the person to whom they are attached. You are also allowing the other person to inadvertently give you some of his/her negativity. You might even get entangled in a net of unhealthy (unfulfilled) expectations to and from the other person, whereby no matter what each of you does or says in the relationship, the other one gets hurt and angry. So allowing these cords to exist makes communication difficult between the two people, limits the high-vibrational exercising of each of their free wills, and restricts the personal growth of each individual entangled by these cords.

Some other examples of good intents forming limiting entanglement are:

➢ A husband going through tough times at work projecting all his stress and anger onto his wife; and the wife gets so worried about her husband, that instead of being the fresh breeze that cools him down—instead keeping her high-vibrational center so she can lift him up, she gets sucked into the whirlpool of his stress and worry.

➢ A parent being worried about his/her son/daughter. The worry comes out of love. But since worry is a close relative of fear, the negative expectation can actually transmit a negative vibe through the entanglement cords into the consciousness of the son/daughter, and out into the Universe. Therefore, the worry energy itself can actually harm the son/daughter, and bring about the very thing the parent is worried about.

➢ A friend asserting their will on how to help you get out of a tough spot in life. Their intent may come out of their love for you. But the best solution for your situation may be different from your friend's here-now level solution. And your despair in such a situation may lead you to rely on your friend's limited view, which forms limiting energetic entanglement cords between the two of you, thereby preventing you from tuning into your Soul's wisdom.

➢ A son or daughter being afraid of not being loved enough their parents.

➢ An empathic healer being too invested in his/her patient's healing, and the patient becoming overly dependent on the healer, can create energetic entanglement cords between the patient and the healer. Being empathic towards a friend or a family member can create such entangled energetic cords that the empathetic person can literally feel the physical pain of the sufferer. This happens to me occasionally.

You can see from these examples that dissolving these entanglement cords serves to promote healthier relationships with the people in your life, or in some cases, to peacefully sever your ties with individuals that no longer serve the highest purpose in your life.

However, let's distinguish here: There are many healthy energetic connections between people that are not considered cords, such as the energetic love connection between two people. When energetically cords cutting, you are not cutting the Light-Love energy that connects you with your loved ones and with all of Creation. You are only dissolving the darker entanglement cords that are binding the two of you in an *unhealthy* relationship. Although cord cutting is sometimes an act of defense against unwanted lower vibrations that are hindering you in some way, you are not necessarily severing your ties with the person you are cords cutting with. You are only dissolving the negative entanglements that are causing the relationship to be tumultuous. By cutting cords, you are actually healing the relationship. For the true nature of a harmonious relationship is walking through life side by side, knowing and honoring your differences, loving each other unconditionally, holding space for one another to grow, and supporting each other's independence and greatness. By eliminating the darker entanglement cords, you are actually allowing a stronger Light-Love connection between the two Souls to shine, and the Divine energy to heal you, the other person, and the relationship.

Meditationally, entanglement cords look like entangled dark roots of two trees, whereas the love connection energy between two people looks like a white Light, usually connecting the heart chakras or the crowns (although if the light connects the crowns, then the other person is undoubtedly a Soulmate). So in a healthy relationship, the two of you will meditationally look like two balls of light, each free from any entanglement. This state of freedom leaves room for each of you to grow, and creates mutual resonance of bathing in each other's Light. It also allows each of you reclaim your True Self, which is the key to magnetizing prosperity into your life.

Besides restoring relationships with people in your life, you can also do Cord Cutting Meditation to dissolve an unhealthy relationship with a company or any element in your life that you feel is limiting the free expression of your True Self. So this meditation also serves as a way to remove any negative themes from your life and to disallow them any further influence in your life.

But one thing to note here is that when you do Cords Cutting Meditation to heal your relationship with a *person* in your life, you may need to do the meditation more than once. And here is why: At the moment that you finish doing the meditation, all entanglement cords with the other person will indeed be severed, and you will feel freer. You will probably also see a positive difference in your day-to-day interactions with this person. And the relationship may stay on this higher note for a while. But the other person also has free will. Therefore, if the other person is stuck in a low vibration, than that low vibration (fear, worry, etc.) will eventually lead him/her to revert back to their old behavior, and they will probably try to attach new entanglement cords to you. At that point, you can either allow or disallow it. Sometimes it is a person that you so deeply care about, that when they go through drama, you almost can't help but open your companionate heart to them, which could leave you energetically open to the attachment of new entanglement cords. And then, you will have to do this meditation again to dissolve the cords. For example, let's say that the other person is your mother, who is always pushing you to get married so forcefully, that her nags have become a stressful element in your life, straining your communications with her. In that case, after Cord Cutting meditation, your communications with her will probably go smoothly for a while; she might even give you a break from the nags. But as soon as you indulge her and you get sucked into a defensive argument (which takes away your personal powers) about your dating life, guess what: as evidenced by the knots that the conversation probably formed in the pit of your stomach, you've just allowed her to attach new energetic entanglement cords to you. On the other hand, if at the point of the conversation, you remain neutral and set healthy boundaries (firmly yet peacefully and kindly), than new cords will not be attached. But more often than not, our compassionate loving nature leads us to open up, and we completely forget to be kind to ourselves, and to maintain our position of peaceful strength. It is when you emotionally allow yourself to get sucked into the dramas, or into the points of view of other people in your life, bending over backwards and defending your position (when in reality, if you come from a place of Soul Truth, no defense is necessary) that you allow them to attach new energetic entanglement cords to you.

The good news is that you can repeat the meditations as often as you need to, and it feels so good, that repeating it is no big deal. In periods when I am dealing with many relationship issues with close friends and family, I find myself doing this meditation almost daily. We can't go through life thinking, "oh, I'm so lofty, I can't allow any energetic spec of dust to touch me." Life is messy sometimes, as it is about experiencing, especially your (love) relationships with people. So it's ok to let your relationships with people get involved and emotional. This meditation helps to periodically clean out the cords of low vibrational energy, so you can drive your relationships onto higher grounds. And of course, as we've explored in *Prosperity From Your Soul*, the more harmonious your relationships are, the more you can stay on track of your Ideal Lifepath of prosperity.

The Meditation:

Choose a quiet space for yourself for this meditation. Cleanse, protect, and bless your space as discussed in Chapter 1 (Clearing & Protection). Light candles or incense set with your prayerful intent; play relaxing non-verbal music; and call upon your Spirit Guides, guardian Angels and the Archangels to help you in this process or any other deity that you believe in and feel comfortable with. Since cord cutting is particularly the domain of Archangel Michael, it may behoove you to call upon him to help you with this meditation. Set the intent that you wish to communicate directly with your Soul Self and draw on Its wisdom and power.

Sit comfortably cross-legged (or in your chosen meditational pose) on your meditation pillows, with your spine loosely erect, your shoulders relaxed down, and your chin slightly tucked in. Close your eyes, and start deepening your breath…

Start with Zohar Breath Meditation (Chapter 2)… Deeply inhale Divine white Light into the back of your heart chakra… let that light fill your entire being… and deeply exhale the white Light from the front of your heart chakra… Continue breathing Divine white Light in and out of your heart space until you feel the supreme peace and clarity of your Soul's presence …

From within the peaceful space of dwelling in the consciousness of your own Soul, call upon the Soul of the other person to be present, and envision the two of you as two ball of light (if you can't visualize, speak your intent to call upon the Soul presence of the other person)… In the beginning, you will become intuitively aware of the existence of darker energetic tentacles extending between the here-now (human) aspects of the two of you, which are forming entanglements that are restricting the bright Light of each of you. In cases where the relationship is very tumultuous, the entanglement cords may form quite an intricate network of entanglements, much like a tangled jumble of steel wool, or like the intricate dark root system of two trees that have become entangled with one another. Do not get scared or disgusted by the presence of such dark energy around you. We all have those energetic entanglements with some of the people in our lives. Trust that you are being protected and helped by your Spirit Guides and Angels (or other deity whose help you have invoked) in this process, and know that you have the power to dissolve these entanglement cords, by virtue of your God given free will.

Sitting in the energetic presence of yours and your friend's Souls, continue deeply breathing Light in and out of your heart space… but now envision (or verbally commend, if you can't visualize) inhaling blue Light to engulf your aura, and exhaling-projecting some of that blue light towards the aura of the other person… This is the Divine Light ray that has the power of clearing, dissolving negativity, protection, as well as enhancing communication. As you inhale, draw more and more blue Light ray into your aura until it is glowing, radiant, and strong… and as you exhale, send-project the blue Light ray towards the entanglement cords and onto your opponent/friend… As you exhale and project the blue Light ray to your opponent and the cords, realize that the blue Light that surrounds you is not being depleted, but instead, both of your auras are getting brighter and brighter with the blue Light that is radiantly engulfing the two of you now. As you continue this breath—inhaling-drawing more and more of the blue Light ray into you and your aura, exhaling-projecting the blue Light towards the entanglement cords and your opponent/friend—you'll gradually see the entanglement cords weakening and then dissolving completely. Keep drawing more blue Light into your aura with every breath… until your aura is brilliant and big.

Now, check if there are any tentacles of energy that you have sent out, giving away your personal energy (and if you are not a good visualizer, than the message may come to you as a clairaudience, clairsentience or claircognizance). Sometimes, as in the case of unrequited love, we willingly give out our personal Ki, without realizing the unhealthy imbalance, and the drain on our personal power resulting from that act. So stay in the consciousness of your Soul (do more Zohar Breaths), and affirm your free will to recall all energy cords that you have sent out, and to reclaim your personal power. If there is actually some energy that you need to reclaim, you will meditationally see it returning to you, and you will suddenly feel more empowered, calmer, more centered.

As you continue inbreathing the protective blue Light and projecting it to your friend/ opponent, bow to his/her Soul, and talk on a Soul-to-Soul level… Humble yourself and ask for forgiveness for all transgressions on your part in this or any other lifetime. For even if he/she is the aggressor in this lifetime, the problem between you may have started in a previous incarnation when you were the aggressor. Thank this person for being part of your life and affording you the Soul-lessons he/she did. Remember that the antagonizers in your life are often the people who push you to excel and reclaim the radiance of whom you Truly are.

You may say (projected thought) something like: "Beloved XYZ, I am sorry that in our individual process of evolving, we got so entangled with each other that we have not been able to see each other clearly, and to see each other's True greatness. I am giving you back all energy cords that you have attached to me. I forgive and release you of all karmic ties to me. I release you into your own God Light. I ask the Angels to engulf you in total Love and abundance energy. Please realize that all of your needs are being met by the Divine, therefore, there is no need for you to attach cords to me. I ask that all energy cords I have sent out return to me permanently now. I ask that you please forgive, bless, and release me into my own God Light now."

As you say that, now inbreathe the pinkish-white Light (Divine Love) through your crown… let it flood your heart and engulf your entire being… and as you exhale project the pinkish-white Light-Love from your third and forth chakra to the other person… Do this either by visualizing or by speaking that intent.

Divine Love is the most powerful energy that Exists. It has the power to dissolve all cords and any ill intent, and transmute the energy into a higher vibrational one. In fact, even in cases of psychic attacks, the best defense against psychic attacks is to send Divine Love towards the attacker. This stops the ill will on its tracks, dissolves its negative energy, and sends healing to the attacker so that he/she doesn't feel the need to psychically attack anyone any more.

So continue to inbreathe Divine Love until it floods your entire being and aura... continue to exhale-project the pink Divine Love energy to engulf your friend/opponent's entire being and aura... until you meditationally see all entanglement cords between the two of you dissolve. You will then see all your energy tentacles return to you, and all energy tentacles belonging to the other person return to him/her. At the end of the meditation, see each of you as a bigger and brighter light-ball. Finally, envision this person in his/her own God-Light, and see yourself in your own God-Light, blessed, happy, light, and absolutely free.

Ground yourself back into ordinary reality, as we've learnt to do in Chapter 2.

Meditation to Remove Childhood Trauma

In an ideal world, everyone's thoughts, feelings, and actions would be completely guided by their Souls; we would all be dwelling in our heart-centers; and would all communicate via Soul communication. But our here-now reality is not always ideal.

Metaphysically speaking, your mind could be understood as a river of consciousness that flows from the Infinite, through your individual mind, which finally translates into your brain's chemical processes that facilitate your human-level logic, emotions, and actions. Life-energy, ideas, Creative energy, and Its manifestation into blessings in the reality of your life can all be thought of as the water of the river. And the river could have many different shapes. It can flow through different routes; it can be narrow or vast. But if you have boulders and rocks blocking the flow of the river, than you are not fully enjoying the stream in the way that it was intended for you—you are not fully tapping into your Infinite Funnel of Abundance. The rocks could be moments in your childhood and throughout your life that were traumatic, and had caused your subconscious to draw an illogical conclusion and put a block around something. These blocks, even though their roots originate from the past, have forced your mind to find an alternate route, and thus a defense mechanism is born. As we have discussed in *Prosperity From Your Soul*, not all defense mechanism still serve your highest purpose, as you have already risen above the need for most childhood defense mechanisms. You have learnt the Soul lessons afforded by the limitations they pose, and so it is time to remove and dissolve them.

This is the only meditation in this book in which you are led to actually recall the traumatic events that became the root cause of a particular issue/block. However, you will recall the event from within the protective Light and higher consciousness of your Soul. Therefore the events will not feel traumatic, and you will not experience any discomfort. The idea of this process is for your Soul to conduct this meditation. Your Higher Self aspect of your Soul—the most objective and wise observer within you—is in perfect position to *command* your subconscious mind to reveal the source of the problem, correct false impressions and conclusions, remove the trauma, deprogram all limiting conditions associated with it, and restore the perfect flow of Spirit within you. Psychologists tell us that most negative conditionings are created by a false conclusion to an imperfect situation, for example, a mom yelling at her five-year-old child, not because he/she is unworthy of receiving love, but because mom was stressed out that day.

An example from my own life is a simple event in which during one afternoon, my older brother had pulled my hair backwards, and was holding my head back with that force. My conscious mind did not even remember the event; and I'm sure my brother didn't really mean anything vicious by that act. We were just quarreling as kids do. But my subconscious mind had created a postural holding pattern (more about holding patterns in *A Lifestyle of Prosperity From Your Soul*) that caused half a lifetime's worth of neck and shoulders pain. So one night, I used this meditation to remove the trauma, and my neck and shoulders have been considerably better since.

This process is as powerful as a session with a hypnotherapist. The only difference is that in this meditative process, you are the one that's in charge of the process and of your mind, so that you only go as far and as deep as you are comfortable going at any given time. I am a big believer in the do-it-yourself method. No psychologist or hypnotherapist can know you better than you know yourself. Your mind is very powerful. So there is no reason why we couldn't harness it to help remove childhood traumas. And when you yourself are in charge of the process, your psyche will give in more, and it will become much easier than when someone else does it for you, no matter how skilled they may be.

When It Happen Naturally:

When your physical body is still, but your mind is alert, the stage is set for you to tune into your subconscious. This meditation is an auto-hypnotic state. But don't get scared from the word autohypnosis, as it is something that happens naturally every night, when your body is in total relaxation just before falling asleep, and your mind is still awake. This is the perfect time to tune into your Soul Self, and use Its perspective to cleanse your subconscious of all trauma and energetic blocks that might be hindering your path to an all-inclusive prosperity.

The Meditation:

Clear, protect, and bless your space as shown in Chapter 1.

Get yourself situated for complete relaxation, as if you are about to go to sleep. This means turning off all outside disturbances, and emptying your bladder. If you're doing this as you go to sleep, brush your teeth and do your bathroom nightly routine prior to starting the meditation. Dim or turn off the lights, so you can perfectly relax.

Make mental note of one to three issues in your life that you'd like to work on during this session. These usually start from the awareness of a current issue in your life that you'd like to change, which you suspect may have deeper roots. They could be bad habits you would like to change, attitudes of "I can't" you'd like to deprogram from within yourself, or childhood traumas that you can remember. At this point, you are not required to know the root cause of the issue yet, just that it is something you'd like to change in yourself. The root causes will come to you during the meditation.

Intend for your Soul to be in charge of this meditation. Tell your mind that as you go deeper to "see" the source of any issue, you will be viewing it from the safe, protected and peaceful perspective of your Soul. Envisioning yourself in a bright bubble of Light, and "seeing" the Light actively feeding off of the Divine funnel of Light will help you to actually *feel* protected during the meditation.

Lie down and start some deep Zohar Breaths (see Chapter 2) to tune into your Soul's awareness. Let your eyelids become heavy and close, and become very relaxed… Do Zohar Breaths until you feel the supreme peace and clarity of your Soul's presence… Then let your breath relax some into a natural deep breath… Continue this relaxation until you feel that you are starting to tune out all outside noises… until you start listening only to the "sounds" of your Soul, internally viewing only what your Soul wants to show you… Be very conscious of maintaining a meditative balance and not falling asleep—let your Higher Self continue to be the observer that's in charge of the process.

Now, envision yourself lying on an air mattress floating on a beautiful turquoise river on a warm spring day. To the side of the river is paradise-looking scenery—whatever paradise means to you. Allow yourself to fully relax and enjoy the nurturing oasis you're in…

Now start a countdown from 10 to 1. As you countdown, "see" your air mattress floating down the river into your past. (Honestly, the visualization of the air mattress going downriver is the most powerful, but if you can't visualize, than just proceed to the countdown, and speak your intent that with every number that you count backwards, you'll be becoming more and more calm, going deeper and deeper into your subconscious, and delving deeper and deeper into the past event that you need to recall to dissolve the trauma.) As you float downriver, a pleasant fog is surrounding your river. With each count, see yourself going down the river as it descends downhill with the terrain, and as you do, feel yourself going deeper and deeper into a more relaxed subconscious state. Tell yourself that when you reach point 1 of your trail, you will recall the moment in your past (from either your present or past lifetime) that instigated the specific issue that you intend to heal. As you count, continue utilizing Zohar Breath to keep yourself tuned into the perspective of your Soul. As you reach the lower numbers of your countdown, see the fog gradually starting to clear, until when you reach point 1, the scenery is completely clear, and you are able to see the events very clearly. When you get to that point, trust your Soul to provide you with a protective Light and to guide you to fully understand the events from Its highest perspective. Now that you've gotten to point 1 of your countdown, (mentally) step off the air mattress secure it to the riverbank, and see yourself floating above the scene, engulfed in the protective bubble of your Soul-Light (or if you're not a good visualizer, than just command your mind to show you the scene or otherwise inform you of the events that you need to recall).

Now trust the first impressions and images that come to your mind, even if you don't consciously remember the incident. Whatever comes to mind in response to your question-issue has obviously stuck in your subconscious for a reason. It doesn't have to make sense. It could be an event that seems trivial to your adult self. Trust it anyway. If no images/impressions comes to mind right away, that's ok too. Just continue Zohar Breaths for a while longer, and bask in the peace of your Soul's presence. Then ask your Soul again to show you the root cause of the issue… until clear messages or images come to mind… At first, you may only get fractions of images, clairaudience messages, or just a general feeling. Know that this process is a valuable cleansing and healing of your subconscious. So spend a bit of time now recalling or looking carefully at all the details of the scene/event. As you continue to practice this meditation, you'll start getting clearer and clearer images, as if you're floating above an actual scene, in which your younger self (or past life self) is participating. Continue trusting the images and impressions that come to you, whatever they are.

Envision your Soul Self hugging and projecting Light and unconditional love towards your child self who is experiencing in the event. Give him/her the wisdom you have now from your higher vantage point. If a wrongdoing was indeed perpetrated on your younger self by others, give those others the karmic responsibility for their actions. You are not here to fix their karma. You are here to heal the injury that their actions have inflicted upon your tender child self. Seeing the righteousness of your own actions from the perspective of your Soul Self can help your healing. And as part of the healing process, your Soul can also shed light on any Soul lessons you may have learnt from the incident. But the core of this process is about nurturing and healing the tender child within you. So from the perspective of your Soul, give your child self all the Love, and all the protection and reassurance he/she needs to feel safe and let go. Assure your him/her that You (Soul) will be with him/her all the days of his/her life to protect him/her and love him/her. Give your child self all that it needs as if it were your baby. If you are a reiki practitioner, you can see yourself sending distant healing and the reiki symbols to your child self. Spend some time doing this healing of your child self… until you can see-feel your child self being safe, happy, and loved.

Continuing Zohar Breaths, use the authority of your Soul to command your subconscious human mind to remove any and all negative conditionings and energetic blocks that originated from this event. Ask your mind to continue working on this particular issue while you sleep. You may wake up feeling all new in the morning, or it may take your mind up to two weeks to rewire the circuitry in your brain to facilitate the new life force flowing into those areas that were blocked until now.

Use the power of your free will to command any and all blocks to be removed from your Infinite Funnel of Abundance. See the river of your Creative energy flowing perfectly, abundantly, and joyously through your Infinite Funnel of Abundance; and see yourself as perfectly flowing with Light, love, beauty, health, happiness, and abundance.

If You Want to Work on More Than One Issue in Each Session…

Let your Higher Self (who is leading the session) recall the next issue you wanted to work on. To facilitate this memory, envision untying your air mattress from the riverbanks, lying on it comfortably, and letting the river take you to the next destination—the next event in your past that has triggered a life issue that you wish to work on… See the riverbanks get foggy again…. And start counting down from three to one…

When you get to point one, again see the fog dissipating, and you are able to see the events very clearly. Step off the air mattress and secure it to the riverbank, and see yourself again floating safely above the scene, protected by the Light of your Soul. Trust the images and impressions that come to you.

Repeat the steps described above… communicate with your child self, and give it your Soul's healing Light-Love, nurturing, and reassurance. See all negative or heavy energy dissolved, and command your mind to deprogram all negative conditionings, and project Light to dissolve all energy blocks that originated from the event. At the end of each theme that you work on, see yourself free from each traumatic event, and feel lighter and more peaceful after each block is removed. The ease of visualizing yourself free, especially your ability to *feel* lighter, is your indications that you have finished the healing process.

It is especially important that you see your child and your adult here-now self, both connected to your Soul Self and with the Divine Infinite Funnel of Abundance in a free and unobstructed way.

Conclude the Meditation:

At the end of the meditation, "see" yourself still in the bubble of your Soul Light, lifted up into the Heavenly realm. Bathe your total Self in this Heavenly Light for a while. See and feel all parts of yourself—past, present and future—integrating the positive results of the healing you've just given yourself, and completely being nurtured and balanced by the blissful Heavenly Light place that you are in.

Now, if you are doing this meditation at night as you fall asleep, just "talk" your mind into giving you a very restful peaceful sleep, so that you may wake up feeling perfectly refreshed.

If You Are Doing This as a Meditation During The Day –

See yourself descending from the Heavenly Light place ever so softly, bringing with you Its healing and Abundance energy, and grounding it into your here-now reality. Deepen your breath once again, and become aware of all of your body parts. Instruct your mind that as you count from one to five, you will become more grounded into full body awareness and full wakefulness:

1. As you breathe deeply, feel the support and nurturing of our Earth-mother beneath your meditation mat. Envision that your feet have roots, grounding you into the center of the earth.
2. Gently start wiggling your toes and fingers, becoming more aware of your body. Then make small circles with your wrists and ankles.
3. Feel refreshed and ready to wake up, like you have just woken up from a refreshing nap. Stretch your arms up over your head, your legs down to elongate the body, and point your toes away from the body in a big stretch.
4. Becoming more and more awake and alert, bend your right knee up over the straight left leg, and stretch it to the left so that it touches the ground (or bed) to the left side of the body—big indulgent cat stretch… now stretch the other way.
5. Rub the soles of the feet together, rub your palms together… this will help ground you and reset the nervous system.

Open your eyes, and feel refreshed, awake, alert yet peaceful, and perfectly joyous!

Lifting Cellular Memory Meditation

Cellular memories are energetic imprints of suffering that we carry with us from earlier on in our present lifetime, or from past lives. Some cellular memories become evident in terms of physical propensity for suffering, like for example, my ankles, which as a child and young adult I always used to twist in a very painful way. As soon as I became privy to this meditation, I did it to lift any and all cellular memory relating to my ankles, and I haven't had a twisted ankle since. Some cellular memories, if you allow them, could crystalize into limiting conditions, which weigh you down and keep you from co-Creating your most auspicious Lifepath. For example, if I didn't do this Lifting Cellular Memory Meditation often, I would have let my propensity for migraines get the better of me, and I would never have written this book series or created any of the wonderful retreat courses that are associated with it—it would have been like I'd given up on living my Ideal Lifepath.

Having cellular memories does not reflect badly on you, since your Soul is pure now, at its inception, and at every point in between. And as we have discussed in *Prosperity From Your Soul*, each Soul is also completely healed from all suffering, when it goes into the Light after each lifetime. However, most Souls *choose* to go through many physical incarnations to facilitate their growth. Sometimes, if there are lessons or experiences that the Soul has begun but not completed in the last lifetime, than as It plans Its next incarnation, the Soul *chooses* to take with It (ingrain in Its human persona) into the next physical incarnation some cellular memory that relates to the suffering of the incarnation when the lesson/experience began. This is done by Your own choice (at the highest level), to give yourself a chance to complete the learning experience, and gain the Soul growth afforded by it.

However, once you graduate the lesson associated with each cellular memory, you may discharge and dissolve it, since it no longer serves any purpose in your life. That is what this meditation is all about. Once you have dissolved these cellular memories that no longer serve your highest wellbeing, it gives you an instant ability to rise above any challenges associated with them, reclaim your natural health and happiness, and restore the free flow of abundance into your life. And like everything else in the process of co-Creating your Ideal Life, lifting cellular memories is achieved by merging your God-given free will with Divine Grace.

Preparing for the Meditation:

When you attend RezoDance sessions, your trained facilitator will provide a perfectly blessed space to empower and facilitate your process. When you do this meditation on your own, it is important that you cleanse, protect, and bless your space according to the suggestions given in Chapter 1 (or in whatever other way you choose).

Invoke the help of your guardian Angels, Spirit Guides, the Archangels Michael and Raphael, or any other deity you believe can help carry out your healing intent. Your invocation will also help set the intent for the meditation, and insure that Divine help is there to facilitate your process. You may wish to light a candle or incense that you've blessed intently… set up blessed crystals around you… or whatever ceremony that you believe blesses your intent for this meditation.

Sit comfortably cross-legged (or in your chosen meditation position) on your cushy meditation pillows, with your spine loosely erect, your shoulders relaxed down, and your chin slightly tucked in… Close your eyes… and start deepening your breath…

The Meditation:

Start with Zohar Breath Meditation…

Once you get to dwell in the supreme peaceful clarity of your Soul, envision (or verbally invoke) a deep blue-magenta Light powerfully swirling down from the core of the Divine, down through the crown of your head, filling every part of your body and aura… This is the Light of Archangel Michael, who is helping you uplift, cleanse and purify all cellular memories of past suffering, breaking any bondage, and clearing any wrongdoing. "See" (or verbally direct) this blue-magenta Light especially directed at any areas in your body that you have always had issues with (areas that have the propensity for, or in which you've had injuries/illnesses)… Intend that this Light penetrate and dissolve all cellular memories of any past suffering that might still be affecting this area… Visualize (or verbally command) any bondage, which exists on ethereal levels, lifting off and dissolved by the power of your intent and with the help of this deep blue-magenta Light… Affirm that any contracts or agreements of poverty, seclusion or suffering, which you may have unwittingly made in past lives (in all directions of time), be null, void, and dissolved by this Light… Continue breathing in this blue-magenta Light through your crown… let the light amplify at your heart center… and continue projecting it into every area of your physical body, your energetic Light Bodies, and into every area of your life that needs this healing…

Allow your higher intuition to guide the flow of this process. In other words, where you "see" the blue-magenta Light focusing may not be a cognitive process. Let it go where it naturally wants to go—where it feels right for it to go. Just go with the images that arise. You may even make motions with your hands, conveying the lifting and clearing all of any gunky energy, uplifting any restrains that may have been there since a past life. For example, if in a past life you were killed or injured by a dagger, than despite the fact that the physical dagger is of course not there any more, the energetic imprint of the injury may still be there as a cellular memory, if the loose remembrance of the event has the potential to facilitate more growth. So making arm movement that convey taking a dagger out of your body helps affirm your free will to remove the cellular memory of this suffering from your energetic bodies. In the same way, conveying arm movements could be of undoing restricting chains, or anything else that come to mind. You don't have to recall the whole past life in detail, or go through its suffering all over again. Just go with arm movements that you feel naturally and instinctively guided to do. I know that initially, you'll probably feel quite ridiculous with yourself doing these arm movements. But these conveying arm-motions help tune your powerful mind into clearing and dissolving of all those heavy cellular memories, and their resultant blocks. Your Soul has always been blessed with the Light-Power to uplift and dissolve these painful cellular memories. You (your here-now self) are just now learning how to assert your free will to do so. By the act of visualizing the deep blue-magenta Light, you call upon the clearing and dissolving aspect of Divine Light; by taking deep breaths, you are allowing that Light into your bodies (physical and energetic); by your visualizations, you are asserting your free will to draw more blue-magenta Light comes into your crown, to be amplified at your heart center with each inhalation, sending the Light to spreads into all areas of your being that need clearing and with each exhalation; by your conveying arm motions, you are strengthening the assertion of your free will how to direct the action of this Cosmic Light ray.

Take your time doing this clearing… Keep inhaling blue-magenta Light – swirling into your crown, and amplified at your heart… keep spreading the blue-magenta Light into all areas of your being that need clearing with every exhalation… It is important that at the end of this process, you feel lighter and brighter and filled with light.

Now envision (or verbally invoke) emerald-green Light coming from the heart of God to fill all the spaces where suffering was lifted from… As the emerald-green Light of Archangel Raphael (the healing Angel) fills all the voids with healing energy, you will begin to feel very nurtured, cared for, and healthy, like a clean slate in life has been given to you. Let this emerald-green Light wash over you inside and out… until you feel completely healed and nurtured.

To end the meditation, envision yourself in a bubble of Divine white Light. You may see yourself in a perfect lotus position (even if your physical posture is sitting with your legs spread out wide in front of you), or free and floating like your angelic Soul Self. Go with the images that come to mind—whatever image feels most blissful, free, perfectly healthy, and light, like your Soul Self. Now that you have reached this lightness, basking in the white Light, you'll probably feel so nurtured, happy and good that you won't want to end the meditation.

Take a few deeper breaths… This time, envision roots of light extending from the soles of your feet to the center of the earth, helping to ground into your life all the blessings and new Light that you have invoked by this meditation, and keeping you in a Light vibration.

Lightening Bolt Meditation

One condition that can limit your energetic resonance with (and therefore the co-Creation of) your highest wishes is having too strong of an empathic connection with suffering experienced by the people close to you, either geographically or spiritually—members of your Soul-group, which could include blood lines, as well as spiritual friends, romantic partners, neighbors, and even teachers/students. As we have discussed, empathy is a wonderful thing when it comes from a strong and radiant aura, and from the Divine that's flowing through you. But as it happens often, most of us unknowingly take on some negative energies (sadness, stress, and even the energy of some body aches) and limiting conditions ("I can't" attitudes) from our environment—people we share close geographical proximity to, and the people of our core Soul-group, with whom we have deep empathic connections. Sometimes, especially if we do not recognize that these negativities actually come from others, they can become energetic imprints in our bodies and lives, which can prevent us from co-Creating our Ideal Life. The good news is that these limiting themes are easily cleared by this meditation.

The Meditation:

Clear, protect, and bless your space, in preparation for this meditation, using one of the methods you've learnt in Chapter 1. Light incense or candles that you've set your prayerful intent... Call upon your Angels, Spirit Guides, Archangels, or any other deity you believe in, to help facilitate your meditation. Sit comfortably on your meditation cushions, with your spine loosely erect, your shoulders relaxed down, and your chin slightly tucked in. Close your eyes, and start deepening your breath...

Now envision (or verbally invoke, if you can't visualize) the most brilliant Divine white Light coming from the core of the Divine, and engulfing your entire being instantly... Know that this brilliant Light can blaze through any blockage, and affect healing on all levels. As you breathe deeply, envision that you are internalizing the essence of this brilliant iridescent Light, and becoming One with It...

Inhale the brilliant Divine white Light into your core (solar plexus and heart)... Exhale and visualize (or verbally direct) the brilliant iridescent Light expanding to enwrap your entire being and aura... Take your time just inhaling-feeding yourself with the scintillating Light, and exhaling-expanding the Light to heal and strengthen yourself and all of your Light Bodies... You need to truly feel empowered by the most powerful Light of your Creator before you can proceed to the next step of this meditation.

Because of your Soul's connection with the other members of your Soul-group, you are permitted to send them healing energy to clear all suffering and limiting conditions. And you are now empowered to do so by the strength of the brilliant Divine white Light that you have invoked. However, if you are also sending this Light to people who are not members of your Soul-group, but whose low vibration affects you only due to their daily close geographical proximity to you, than in order to honor their free will, you need to intend that they receive only as much of the benefits of the Light as their Higher Selves deems appropriate for them at that time, and receive the rest of the healing at a later time when it is most beneficial for them.

So now envision (or think of) around you a circle of all the people in your life (Soul-group members, people in close geographical proximity, or otherwise people you care about) whose energies (of stress, unhappiness, etc.) have ill affected you or brought you down. Remember that you are still engulfed in the most powerful brilliant Divine white Light—you are still nurtured and protected by the Light. Continue inhaling the brilliant Divine Light into your core, but now as you exhale, project (either by visualization, or if you can't visualize, than verbally direct) the amplified Light from your heart center into all the people in your circle... See the Light radiating from your heart center out like hundreds of lightning bolts projected to these people, energetically blazing through and dissolving all negativities, and healing all of their suffering that may have affected you and your life. You may continue this process for a while... inhale the scintillating Divine which Light into yourself... exhale and project the Light as healing lightening bolts to the people in your circle...

At the end of the meditation, visualize (or verbally affirm that) all people in your circle, including yourself, free from all suffering and bondage, healthy, and happy. Once you have finished an internal processing period, which usually follows this meditation, you will feel lighter, freer, and more ready to co-Create your Ideal Lifepath.

The meditations in this chapter are very powerful, and may induce very powerful purging on all levels. And purging is good, since it makes room for plenty of fresh Creative energy to pour into your life through your Infinite Funnel of Abundance. But since purging too quickly can have some uncomfortable emotional or physical manifestations, these meditations are designed to be gradual and harmonious. As you may have noticed, all the meditations given here actively bring in Divine Light to empower you before, during, and after lifting each negativity, so that the healing of those internal spaces is immediate and automatic, leaving you feeling lighter, freer, and a more empowered after each meditation.

That being said, Rome wasn't built in one day. Everyone is different when it comes to the load of their energetic baggage, and their ability to handle the purging process. Realize that having a heavy load of energetic baggage is not necessarily a badge of shame. Everyone who's had much life experience would almost inevitably have those energetic blocks, unless he/she is a saint. These blocks simply need to be lifted in order to allow you to become the conscious co-Creator that you were meant to be. So if you have a heavy load to clear, it may be wiser to start cleansing only one issue per day, allowing for plenty of time for processing after each meditation. You can return and do a each meditation again and again… until you finish cleansing all that needs to be cleansed, and you feel lighter, freer, and ready to reclaim your Ideal Lifepath. Allow your Soul to guide you on how long and how deep to go in each meditation. No guru can guide you on what is right *for you* better than your own inner wisdom. Throughout the process, be very kind and forgiving to yourself. Allow yourself plenty of downtime for processing, and plenty of nurturing on all levels. Incidentally, self-nurturing is the subject of our next chapter, and is one of the pillars of manifesting prosperity in your life.

Chapter 5

Living in the Infinite Funnel of Abundance

In the last two chapters, you and I have walked together the path of dissolving all that no longer serves your highest wellbeing, and removing all energetic blocks that might have been keeping you from your Ideal Lifepath until now. You probably are already starting to feel lighter, freer, and more ready to reclaim your Ideal Lifepath. You might even be starting to see some auspicious synchronistic events happening in your life. Indeed, now that you have gone through this profound clearing, there is room for fresh Creative energy to flow into your physical body, your energetic self, and your life. However, in order for auspicious synchronicities to *consistently* lead you towards your Ideal Lifepath, and in order to boost your co-Creative powers to the next level, you need to consciously and actively connect to the Infinite Funnel of Abundance—on a daily basis. This stage in our seven-stage process of co-Creation is about strengthening your connection with the Infinite Funnel of Abundance, by tuning into the Divine vibration of kindness, gratitude, joy, and generosity, which is the vibration of Divine abundance.

In order to truly tap into the Divine energy of Creation, the kindness, gratitude, joy and generosity that you express need to be genuine. True kindness needs to be deeply felt within the core of one's being to be genuine; generosity need not come out of lack, but out of being filled with Divine blessings to overflow; and gratitude needs be a song of the heart, sung with joy! And since you have just finished doing some pretty deep work on yourself, it may be difficult for you to just jump directly from that powerful "housecleaning" to swimming in blissful gratitude and generosity. Just as when fever leaves the body, one might experience shivering and fatigue, so too, after energetically ridding yourself of all lower vibrational energies, you may feel tired, and in need of nurturing. And that's as it should be. It is natural to feel the need for nurturing in your cocoon before you become a butterfly. Your body, mind, and emotions are stabilizing and healing—regrouping before soaring. And you need to honor that process, because before you can *truly feel* the bliss of gratitude, generosity and kindness, some self-healing and self-nurturing is in order. In a way, how high you soar later depends on how well you nurture yourself at this stage of the rebirthing of your life.

With that in mind, the first part of this chapter is devoted to your process of nurturing and recharging your Ki batteries from Nature. The second part is devoted to getting you into a mindset, a feeling, and a vibration of gratitude and generosity, which as we have discussed in *Prosperity From Your Soul*, are keys to becoming a more effective co-Creator of a prosperous life. At the end of the chapter, I give you the Infinite Funnel of Abundance Meditation, which is a very potent energetic-vibrational tool to co-Creating a successful life.

When it comes to generosity practices, remember that the actual giving to others does not have to be significant, although it can be if you want it to. It could be simply buying someone a cup of coffee, giving a nicer tip to your server, or just being generous with your kind smile and open heart. So for example, if you give $100 to a homeless person, but feel burdened by that giving to the point that you find yourself cursing all day for having done it, than that's not going to achieve the co-Creative results you seek. It's much better to give just a dollar to that homeless person, if that is the amount you can give *with an open heart and a kind smile*. The important thing is to *feel* fabulous about the giving, and to use that giving to get yourself into a mode of feeling that you can afford to be generous because you are connected to Infinite resources. It is important to get yourself in a vibrational mode of feeling that every kindness you bestow upon another is rewarded by more kindness coming to you through the Infinite Funnel of Abundance.

The consciousness of generosity, kindness and gratitude is important. But mind-energy in and of itself has only a fraction of the vibrational energy that *feelings* generate. Feelings, which are generated by a mutual resonance between your physical body (hormones, neurotransmitters, nervous system, peptides, etc.) and your energetic bodies (namely, your Astral Body), are the force that shifts your entire vibrational essence into likeness and attractive resonance with the prosperity seek. Although emotions do have an anchor in your physiological body function, their more profound influence is on your energetic vibration. Emotions become an energetic vibration, which resonate throughout your energetic bodies and seep out into the Universe. In other words, emotions are the very force that transmits your co-Creative intents into the Universe, and creates a mutual resonance between you and the abundance you seek. The actual actions of generosity and gratitude are just extensions of these feelings into your physical reality—anchors, if you will. At the beginning of the co-Creative process, actions can be the means of driving your emotions and energetic vibration into likeness and resonance with what you want. At the final stages of the co-Creative process, when the manifestation of your request is imminent, inspiration for action would be the means for driving you into a position to reap the rewards. But either way, both action and purely cognitive processes are only extensions of where the real process of co-Creation happens—in your energetic bodies and their resonant connection with the Universe. So it becomes apparent that a true shift of your feelings and energetic vibration is in order. And that shift can be easily achieved by the meditation processes included in this chapter.

Self Nurturing Meditation

This is a simple meditation that can be done in a relatively short time. It will help you start your healing process, and instill a deep feeling of nurturing, peace, and self-worth within. It is this deep knowing that you are worthy of every blessing that then enables you to co-Create those blessings in your life.

Preparing for the Meditation:

Select a quiet space in which you will be uninterrupted for the duration of the meditation. Cleanse, protect, and bless your space in accordance with the processes given in Chapter 1 (Clearing and Protection). Put on music that is very inspiring and that you consider nurturing and elating... This may be devotional music to the deity you believe in, earthly music with womb-of-the-earth sounds, or other non-verbal music. For this meditation, I really like yogic music sung by Singh Kaur & Kim Robertson called Crimson Collection 1. It is very gentle music with Celtic harp and a mantra that helps heal the heart and magnetize miracles into one's life. You should put whatever music inspires heart nurturing for you. Light incense, or a candle with an aromatherapy dispenser with essential oil of rose and frankincense (rose invokes Divine love and nurturing; frankincense enables you to go deep within). Before you light them, bless the incense or candle with your intent for nurturing and healing.

The Meditation:

Sit comfortably on your meditation cushions, with your spine loosely erect, your chin slightly tucked in, and your shoulders relaxed down. Have your eyes nine-tenth closed, one tenth open, as if your eyes are looking downwards, projecting the Divine nurturing Light onto your heart space. Put your open left palm over your chest (heart chakra), and your open right palm on top of it. Sit quietly and listen to the uplifting music.

Now start deepening your breath... Envision that with every inhalation, Divine pink Light comes in through your crown, and fills your heart center; and with every exhalation, the pink Light spreads throughout your entire being. If you can't visualize, than verbally affirm the action of the pink Light. This pink Light is the Divine vibration of Love. Allow yourself to bathe with it completely.

As with any meditation, initially some thoughts will come up. And that's OK. Continue letting those thoughts go as they surface. Continue bringing your awareness back into inhaling Divine pink Light through your heart, making the Light within your heart center a bright Love oasis, projecting the Light to spread, permeate and nurture your entire being with each exhalation... until your whole body and aura are engulfed in this nurturing whitish-pink Light of Divine Love. After a while, your mind will become quiet, and a small oasis of Divine loving Light will glow within your heart center. As your hands, still over your heart center, help convey the feeling of complete nurturing, envision the internal space of your heart chakra as glowing with the most beautiful loving pinkish-white Light. Within this loving oasis, completely embrace all that you are and all that you're feeling at this moment... every aspect of you. Forgive yourself all of your self-perceived shortcomings, release yourself of all karma, and most importantly, release all judgment you might have been passing on any aspect of yourself. Let it all go, and embrace all that you are. Place everything that you are within this flame of Divine Love-Light that is within your heart center now, and allow yourself to receive all the Love that you deserve.

Towards the end of the meditation, envision that as you exhale the white-pink Light, it completely surrounds you — your aura — the room you're in — the house — and even your neighborhood with the pinkish-white Light of Divine Love that you have just allowed yourself to receive.

To ground, take a few deeper breaths and envision roots of Light connecting the soles of your feet and your perineum with the center of the Earth, anchoring this new Love energy into your physical existence. You may gently caress your feet. Envision the Light around you forming a very bright and shiny aura… until you feel refreshed, awake and alert, yet very peaceful.

Nature Meditation

Everything in our reality is a continuous flow of Oneness. And just as our Divine Creator is not separate from us, so too, Mother Nature and her elements are not separate from us, or at least they were not meant to be. However, in the reality of our everyday lives, we all get caught up the conveniences of modern living. Most of us get up in the morning inside a home that is very separate from the smell of the sage and the singing of the birds. Then we spend eight plus hours a day inside an office built from glass and steel, which do not in any way resemble the view of the mountains (trees, ocean). Our living and workspaces are generally illuminated by artificial lights that are very far removed from the glistening sun on the trees and on the ocean. And throughout our day, we breathe air that is recycled through air conditioning systems, which contains very little of the freshness of the cedar and eucalyptus, and even littler of the natural feel of the wind on our faces. And by the end of the day, most of us are exhausted, and go back to our air-conditioned/heated homes, where we eat microwaved frozen dinners that contain very little of Nature's wholesome goodness. But with all good things that could be said about the convenience of modern life, mankind was never meant to be separated from the natural world, since the Nature was designed to heal us. Even Genesis describes all the animals and vegetation as the gifts given by our Creator to heal and nurture us. And there are several levels to understand this.

On the level of the physical reality, environmentally speaking, plants take the byproducts of our metabolism and convert them back into fresh products we can use. For example, plants convert carbon-dioxide to oxygen through photosynthesis. They can also draw toxins from the earth through their roots, and convert them to less toxic substances in their leaves through the process of phytoremediation[1]. Biologically speaking, plants are the lowest species in our food chain, which means that they supply clean nutritional energy not only in the form of plant-based foods that we eat. They also are the base foods that all animals feed of, directly or indirectly. And as the new research field of nutritional medicine will tell you (which we will explore in *A Lifestyle of Prosperity From Your Soul*), natural foods are perfect as they are. They were designed by an all-knowing Creator to contain every nutrient we need. But plants are designed to do more than just supply oxygen, eliminate toxins, and feed our stomachs.

On the bridge between the physical and metaphysical, getting a full breath of fresh air filled with the smell of your natural environment (ocean breeze, cedar, eucalyptus, sage…) triggers a subconscious response inducing a state of calm-yet-alert centeredness, which is our natural state of being. On spiritual-energetic level, plants are storage houses and amplifiers of Divine energy. Recall from *Prosperity From Your Soul* that plants' spirits (Ruach) are not tainted by the primal-instinctual Nefesh that so often biases human emotions. Therefore they are direct channelers of a very distilled form of Divine energy. Since plants directly absorb, ground and amplify the Divine energy as they grow, they can project to you a more grounded version of it, which is easier for us-humans to relate to and absorb. It's like your favorite radio station always broadcasts its programs. But unless you are in the vicinity of a radio receiver, it would be difficult for you to receive and enjoy the program… In the same way, when you immerse yourself in the beauty of nature, plants lovingly emit to you a very grounded "ready-to-use" aspect of Divine energy.

On a metaphysical level, connecting to all the highest life forms on Earth (and beyond) can be a source that replenishes your lost energies in the most natural way, and reconnects you to the life-giving Source of all healing. Through this communion with Nature—as a reflector of the Divine Creative energy, you can find the joy of simple moments, so that you can once again feel generous, kind, and grateful, flowing with ease into every moment in life. Also, since plants are always plentiful and nature always bountiful, what better way to reclaim your attunement with the vibration of bountifulness, then through communion with nature? In my own personal evolution, I have found Nature Meditations (described below), and Nature Walk (*A Lifestyle of Prosperity From Your Soul*) to be wonderful tools to lift off even the most intense stresses, to rebalance myself, and to get me into a blissful state. It always makes me feel perfectly whole, like all is right with my world. I invite you to try them, modify them as you feel inspired, make them your own, and most of all, enjoy!

The Meditation:

Find a place of nature that "speaks" to you. This could be a meadow, a beach, a secret garden, or even just your back yard. Sit in a comfortable position, or lie down on the ground if you are more comfortable that way. Close your eyes and get even more comfortable… Start comfortably deepening your breath, so that each breath is comfortably deeper than the one before.

Now envision or think of all the beautiful parts of your environment emitting glowing dreamy colors of energy to you. Envision (or pensively intend) that with every inhalation, you are absorbing their beauty, radiance and vitality, and with every exhalation, you are giving away your stress and troubles, to be neutralized by Nature. Keep breathing natural-deep breaths. Keep absorbing all the energy you need from this natural environment. If you are magnetized to a particular color or a particular element that day, commune with that element in your mind… Let your consciousness take you where it may with this communion. If you feel a particular affinity to the green grass, than "see" yourself especially absorbing its energy to the point that you become the green grass. Become the freedom of that seagull that's magnetizing your attention… become the lightness of the billowy white clouds above… become the stability and ancient wisdom of the tree… become the beauty of the flower… become one with whatever element is calling your attention and making you feel joyous.

Consider taking off your shoes and planting your feet in in the sand (or dirt), or running free in a field, stretching your arms out wide to feel totally free. Or if you are at the beach, if the ocean water is calling you, dip your feet in the water. Don't think about how other people are going to view you in this moment. Don't think about time constrains, or physical limitation. Just engulf yourself in whatever nature element is "calling" you. You can either do whatever you feel inspired to, or you can envision yourself doing so. So for example, if you can't run as free as the wind, than close your eyes, and meditatively envision that you are doing so, or feel your oneness with the lightness of the wind. You can't fly like a bird, but your spirit can fly even higher and freer. This is more than just an indulgence. This is *your* time to *Truly* commune with nature, refill your batteries with all of her healing energies, and restore your balance, health, and happiness.

Always end the meditation with gratitude. Feel and say thanks to Nature, to your Soul, God, your Angels, or any deity that you feel may have helped you heal during this time. Stand up and envision Divine white Light run through and engulf all of you from head to toe. Envision Light roots extending through the soles of your feet, the palms of your hands, and the center of your body towards the center of the earth, or if you can't visualize, than just commune with the earth element of nature. This will help stabilize the energy and ground you so you can safely drive (or walk) home.

Indoors Nature Healing

Most of us are fortunate enough that we can go out into nature and do these awesome meditations and walks. But even if you live in Maine and it's the middle of winter, or if you suffer a severe health ailment that has you are bed-ridden, you can still enjoy Mother Nature's healing through the window of your mind. And again, if you can't visualize, than speak your intents and keep your thoughts on the elements of the meditation, and it will work almost as well.

Find a comfortable meditative space that is near a window that could be opened at least partially (preferably a window that faces a garden or nature area). As you settle in a comfortable position (I like to do this one lying down on my back), close your eyes, and take some deep breaths, taking in all the earth smells coming in through your open window. As you inbreathe the fresh smells of the earth, envision being healed by Nature and absorbing her nurturing energies. When a slight breeze comes in through the window, envision that it is bringing you more of the Divine breath of life. Envision the beauty of all the vast spaces of nature that this wind brings with it… become that wind, and feel the its freedom, caressing the grass and all that it touches… When you hear the birds singing outside your window, become infused with their healing songs. As you inhale the freshness of the earth, become one with the Earth-mother, and let her ground, strengthen and nurture you. Become one with the vitality and life-force of the vegetation outside your window. Just allow the Earth-mother to give you all the healing and strength that you need, through your bedroom window.

As you tune deeper into yourself and your oneness with Nature, envision that you are lying in a comfortable basket under the open skies, and a humongous beautiful bird is picking you up like a stork carrying a baby in a soft blanket. The bird that you see in the eyes of your mind can be your animal totem, or some mythological creature. Just make sure you feel safe and good with that bird, as she is taking you to a high healing place. Envision the bird carrying you through the skies until you feel absolutely free and lighthearted. It takes you through the most beautiful sights of the Earth… into your own sacred healing place. This could be a place you have visited in real life or in your dreams; or it could be a place you'd never seen before, but you feel totally peaceful and nurtured in it. Most people see this healing place as either a high-elevation place, or an incredibly luscious and beautiful place. Let the vision come to you. The important part is to let your Mind Body take you to this place that has magical healing powers for you. Now that you are in your sacred healing place, you are one with the place itself in all of its magical healing powers. As your healing place is helping you reconnect with your Soul Self, envision yourself completely healed by Divine Love and Light, grounded and protected by the Earth-mother, infused with the life force of the flowers, trees and lush vegetation, enlivened with the joy of living water. You are now One with all the elements of Creation. Breathe in their virtues, and absorb their beauty. "See" this sacred healing place as beautiful and as magnificent as you wish. Allow yourself to be in complete peace in your special healing place. Take your time, receive all the gifts that the Universe wants to give you, and internalize them as you breathe.

When you are ready, call your bird-spirit to pick you up and take you back to your own reality. As you start returning to your reality, take a few deeper breaths and consciously bring your awareness to full body consciousness. Wiggle your toes, and make small circles with your ankles and wrists. You can rub the soles of your feet together to further ground yourself. Stretch and feel perfectly healed, refreshed, and balanced.

Sunset Meditation

This is an effortless meditation, not one in which you have to actively engage your mind in order to let go of the brain-fucking noise. Since it is a meditation of beauty and pure joy, Nature will do the job for you.

Dress in your most comfortable clothing that make you feel at home, but sensual and tuned into beauty. Go out to a beautiful place in which you can watch the sunset (for me it is a beach, with the sun setting to the ocean). You can do this meditation sitting up, or standing with your legs spread about shoulder width apart, and your knees straight but unlocked. This stance will give you a comfortably grounded base. Take off your hat. Take off your sunglasses, if you can. Do a few soft wavy movements to further relax your body. Now start comfortably deepening your breath into natural deep breaths… Relax your eyes into an unfocused soft gaze, so that you can hazily watch the sun low in the horizon. The keys to sustaining this meditation effortlessly are the hazy, off-focus viewing, and the breath.

Relax and breathe in the beauty of the sun in all of its colors in the skies… You may see the red orange of the skies, the yellow white of the sun ball, the shades of blue created in the skies. The colors may then merge and you may be able to see green as the yellow of the sun smudges into the blue of the skies. You may see the skies turn into a darker blue and mix with the red haze layers in a swirl of indigo and magenta. Breathe in all this beauty and envision that all of these colors are feeding-healing all of your chakras and all of your light bodies… Just let go, absorb this beauty, and let it engulf you… Let all thoughts go and immerse yourself in the beauty and freshness of the air as you continue to breathe in this beauty and let it nurture every part of you.

As the sun disappears below the horizon, ground yourself by envisioning that you are the channel connecting the Heavens and the Earth. Envision the Divine Light extending from the heart of the Universe, through your crown… your heart… and out the soles of your feet to the center of Earth. As you have just absorbed the energy of all colors of the rainbow through our sun-star (as a conduit of Divine energy), your body and aura are glowing ever so brightly with Divine Light surrounding your entire being. You'll feel blissful yet grounded, strong, peaceful, and absolutely joyous!

Gratitude Meditation

Now that you have spent some time healing and recharging yourself with the last few meditations (and you can repeat them as many times as you feel the need to), you are ready to more fully tune into gratitude. This meditation will help you feel grateful for all the blessings you have already co-Created into your life. Since gratitude is one of the main pillars on which all-inclusive prosperity stands, as you become able to truly *feel* gratitude for your life, your vibrational essence will also shift into likeness and resonance with the Divine, thereby strengthening your ability to tap more powerfully into the Infinite Funnel of Abundance, and ground Its blessings into your life.

Select a space in which you can be undisturbed for the duration of this meditation. Use the practices listed in Chapter 1 to cleanse, protect, and bless your space for the meditation. Make the lighting of the room soft and soothing. Put on music that makes you feel nurtured like a child. Intend that this music will nurture you in the deepest way, and connect you to your Light.

Now sit comfortably on your meditation pillows, with your spine softly erect, your shoulders relaxed down, your chin slightly tucked in, and your eyes closed. Put your hands in your lap, palms up in a receiving mode. Gradually deepen your breath… start by doing some Zohar Breaths, inhaling Divine white Light into the back of your heart space, letting it fill your entire body, and exhaling Divine white Light through the front of your heart chakra…

When you reach the place of peace and stillness, envision that as you inhale, you draw in more of the Divine Light to nurture your entire being… as you exhale, the Divine white Light projects out through your now glowing heart-space… and surrounds your entire being with a bubble of the brightest white Light… Envision that with every breath, your aura becomes bigger and stronger, until it is a huge bubble of scintillating white Light. This scintillating white Light could be as big as a house, or bigger. If you can't visualize, than carry the thought of those intents as you breathe.

Now envision (or think of) all the things and people that you are grateful for ethereally manifest within your aura-bubble of scintillating white Light… As you continue this breathing and projecting this Light all around you, your aura will become bigger and bigger, allowing you to place within its Light more things and people that you are grateful for… until you "see" the entire room… and then the entire city you live in full of your glowing aura, and within it, the images of all things and people that you are grateful for. Envision (or think of) all the blessings currently in your life also glowing in their brightest Light. Envision all the people you've placed in this bubble smiling, peaceful, and happy in their own bubbles of Light… until you begin to see each blessing that's in your life in its own Divine Light, but connected to your bubble of Light, and supporting you in your highest mission in life.

As a manifestation tool, you may extend the meditation to envision within the scintillating Light of your expanded aura all the things that you wish to co-Create into your life, as if they are already manifested in your auric bubble of scintillating Light. This will magnetize those things and people to you and help them manifest into your physical reality.

This is a very blissful meditation that you'll find that you just want to keep on doing. To end the meditation, take some deeper breaths, massage/caress your feet, and envision roots of Light extending from the soles of your feet to the center of the Earth.

Gratitude Practices

Living in a state of grace is more than just doing a gratitude meditation once in a blue moon. It is an attitude towards life that can make the smallest of moments in life sparkle with joy. Now I know that it's not always easy to find something to be grateful for in the hectic reality of your life. You can start by adopting a few simple practices that can help refocus your energies into a joyful gratitude vibration each time you do them. For example, you can adopt a habit of counting your blessings as you wake up each morning, and before get out of bed. Never mind how much you don't feel like getting up yet. Let go of all troubling thoughts about the challenges of your day; just find at least three things that you are grateful for in those moments.

Another helpful practice is to pick one meal a day in which you pamper yourself even if you are eating alone. This could be done at dinner, when most people are at leisure, in a leisurely lunch, or even at breakfast if you have the time. Set up a nice table for yourself, with a tablecloth, a linen napkin, and your nicest dishware. Put on your favorite music that would get you into your "I'm Fabulous" mood. You can even light a candle that you've blessed. Set it up so that it makes you really feel that you are a beloved child of God. Before you start eating your meal, take a few moments to count your blessings. Just close your eyes for a moment, take a few deep breaths, and make a little mental list of what you're grateful for in that moment. At first, this may seem forced, like a meaningless mental list. But if you really take your time to breathe gratitude into each realization, the list will grow to be a true reminder of all the blessings that are already in your life... until you begin to truly *feel* grateful! Don't worry if the feeling of gratitude takes time to come. At first, it'll be just a fleeting moment of tuning into the true feeling of it. With time, you will be more apt at tuning into gratitude, and the feeling-vibration of it will sweep over you more frequently and more profoundly.

There could be many other practices that could help you feel gratitude. Whichever practice you choose to adopt, when you find a way to live your life with an attitude of gratitude, you'll start connecting with every element within it with joy and with hopeful eyes, and you'll vibrationally attract more blessings into your life.

Generosity & Kindness Meditation

As important to co-Creation as kindness and generosity are, like gratitude, they are not always easy to *feel*, in the hectic reality of life. The key to being able to feel it is to know that kindness and generosity to others should be a natural extension of being kind and generous to yourself. Because you shouldn't be forced to give to others what you feel you don't have enough of. Since the best Source for all of this generosity is the Divine Her-Himself, the abundance should pour into you and your life until you feel filled to overflowing with Divine goodness. But understand that this is really a matter of feeling. Say that $10,000 just landed in your lap. But if you don't feel connected to the Divine Funnel of Abundance, you will fear that this was a one-time thing, and as a result, you will hoard the money rather than share or even spend it on something you like. I'm not saying that you should blow the money on something unimportant, just in a whim. The point it that only when you *know* that the Divine will keep precipitating goodness on you, do you truly *feel* safe enough to be generous to others. And only then will you truly feel the need to give to others out of the goodness of your heart. When you feel this urge to give to others out of your overflowing heart, that is when you are connected to the Infinite Funnel of Abundance and to everything in your reality as One. And you are then ready to co-Create wonderful things into your life. This meditation will help you tune into that feeling.

Prepare Your Space for the Meditation:

Choose a safe quiet place, in which you can be uninterrupted for a few minutes. Cleanse, protect and bless the space using the tools listed in Chapter 1. Put on relaxing non-verbal music of the heart—music that opens your heart and makes you feel inspired. You can light a candle or incense that you've blessed with intent.

The Meditation:

Sit comfortably on your meditation cushions, with your spine loosely erect, your shoulders relaxed down, your chin slightly tucked in, and your hands in your lap, palms facing up in a receptive mode… Close your eyes, and gradually deepen your breath…

Envision (or think of) the most nurturing Divine golden Light come into you through the crown of your head. And as the energy of nurturing kindness comes in, envision that it pours in slowly and indulgently, almost like honey, through your neck, over your heart, and your entire being… Bathe for a while in this golden Light of nurturing kindness, and let it fill you completely… As you inhale, let the golden Light come in through your crown and pour into your heart… and as you exhale, let the power of your heart magnify the Light exponentially to nurture your entire being… If you can't visualize, than speak your intents as you breathe, and then carry the thought of the golden Light nurturing your entire being.

After a few moments of bathing yourself in the golden nurturing Light, there will be so much of that Light that you'll naturally want to make more use of it. It's like honey endlessly pouring into a jar; after it fills the jar, you need to find more jars to put the endless honey in. So envision (or think of) all the people that have crossed your path recently and that you wish to bestow kindness on. You can envision them one at a time, or surrounding you in a sacred circle. Envision that the Divine nurturing golden Light is still pouring into you through your crown with each breath, still flooding over your heart, and still nurturing your whole being; but now envision that you are projecting (or verbally directing) the *overflow* of the golden Light (kindness, generosity, nurturing) through your heart chakra, out to the objects of your kindness... until they are completely basking in that Light... Continue inhaling more golden Light through your crown, and exhaling-projecting the access Light to the person receiving this kindness... until you "see" both of you sitting in perfect lotus position, perfectly serene, and bathed in Divine golden Light of kindness, generosity, love, happiness, bliss, and abundance.

Ground yourself by gently massaging your feet and envisioning light roots extending from the soles of your feet into the center of the earth. Take a few refreshing breaths. You may even do a couple of minutes of Grounding Breaths (see Chapter 2).

Infinite Funnel of Abundance Meditation

As you already cognitively know, your breath, your life, and all that you have is given to you as the most beloved child of your Creator. Although you and your Creator Truly are One, it is easier for us as humans to envision your connection with the Divine as being at the receiving end of a funnel—Her-His Infinite Funnel of Abundance. And of course, the more open you are to the Divine's flow within you, the more freely blessings will flow into your life. But as you also know, it isn't cognitive knowing that really helps you strengthen your connection with the Divine. It is a deep knowing-feeling that raises your vibration, strengthens your connection, and allows the free flow of abundance into your life.

This meditation will help you feel and vibrationally reconnect with the Infinite Funnel of Abundance. It is, therefore, a very important meditation to the process of co-Creation, the ace in the hole, so to speak. The meditation will gain even more potency when you do it again at the end of all the meditational processes of the next few chapters, once you have fully tuned into the details of your Ideal Lifeplan. But it is never too early to start permanently anchoring yourself into the Infinite Funnel of Abundance.

Prepare Your Space for the Meditation:

Select a safe quiet place, in which you can be uninterrupted for the duration of the meditation. Cleanse, protect, and bless the space using some of the practices listed in Chapter 1. Put on some relaxing non-verbal music. You can light a candle or incense that you've blessed with intent.

The Meditation:

Sit comfortably on your meditation cushions, with your spine loosely erect, your shoulders relaxed down, and your chin slightly tucked in... close your eyes, and start deepening your breath...

When your breath gets relatively deep do three significant "tuning-in" breaths: Inhale deeply and bring your arms up into a V above your head; hold your breath for a moment, and envision (or verbally affirm) that between the V of your arms is the receiving end of the Divine Funnel of Light and Abundance—is the funnel through which the Infinite pours all of Her-His blessings to you. In this brief moment that your arms are up and your lungs are full of air, tune into all the Divine blessings that you wish to bring into your life right now, and envision them descending into you as a funnel of Infinite Light. If you do not yet know what you wish for, just envision Divine Light between your arms, and set the intent that with this movement, you are tapping into the Infinite resources of Heaven. After that brief moment, exhale as you sweep your arms down to the side of your body, envisioning (or otherwise affirming) that you are actively pulling the Infinite Funnel of Abundance unto you—as if you are wearing it like a dress. Envision that as the Light pours into you through the Funnel, all of these blessings merge with your aura, making it Infinitely bigger and brighter, and are ready to manifest within your physical reality… Repeat this tuning-in breath with the arm movement 3-5 times.

Then, continue sitting on your meditation cushion, and envision (or verbally affirm) that you have fully merged with the Light coming through the Infinite Funnel of Abundance. Affirm that with every inhalation, you feed more of it into you, as if you are actively "sucking" it in… and with every exhalation, you exhale the Light to enhance your aura, your living space, and every aspect of your life… As you envision (or carry the thought of) yourself and your aura becoming bigger and brighter, fed by the Light of the Infinite, your aura will become so big, that it extends to the whole city you live in… When you feel that you have absorbed a good amount of Light, and that you have expanded yourself enough for the time being, you may start "seeing" (or otherwise becoming aware of) forms and things within your expanded aura. The things that you see (or become aware of) may be specific things you wish to manifest, like cash or a new house for example, or they may be symbolic things, like glowing gold coins. Whatever they are, it is important that you "see" them manifest as easily as if they just "poof"—appear. It is important that you feel like they are of the essence of the Divine Light, and that they make you feel joyous. Throughout the process, continue visualizing yourself bathing within the Divine Funnel of Abundance… continue drawing Its blessings into you with every inhalation… continue exhaling—channeling that Light into your aura, and envisioning the blessings you wish for manifested into a sphere of Light that represents your life…

After a while, you will start feeling very peaceful, but at the same time hopeful and charged with vitality and positive energy. It is a vitality energy that comes from a deep knowing that everything is going to be alright, that all the abundance you seek is and will be given, that you are cared and provided for, and that the best manifestations in your life are yet to come. And this knowing is not a cognitive knowing, but a deeply felt knowing that you are One with the Source from which all prosperity comes. When the meditation has led you to these feelings, it is time to return to your here-now consciousness, and ground yourself. For you have, at that point, restored your original unobstructed connection with the Infinite Funnel of Abundance, and with it, your vibrational potency to actually co-Create that abundance in your life. It is good to do this meditation often, so as to restore that great feeling on a daily basis, and perpetuate your attractive vibrational resonance with the abundance you seek.

Without dissolving the Infinite Funnel of Abundance, envision (or carry the thought of) a large pyramid of crystal clear Divine Light all around you and your life. Relax your breath to a natural breath, and feel the pyramid of Light stabilize and ground all the positive effects of the meditation into your here-now reality. Take a few moments doing this. Allow the pyramid of crystal Light to bring all of your senses into balance and stability, and envision that the pyramid crystalizes all the blessings that you saw in your meditation, into physical manifestation. When the meditation comes to its natural ending, you'll feel peaceful, centered, yet happy and zesty, excited to go on and bring all these blessings that you saw into full fruition in your life.

Through the meditations in this chapter, you have restored much of the energy of your Original Self, and have begun to experientially ground the radiance, zest of life, and joy that were always meant to be yours. You should now be in a state of easily connecting to all the elements of your life with love and joy. It is a state of hopefulness and of deeply knowing that positive changes are coming your way.

Although you have shifted your awareness considerably, and are beginning to be much happier in your life, you have not yet started to co-Create real changes in the physical circumstances of your life. And before you take any physical steps, you'll need to tune into the Ideal Lifeplan that your Soul has laid out for your life. In the next chapter, I will help you tune into what makes you happy, the essence of your Soul, and the details of your life-mission, all of which lays the foundation for tuning into your Ideal Lifeplan, and constructing a real life plan to co-Create it.

Chapter 6

The Ideal-you

Just as there are Infinite resources for wealth, there is also an infinite number of paths that can lead to health, happiness and prosperity. We are each unique. Our talents are different; what makes us happy is different; and our True calling in life is also different. What makes Joe happy may not necessarily make Mary happy. For example, I was never meant to be a five-star basketball player, and Michael Jordan was probably not meant to be a reiki master; and neither one of us was destined to be a prima ballerina. So with all of the free choice that we were each given, we each also have our own unique path that is destined to take us through life in the most auspicious way. This is the Lifepath that is Ideal *for you*, and will easily bring you the best health, provide you with the most easily flowing abundance, and make you happy in each moment. It is the Lifepath that makes your heart sing with joy. But do you actually know what it is that makes you joyous to the very core of your being? Do you know what makes you so happy that you can't help but secretly wiggle your toes in pleasure?

Ah… Many people walk through life somewhere between their hectic lives and their deep desire to be happier. But most of us forget what it is that actually makes us happy. We forget what our hopes and dreams were. They become something tucked away somewhere in the back of our minds, until one day we completely forget what they were. Then we are left with only a dim memory of having once known what makes us happy, like having the memory of the memory…

In the next chapter, we will delve deeply into meditations that will help you tune into the specific details of your Ideal Lifeplan, having a complete Internal Experience of what it would be like to actually live your Ideal Lifepath of prosperity. In the course of the next chapter, you will also devise a plan, anchored in physical reality, to make your Ideal Lifepath happen. But since your Ideal Lifeplan relies on your Ideal Lifework, which in turn depends on your Truest passions and talents, than in order to be able to tune into your Ideal Lifeplan, it is essential for you to first experience your True essence. What is it that Truly makes you happy? What were your heartfelt hopes and dreams as a child and throughout your life? What is your innermost Self like? What does It want? And what does it hope to achieve in this lifetime? When the answers to these questions resonate deep within every part of you (not only cognitively, but also emotionally and vibrationally), then and only then, will you be ready to tune into the True mission of your life—the mission that makes your innermost heartstring resonate with joy, on which your Ideal Lifepath of prosperity is based.

So in this chapter, I will help you tune into the very essence of your being. You have already started to tune into guidance from your Soul, when you started doing Zohar Breath Meditations. The meditations in this chapter will deepen your connection with your Soul, and help you tune into Its vibrational essence and into the *feeling* of Its Ideal plans for you and for your life. For once you fully tune into your True talents, desires, and wants, it will become much easier to tune into the Ideal Lifepath that will lead you to a lifetime of health, happiness, and prosperity.

Meditation to Invite Divine Guidance

One of the first steps to getting to know the real you is asking for Divine guidance, and being open to receive it in the deeper sense. As you already know, since the Universe works by free will, higher guidance—be it from your Soul Self, the elements of nature, Angels, God or any other deity you may believe in—cannot come to you unless you allow it, and invite it into your life. So this simple meditation opens up the channel of communication between you and the Divine, in a more profound way than your average daily life. Once that channel is open, we can build on that with more specific meditations later in this chapter.

Find a nice quiet place, in which you will feel safe and be uninterrupted during this meditation. Use the practices listed in Chapter 1 to cleanse, protect and bless your space, in preparation for this meditation. Put on some relaxing non-verbal music that you know will put you in a very relaxed state. You can light a candle or an incense that you've blessed with the intent of the meditation.

Sit comfortably on your meditation cushions, with your spine loosely erect, your shoulders relaxed down, and your chin slightly tucked in. Close your eyes, and start deepening your breath… Now envision (or invoke) the brightest Divine white Light, coming from the center of the Universe, engulfing and forming a column of Light around you. This is an iridescent pearly Light, which embodies God's purest wisdom, self-acceptance, and coming into one's own God Self. Being engulfed in that Light feels very nurturing, like in that moment, it's ok to just be you. Envision this column iridescent pearly Light (or direct it to) surrounding you—crown to feet, and then grounding itself into the Earth.

As with any meditation, in the beginning, thoughts will surface up as your mind cleanses itself from the brainfucking clutter. Just let them all surface, and send all those cluttered thoughts into the column of Light, intending that any difficulty or disharmony would be dissolved by the purity of the Light, and the wisest, highest-vibrational solutions to all issues descend to you from the Light. Send all positive themes into the loving hands of God for further manifestation in your life. Keep coming back to being bathed in the nurturing wisdom of the Light. After a few minutes, you'll reach a point of peace and stillness and begin to feel completely safe in this Light.

It is at this point that you should focus on your breath again… With every deep inhalation, envision (or silently verbally affirm) that you are bringing the Divine wisdom of the Light into yourself through your crown, third eye, throat, heart, and the rest of your being… and with every deep exhalation, envision (or silently verbally affirm that) the wisdom that you have internalized coming into fruition as ideas, feelings, and physical manifestations. Keep inhaling the wisdom and pulling it down through all your chakras; keep exhaling and allowing the wisdom to manifest and take form within your mind and aura.

The way to know if ideas are Divinely inspired (and not a part of the brainfucking noise) is that they bring you deep joy and peace. If a thought or idea makes you start arguing with yourself back and forth, or if it makes you feel uneasy and snaps you out of the peaceful state of the meditation, than it is, no doubt, a part of the brainfucking noise. If, on the other hand, it gives you supreme peace, to the point that you are just happy dwelling in it, than it is inspired by your Soul Self. Use the God Meter and the Joy Meter detailed in *Prosperity From Your Soul* to make sure that these ideas are Divinely inspired. Generally, ideas that are inspired by your True Self just resonate right with every part of you.

This is a very nurturing meditation that you'll just love doing. Yet it is so simple to do. At this stage, what is important is that you invite Divine guidance, healing and Love in, by visualizing Her-His column of Light engulfing you and by breathing it in. It is this invitation that is the objective of this meditation. So at this point it is not necessary that the Light you exhale take form as any specific ideas yet. It will probably take form later, when you repeat the meditation again, after you've tuned into your Ideal Lifeplan in the next chapter. However, many times you'll find that as you start this meditation, and start absorbing the essence of this iridescent pearly Light-ray through your chakras, the essence will take form, and ideas will start coming through, sometimes even after you finish the meditation and go about your day. It may be helpful to keep a pen and paper with you, so that you can write some notes of all the ideas that come to you.

Meditation on What Makes You Happy

While the very essence of your Soul may still be somewhat elusive for you at this point, many of the activities of your life can easily be definable as activities that are either pleasant or unpleasant for you. This definition can clue you into what actually makes you happy, as a prerequisite for tuning into your Ideal Lifeplan. This meditation aims to categorize the activities of your life into pleasant or unpleasant, and then asks the wisdom of your Soul to show you how to arrange your life so that all of it can become more pleasant. This insistence on spending as many moments in your daily life doing pleasant things is more than just an indulgence. At this point of your co-Creative new path, especially after you've worked so hard to eliminate all negative motifs from your life (in Chapters 3 & 4), it is especially important to limit the time you devote to unpleasant activities, and to fill your days with joyful activities, as a way to keep you connected to Universal joy and tapped into the Infinite Funnel of Abundance.

Be aware that if you've tucked away your hopes and dreams a long time ago, your Ideal Lifeplan may not pop up like a brilliant idea as soon as you close your eyes and decide to meditate. In most cases it is a process. That is why I'm giving you all these different meditations, to help take you through this process step-by-step. So be patient and kind to yourself as you go through it.

The process of this meditation involves posing questions from the perspective of your here-now self, then delving into Zohar Breath Meditation to tune into the answers from the perspective of your Soul Self, and perhaps jotting down whatever comes to mind. The writing here is automatic, which means without stopping to think about it, and without filtering anything through your logical mind. Just writing down whatever comes, as if it is coming straight from your subconscious, or in this case, straight from your Soul's consciousness. It doesn't have to be longhand writing, either. It can be just some keynotes on images you saw, clairaudience messages you received, feelings, etc. The writing may help you not only remember the answers that came to you, but also analyze them get more a-ha moments later, after you get back to ordinary consciousness.

Prepare Your Space for the Meditation:

Select a quiet place in which you would be undisturbed through the meditation. Cleanse, protect, and bless your space in accordance with some of the suggestions given in Chapter 1. Set your intent for this meditation. You may light candles or incense that you've blessed with the intent of the meditation. Put on some music that is inspiring but neutral.

Before the meditation, take a large piece of paper, and divide it into two columns. On the left column, write a list of (daily, weekly, monthly) activities you've engaged in during the past few weeks or months. Write the pleasant activities on the top part of the left column, and the unpleasant activities on the bottom of the left column. Set the paper and pen besides your meditation cushions, so that you'd be able to get to it during the meditation.

The Meditation:

Sit comfortably on your meditation cushions, with your spine erect yet relaxed, your shoulders relaxed down, and your chin slightly tucked in. Close your eyes, and gradually deepen your breaths. Start with some Zohar Breaths, inhaling Divine white Light into the back of your heart chakra, letting it engulf you, and exhaling Divine white Light out of the front of the heart chakra. Let all troubling thoughts surface and then let them go… and get to the point where you experience the stillness, clarity, supreme peace, and nurturing Light of your Soul. While staying in the high perspective of your Soul Self, have your here-now self pose these questions (but stay in your Soul's perspective, like you're looking at yourself from above, almost like you're looking at someone else's life):

- How did the pleasant activities make you feel? Happy? Empowered?
- What was it about these pleasant activities that made you feel so good?
- Are any of these pleasant activities related to the True essence of your Soul, or to your Ideal Lifeplan?
- What should you do at this point to maximize your time spent on pleasant activities?
- In retrospect, were all the unpleasant activities really necessary?
- Was there a way to avoid the stress associated with them?
- Was there another way to do the unpleasant activities, which could have made them pleasant?

- ☙ Would doing a meditation or a joyful physical activity (see *A Lifestyle of Prosperity From Your Soul*) before starting the unpleasant activity have put you in a mind frame that is more conducive to having more fun with this activity?
- ☙ How can you get all the necessary tasks in your life be done with only pleasant things?
- ☙ What is the perfect way to achieve all of your life's activities in an enjoyable way?

After you pose each question, go back to Zohar Breaths in order to go back into your Soul's perspective. Don't rush. Just pose each question separately, and then do enough Zohar Breaths until you are back in the supreme peace and stillness of your Soul's presence. While dwelling in the nurturing and supreme peace of your Soul, just wait for an impression to come to you. It may come as a clairaudience message, as a vision, a feeling, or an unexplainable knowing. Just go with impressions you get that feel right. Do some automatic writing to record the impressions and messages that came to you. At this point, one tendency that many novice meditators have is to second-guess the impressions that come, asking, "is this really a message from my Soul Self or am I just imagining things? What if this is just a capricious notion of my here-now self?" Again, as long as you feel that supreme peace, stillness, and nurturing of your Soul-Love, than you are indeed tuned into the consciousness of your Soul; and as long as the message is consistent, crystal clear, and resonates harmoniously throughout your being, than it is indeed coming from your Soul Self or a high-level Spirit Guide.

Now, there are many things you can do to minimize the annoying tasks, and give the forte to the enjoyable tasks. For example, before you start an annoying task, you can eat a breakfast that is particularly enjoyable, put on some relaxing music in the background, or go for a Nature Walk (see *A Lifestyle of Prosperity From Your Soul*). You could decide in advance to only allot a certain amount of time to the annoying tasks, and then go do something fun, perhaps lunch with a friend. And it is always helpful to set your intent that taking care of the annoying tasks will flow as easy as a breeze, and that the main part of the day will consist of your enjoyable activities. After all, the purpose of an Earthly life is not so you can pay bills, slave your ass off, or please your boss, although I agree that some of these activities are necessities of living on this physical earth-plain. Despite their necessity, the unpleasant tasks had better not be the main course of your life! Because *the purpose of your being here on Earth is to experience love and joy, and by that, co-Create more love in the world*. When you understand this perspective, channeling your life to have more enjoyable moments is an important step towards co-Creating your Ideal Lifepath.

This meditation is only the beginning of your awareness of what makes you happy. From a basic here-now perspective, it shows you what makes you happy, and what you can do to minimize unpleasant moments in your life, or perhaps how to achieve the necessary tasks in a more enjoyable way. But from a more metaphysical co-Creation perspective, it is more than just a step. For when you categorize for yourself which activities make you truly happy, it can help you direct your life in a more positive flow towards your True life-mission. And once you direct the activities of your life to revolve around joyful activities, you will be able to spend most of your time dwelling in a vibration of bliss, which will help you reconnect and stay connected to the Infinite Funnel of Abundance.

An example from my own life, a few years ago, at the time that my income was low, the position of the chief pilot of the Los Angeles base opened at the airline that I was working for. Based on my professional experience, I was perfect for the job, had I chosen to apply for it. It would have also meant an early upgrade into a captain's position in the airplane, and a big pay increase, not to mention prestige. I thought long and hard about applying for the position. To help me with the decision, I did this meditation. As I took inventory of which of the activities of my life make me happy, and which make me unhappy, I came to the conclusion that sitting inside a dark office, dealing with company politics, disciplining/reprimanding people, and spending long hours categorizing people and events into computer codes, are all tasks which would have made me extremely unhappy. At that point of my meditation, I realized that being outdoors, meditating, doing reiki, and helping people realize their greatness are the things that do make me happy. It was then that I decided to pass on the position, and go to massage therapy school—a path that opened a whole world of spiritual possibilities for me, and brought me closer to my True life-mission, which I now believe revolves around bringing for you the wisdom of these books, the different courses of Soul Path Retreat, Rezossage (a new holistic massage modality), and RezoDance, to help you connect with all that you can be and all the health, happiness, and prosperity that you can manifest in your life.

Essence of Your Soul Meditation

The Ideal Lifeplan that your Soul has laid out for you before you were born is not just some ethereal idea that is detached from your here-now self. This Ideal Lifepath that your Soul is still pushing you to walk in this lifetime has real roots within you in the form of your Truest talents, your hopes, your dreams, and your deepest heartfelt desires. Your hopes and dreams did not manifest in your mind out of thin air. They materialized within you because they were implanted there by your very own Soul, as the forces that push you to fulfill your Ideal Lifepath. Your Truest talents also didn't come out of nothing. They too were given to you by your Soul, to help you co-Create your Ideal Lifepath. So in a very real way, the seeds for your success are already embedded in you.

Thus, tuning into your early childhood dreams, desires, and talents, which are indicative of your True dreams, desires and talents, can help you tune into the true essence of whom you Truly are, and lead you (in the next chapter) to recapture the details of your Ideal Lifeplan. In this meditation, we will tune into your very early childhood, recall what your natural affinities were, and through these, start tuning in and experience the True essence of your Soul. This is a very important meditation to start the ball rolling in the direction of True abundance in your life.

Prepare Your Space for the Meditation:

Select a quiet place, in which you can be uninterrupted through the meditation. Use the practices you've learnt in Chapter 1 to cleanse, protect, and bless your space for the meditation. Set a pure intent for this meditation to help you tune into the very essence of your Soul and Its mission.

You may light incense or a candle with prayerful intent to help you get into a sacred solitude. You may also invite your Angels, Spirit Guides, or other deities that you believe in, to help you with this meditation. Put on music that you know sends you into the deepest heart space. Have a pen and paper ready by your side, so you can do some automatic writing to record your impressions…

The Meditation:

Sit comfortably on your meditation cushions with your spine loosely erect, your shoulders relaxed down, and your chin slightly tucked in. Have your eyes nine-tenth closed and one-tenth open, as if looking down at your internal heart-space. Gradually start deepening your breath…

Start by doing some Zohar Breaths… After the usual period of cleansing of all brainfucking mind-noise and lower vibrational energies, you will come to the point of experiencing the now familiar peace and Grace of your Soul Self. Continue with Zohar Breaths, and set the intent to go deeper and view your life from the perspective your Soul.

Staying in this perspective, ask your Soul to show you your early childhood and life. Then, without losing your Soul's perspective, have your here-now self ask your Soul:

- ☯ What fascinated you and magnetized you as a child?
- ☯ What were some of the activities you loved to do?
- ☯ What were you very passionate about?
- ☯ Which of these themes are you still passionate about today?
- ☯ What were some of your hopes, dreams, and daydreams as a child or younger adult?
- ☯ What were some of the talents that you, or others close to you, have always known you have?
- ☯ What were the things that you were always just naturally good at—activities and achievements that just seem to 'fall off your sleeves,' and turned out good and successful effortlessly?
- ☯ What are your greatest gifts?
- ☯ What activities, thoughts, or occurrences make you deeply feel the certainty of– "it's ok to just be me," "I am fabulous just because I'm me," and- "everything is absolutely going to be alright?"
- ☯ What is it that reconnects you with that feeling of lightness, freedom, joy and Divine Grace within?
- ☯ What is the most important thing that is closest to your heart?
- ☯ How does all that shed new light on the questions of your life?

Again, after posing each question, get back into Zohar Breath. Keep a strong concentration on the nurturing Divine Light breathing in and out of your heart space… until you are again dwelling in the stillness and supreme peace of your Soul's presence. Then, just wait until inner visions, words spoken clearly, or other impressions come to you. As long as you feel the supreme peace and Grace, you can trust that the impressions are coming from your Soul or your high-level Spirit Guide.

After each answer/impression finishes coming through, do some automatic writing to record the impressions and messages, even if they don't yet seem like they could lead to prosperity, even if it's just a childhood dream to fly to Mars. The connection to your Ideal Lifepath of prosperity will come to you later, as this list crystalizes into a more cohesive plan (in the next chapter). You should do this meditation as many times as it takes to get a cohesive list of all those hopes and dreams that are still precious to you, and all your talents that are related to the very essence of your Soul.

The Ideal-you Meditation

This meditation is a monumentally important step towards being able to zero in on your Ideal Lifeplan of prosperity. In this meditation, we are not yet zeroing in on your Ideal Lifework—your ideal avenues through which you are meant to receive prosperity, or even on your Ideal Lifeplan. But you will begin to bring the lofty and ethereal essence of your Soul into an image of you that you can live up to in this physical incarnation. It isn't just that this Ideal-you is an integral part of your Ideal Lifepath. The cause and effect chain is: prosperity is given to you so that you can reclaim your Ideal Lifepath; your Ideal Lifepath helps you achieve your life-mission (see *Prosperity From Your Soul*); and your life-mission is all about becoming the Ideal-you, thereby enriching your Soul.

The Ideal-you is not exactly your Soul Self; but it is not your current here-now persona. It is your Original Self—the ideal way in which the essence of your Soul was designed to come into manifestation in your current human incarnation, and the way your Soul is still rooting for you to become. This is how you would have been if your Soul were the only one with free will to formulate your personality and make decisions in your life—if your here-now self didn't have any free will; and if you didn't carry any scars of disappointment, non-serving programing, or imbalances and debris in your energetic apparatus. For example, you may tune into the feeling of total lightness, lightheartedness, freedom, joy, happiness, youth, vitality, peace, groundedness, and wisdom… all the wonderful qualities that are generally a part of your Original Self. You probably also have qualities that are unique to you that are part of the Ideal-you. Tuning into and reaching this Ideal-you requires going past your human programing filters, which is tough for your here-now self to do. The only one that can really shed Light on the original image of the Ideal-you is your Soul.

So now, prepare your space for the meditation in accordance with some of the practices discussed in Chapter 1. Sit comfortably cross legged (or in your most comfortable meditation pose) on your meditation cushions, with your spine loosely erect, your shoulders relaxed down, your chest slightly out, and your chin slightly tucked in.

Start gradually deepening your breath… Begin with Zohar Breaths, envisioning the Divine white Light coming into the back of your heart space and filling you up completely with each inhalation, and the Divine white Light seeping out of the front of your chest and engulfing you with nurturing peace with each exhalation. Take your time doing Zohar Breaths until you are feeling very nurtured, and are dwelling in the supreme peace, stillness, and Grace of your Soul. Stay in this peaceful stillness for a while and enjoy.

Now have your Soul show you the Ideal-you. Allow yourself to be receptive and totally go with the images and feelings that comes to you. What does the Ideal-you look like? What does his/her presence feel like? Make sure that the presence you see and feel jives with the feeling of the essence of your Soul that you've seen in the previous meditation. This will usually be a version of yourself that is angelic, peaceful, and lighthearted on the one hand, and on the other hand is very youthful (even if you are eighty years old), optimistic, confident, and very alive. It's the perfect balance between the loftiness of your Soul's essence and being present in your current reality—the perfect buoyancy that we discussed in *Prosperity From Your Soul*.

Initially, you may see the Ideal-you as an image that is separate from yourself. That's OK. Use Zohar Breaths to help you stay in the consciousness of your Soul and hold on to this vision. Do not judge your here-now self for not measuring up to this wonderful Ideal-you. Just spend a few moments feasting your eyes with this beautiful person. Notice and absorb as many details about this Ideal-you as you can. You may see the Ideal-you engaged in certain activities. And if you do, take note of these, as these could be clues for your Ideal Lifepath. In later repeats of this Ideal-you meditation, once you get comfortable and confident that what you see is actually the Ideal-you, you may ask your Soul to also show you some of the daily activities that the Ideal-you is normally engaged in. And when you get a vision of those, they are even bigger clues that will later plug into your Ideal Lifeplan meditations in the next chapter. But for now, the important first step of this meditation is just to *feel* the presence of the Ideal-you, his/her radiance and his/her peace.

After the image of the Ideal-you have fully formed (and this may take several meditations on different days to achieve), and you feel comfortable and uplifted by his/her presence, envision yourself lovingly embracing this Ideal-you, and being embraced by his/her. At the end of that embrace, see-feel yourself merging with the beautiful image of the Ideal-you, like you've stepped into her/his body, and she/he has stepped into your body—the two of you have merged and become one. You are her/him, and she/he is you.

Deepen your Zohar Breaths, until you see-feel a large and radiant aura around you. What does it feel like to be the Ideal-you? What are your predominate thoughts as the Ideal-you? How do your senses feel? Do you see things (colors) more vividly and brightly? Do you smell every fragrant in the air more sensuously? Are you more hopeful? Do you suddenly have a feeling that everything is going to be ok? Is your body in great shape? Do you feel this lightness of "I can do anything?" As the Ideal-you, how do you now react to life situations, and how do these reactions better serve your Ideal Lifepath of prosperity? Completely merge with the image, thoughts, and feelings of the Ideal-you, and have a complete Internal Experience of living as the Ideal-you.

The image of the Ideal-you may take several meditations to perfect… until you are able to tune into an image that resonates favorably with every fiber of your being. Once you "get" that perfect Ideal-you resonance, you should do a brief version of this meditation twice a day, as you fall asleep and as you wake up, in the space between wakefulness and sleep—the time in which it is easiest to imprint your new favorable self-image into your subconscious. When you do this brief Ideal-you Internal Experience as you fall asleep and as you wake up, you don't necessarily have to do all the preparations for an extensive meditation. Just consciously bring forth the image of the Ideal-you that you have already perfected in your previous meditations—the one that resonated harmoniously in every fiber of your being. And the more you can imprint this image into your subconscious, the more completely you'll merge with that image, until one day, without even noticing how you got there, you'll notice that you've actually become the Ideal-you in your here-now reality. And that goes a long way towards manifesting your Ideal Lifepath of prosperity from your Soul.

The meditations in this chapter were targeted at tuning into the real you from the highest perspective of your Soul—what makes you happy in the deeper sense, the flavor of your Soul's essence, and the Ideal-you that your Soul is still rooting for you to reclaim being. All of these are the building blocks of living your Ideal Lifepath. Since your Ideal Lifeplan is based on your uniqueness, your avenues for receiving Universal abundance are also unique, and perfectly tailored to you. Thus, it was necessary for you to get to know the real You as the basis of perceiving your Ideal Lifeplan of prosperity.

In the next chapter, we will rely on the meditations and visions that you have tuned into in this chapter, and help you focus them into a specific, detailed plan to reclaim your Ideal Lifepath of health, happiness, and prosperity.

Chapter 7

Your Ideal Life

This is the part you've been waiting for—the stage in which you'll bring into full focus your Ideal Lifeplan in its exact detail, and devise a specific plan of action to bring it into manifestation in your here-now reality.

In Chapter 8 of *Prosperity From Your Soul*, we've talked about the bridge between your "now" reality and your Ideal Lifepath. In this Chapter, we will go through Stages 4, 5 and 6 of the seven-stage process I've outlined in the introduction to this book: You'll meditationally tune into your Ideal Lifeplan and all of its detail (Stage 4); then you'll get a more specific and comprehensive Internal Experience of your Ideal Lifepath, meditationally engaging all of your senses (Stage 5); and finally, you'll devise a plan of action for navigating your current life into your Ideal Lifepath (Stage 6).

My Ideal Life Meditation

This meditation will help you tune into the original Ideal Lifeplan that your Soul has laid out for you—how your life will potentially look like when you actually co-Create your Ideal Lifepath in this physical Earth plane. And I say "potentially," since there are many possible future-realities that you may navigate your life to, the decision of which reality your life ends up as is, of course, up to you and your free will (see Chapter 6 of *Prosperity From Your Soul*).

Since there are parts of this vision, such as the Ideal avenues through which you should allow prosperity to come into your life, that could potentially be very emotional for your here-now self, we'll be tuning into your Ideal Life in three steps, from the most general and ethereal to the more specific.

Select a quiet place in which you would be uninterrupted for the duration of this meditation. Cleanse, protect and bless your space according to the practices you have learnt in Chapter 1 (or ones that you've come up with on your own). Set the purest intent for this meditation, according to the instructions given for Zohar Breath Meditation. Put on inspiring non-verbal music. Light a candle or incense that you have blessed with the intent to help you tune into the highest wisdom of your Soul. Prepare a pen and paper (or your journal) next to your meditation cushions, in which you can do some automatic writing (remember our discussion of automatic writing in Chapter 1).

Step 1: General Impressions of Your Ideal Life:

Sit comfortably on your meditation cushions, with your spine erect yet relaxed, your chin slightly tucked in, and your shoulders relaxed down. Close your eyes and start deepening your breath… Start with Zohar Breath Meditation to tune into the consciousness of your Soul… until you are dwelling in the supreme peace and Light of your Soul… By now, you should be proficient getting into Zohar Breath Meditation, so the peace, absolute contentedness, Love, Light, and super-clarity that your Soul consciousness affords should be very familiar to you. So just get there first, and then dwell in it for a while…

Now bring forth in your consciousness your natural gifts, talents, wishes and dreams, all of which you have tuned into in the Essence of Your Soul Meditation that you did in the last chapter. Allow yourself to feel strengthened by the essence of your Soul for a while…

Now, without veering from your Soul consciousness, have your Soul show you:

☯ From the highest perspective of your Soul, what is your life's mission for this human lifetime?

Once you've asked the question, go back to Zohar Breath in order to get back into the consciousness of your Soul. Don't try to conjure up the answer from your logical here-now consciousness. The answer doesn't have to come to you right away. So after asking, just go back to breathing Divine white Light in and out of your heart space, until you arrive again at the supreme nurturing Love-Light-peace-clarity of your Soul Self… and wait for impressions to naturally come to you. Keep in mind that the impressions that you get at this point could be very ethereal and not yet very well defined in human terms (such as A., A1, A2, B., C… C3, etc.). And that's as it should be. Remember that your Soul's natural environment is the Heavenly one. So the natural language that the Soul is best versed in is a vibrational one. The more you do these meditations, the more your Soul and your Spirit Guide will learn to downstep their high vibrational language into something that you as a human can understand. With practice, you'll also learn to translate that vibrational language into clear images (clairvoyance), words (clairaudience), and knowings (claircognizance) that make more sense to your human mind. But in the beginning, the messages that you get will usually be ethereal feelings and formless impressions. So just keep being receptive to those impressions, don't try to categorize them yet, and keep the flow of impressions going—don't get too attached to any one impression that comes. Let your Soul be in charge of the communications.

To check the validity of the messages that are now coming to you, without veering from your meditational state of mind, loosely bring into your awareness again the essence of your Soul that you've tuned into. Now sound the answers/messages that came to you against the essence of your Soul, and check for a harmonious mutual resonance. The idea is that your life's mission must (by Design) jive well with who You Truly are.

As images and messages keep coming to you, when you get to a point in which your meditational focus is strong, and you don't feel like the flow of messages would be interrupted, do some automatic writing to record those messages.

The next question that you should ask your Soul Self is:

☯ What was the Ideal Plan that your Soul has laid out for you to best fulfill that mission? (Here again, the answers do not yet have to be specific. It might actually work in your favor if the answers are general, ethereal feelings and impressions.)

Once you've asked the question, use additional Zohar Breaths to get back into Soul consciousness…

Since this is potentially an emotionally charged question, your here-now mind may attempt to throw you out of the meditation and start brainfucking, but don't let it! Remember that your Soul's (and your Spirit Guide's) answers will always be very clear, and very consistent, as opposed to your human brainfucking, which usually starts arguing with itself, confusing you even more, and making you feel edgy. Your Soul's answers will also never assign blame to you or anyone else in your life, but instead, offer the highest vibrational perspective and solutions for the situation. So if in response to your question, you get a jumble conflicting thoughts all arguing with each other and making you feel agitated, than go back to concentrating on the Divine white Light in and out of your heart space, and actively let go of all the brainfucking of all those internal arguments… until you get again into the supreme stillness-Love-Light-nurturing-wisdom and clarity of your Soul. For then, and only then, are you really tuning into wisdom from your Soul.

When you've gotten some impressions of your Soul's Plan for the fulfillment of your life mission, without veering from the consciousness of your Soul, do some automatic writing to record the impressions, even if they are very general. We will use all of your automatic writing notes in the next meditations and in the next chapter.

Now, still dwelling in the consciousness and True essence of your Soul, bring up the image and feeling of the Ideal-you that you merged with in the Ideal-you Meditation in the last chapter… Sound the impressions-answers that you got against the Ideal-you. Dwelling in the persona of the Ideal-you will help anchor the Divine-ethereal impressions that you initially got into more realistic understandings that could begin to be understood by your here-now self. But you are not quite diving back down into here-now consciousness. You should still be loosely dwelling in the consciousness of your Soul; but just have your Soul show you how the Ideal-you thrives when Its plan for your Ideal Life is manifested, and how your Ideal Life really relies on you reclaiming being the Ideal-you. You may do more automatic writing to record the messages you get.

At this point, all the impressions that you get may only be bits and pieces of your Ideal Life. And that's ok. As long as you are dwelling in the bliss of your Soul, trust the impressions, visions and messages that come to you—just allow them to flow into your awareness, even if they do not yet make sense, and even if they do not yet seem connected to a cohesive Lifeplan that you would normally associate with monetary prosperity. Remember that you Soul may have in store for you goodies that your "logical" here-now self cannot even imagine. The dots will be connected, and it will all start to make sense later later – as you complete the meditations, and as you start walking the path of a conscious co-Creator (in the next chapter and in *A Lifestyle of Prosperity From Your Soul*). The important thing right now is that all the impressions that come to you evoke pleasant feelings of joy, peace and love, which resonate deeply within you, for the pleasant feelings are the telltales that the impressions are indeed coming from your Soul and are part of your Ideal Lifeplan.

You may need to do this meditation up to this point a few times before you are ready to go to the next step, until you solidify your vision a little bit, and until your impressions of your life mission and its intended manifestation as your life, however ethereal, is an impression-feeling that you can easily come to dwell in with a snap of the fingers.

Step 2: The Specifics of Your Ideal Life:

Now let's get more specific. If you've done Step-1 several times, than you are probably doing this Step-2 as a stand-alone meditation. In that case, prepare your space again, find your comfortable meditational pose again, deepen your breath… and allow yourself enough Zohar Breaths to be uplifted again into the consciousness and blissful stillness of your Soul. If you are doing it all in one sitting, than just take a few more Zohar Breaths, and allow yourself a few minutes to just bask in the Light and peace of your Soul.

To prepare for this next step in your Ideal Life meditation, go deeper into your Soul's consciousness. Bring forth, the essence of your Soul, your life's mission, and the general impression-vision of your Ideal Life that you've tune into so far. Spend a few moments feeling and absorbing your Soul's joy regarding Its Plan for your life…

Then, without veering from your Internal Experience of your Soul or from the vision of your general impressions of your Ideal Lifeplan, have your here-now self ask your Soul Self:

- ☯ What True passions did your Soul plant in you, specifically to help guide you towards fulfillment of your life mission?
- ☯ What talents and gifts did your Soul give you to help facilitate your mission in this life?
- ☯ From your Soul's perspective, what is the most Ideal way to let those talents and desires come into play in your here-now existence? What activities do you "see" yourself engaging in on a daily basis, which serve your Truest passions and are served by your Truest gifts in your Ideal Life? Have your Soul show you the Lifepath that would best let Its Light shine through in your here-now life. In asking this question, you are not yet looking for any specific moneymaking profession, occupation, investment opportunities, or endeavor. It's fine if you get the beginning of some ideas. But the purpose in this question is to get some impressions of the *lifestyle* that would rely on your True talents and passions.
- ☯ Now bring forth the image-feeling of the Ideal-you, and merge once more with this Ideal-you… If the Ideal-you could live an Ideal Life right now, without any constraints or limitations (if money was no object, and there were no physical/objective limitations), what would that life look-feel like?

⁂ In what ways does the Ideal Life that you've perceived so far make you feel fulfilled? How does it bring your natural talents, hopes, dreams, and earnest-most desires into a lifestyle of happiness and fulfillment? For beyond Love (Love is a given, because it is *the* fundamental building block of Creation), one of the hallmarks of True happiness in life is that you feel deeply fulfilled, both personally and professionally. This means that if you win the grand lottery prize, and have no other goals for your life—if you just sit there doing nothing, and let life pass you by, you will probably not feel fulfilled. That is why your Ideal Lifeplan that your Soul has laid out for you is necessarily one in which you feel fulfilled. Keep that in mind.

⁂ Does this Ideal Life that you "see" right now make you feel the same as you felt when you were tuned into the Essence of Your Soul's Vision Meditation? The 'you' that you see in this Ideal Life vision, is it the Ideal-you that you've merged with in the Ideal-you Meditation? Or is it different? This is your sounding board. If the 'you' that you see in your vision of your Ideal Life is the same as the Ideal-you, and is a direct extension of the True essence of your Soul, than that's how you know you are getting it right.

⁂ If you were living this Ideal Life, would it better the people around you? Would it better your community? The world? This is another telltale: your Ideal Life is usually something that, rather than step on other people to achieve success, is actually beneficial for the people around you and the community, sometimes even the world.

When posing these questions, we are not yet focusing on the how. In other words, if you need three hundred thousand dollars to open your dream endeavor or business, just ignore that fact for now. Once you finish your planning, if your plan is indeed anchored in your Soul's vision for your life, the Universe will find a way to bring you investment money. Keep in mind that as far as the Universe is concerned, while money is a form of energy too, it is not a manifestation endeavor in and of itself, but the means for bringing into manifestation more concrete co-Creations that benefit your Soul and the world around you. So don't worry about money for now. This step is about envisioning the Ideal. And it's not like a high school kid trying to figure out which college he/she has a realistic chance of getting into, and based on that, deciding what he/she wants to do with his/her life. In this process, we are not climbing from the limited perspective of your here-now reality into the Ideal, but are doing the opposite: You are perceiving the Ideal first; then vibrationally magnetizing that Ideal to you by having a complete Internal Experience of it (next meditation), which co-Creates an attractive vibrational resonance with that Ideal; and by the end of this chapter, we'll devise a plan of actions to help pull this Ideal into manifestation in your physical reality. So the only appropriate place to start the process of reclaiming all those gifts that the Universe has in store for you is by first tuning into the Ideal, without regards for the 'now' or for how you'll get there. And Ideal means Ideal. Don't worry about what is logical right now. Don't worry about whether or not you have the money to start that fabulous new business you dream of; where the money would come from to sponsor your time off to write that book you've always wanted to write; where to get the money for the education you want; or how to climb into the position you want. Just let the images, sounds and feelings come in, and don't allow your here-now "logic" to taint them. Remember that if opening a multi-million dollar business is part of your life-mission from the perspective of your Soul, and especially if that business is meant to betters humanity and plant more love in the world, than God will absolutely bless you with all the means necessary to make it happen. So allow yourself to indulge in this vision of a best-case scenario—not what you logically think you can achieve from your here-now perspective, but your dream-life, which is of course more than possible from the perspective of your Soul. The underline here is that your Ideal Lifeplan brings joy and Love to you, your loved ones, your community, and perhaps the world. And it should be joyful for you to dwell in, meditationally. So make sure that what comes to you just feels right in every fiber of your being.

Again, after posing each question, do not let your here-now mind do the brainfucking. Go back into Zohar Breath and into your Soul's consciousness; actively let go of any internal arguments; persist with envisioning the Divine white Light coming in and out of your heart space, and wait until you feel the supreme nurturing stillness-peace-Love-Light-clarity... Then wait for impressions and messages to come flooding into your mind. Detach yourself from where your current life is, and from any self-imposed limitation. As long as you are immersed in the bliss of your Soul, trust all that comes to you which resonates pleasantly within your depth.

When you get to the point in which you feel that the flow of messages from your Soul would not be interrupted, do some automatic writing to record your impressions. We will use those notes in later meditations.

Step 3: Ask Your Soul About Your Ideal Lifework:

Notice that until now, we haven't yet asked about your Ideal Lifework, your profession, business endeavor, or the avenue through which money is to flow into your life. Again, these are very emotionally charged questions, that you should absolutely ask your Soul. But you should do so after you have solidified your Ideal Life vision in steps one and two, and are sure that they are reverberating like a song of the heart in every fiber of your being.

So go back into Zohar Breath... Bring yourself back into the consciousness of your Soul... feel the supreme stillness-peace-Love-nurturing-wisdom of your Soul... Bring into your consciousness the Ideal Life that you have perceived so far, and allow yourself to dwell in it and feel how wonderfully it reverberate throughout your entire being...

Now, without veering from the consciousness of this wonderful Internal Experience or from the nurturing stillness of your Soul's presence, ask your Soul:

- ❧ Within your Ideal Lifeplan, if you reclaim being the Ideal-you, how does your Soul intend for you to capitalize on your Truest talents and passions? The word capitalize is not yet specific only to moneymaking. The visions/impressions that your Soul shows you as an answer to this question could be how your talents and passions have served you well in this life so far, so you can start to understand what activities/occupations you are good and happy doing, what usually plays well in your life like a wildcard, and which ways of doing things typically fail in your life.
- ❧ What is your Ideal Lifework? What were you meant to do in this lifetime, because you do it so well naturally, and because you derive so much joy out of it?

☯ How can your Ideal Lifework be translated into an occupation, vocation, profession, position, an investment, a business, or another moneymaking endeavor?

In this step, it is especially important that once you ask each question, you do not attach or get stuck on any preconceived notions. Make sure that your mind is still and open to new ideas coming from your Soul. To do that, pose the questions from the most neutral place you can muster, and then let go of all expectations, which I know is extremely difficult for the here-now self to do. Zohar Breaths—focusing on Divine Light coming in and out of your heart-space as you breathe—is the only way I know of that could achieve this detached receptiveness to Soul wisdom, unless you have reached enlightenment, or have some other magical way of tapping into Soul consciousness. Use the process that we have at hand: Take some Zohar Breaths… bask in the Light of your Soul… allow It to heal and dissolve any preconceived ideas within you that no longer serve your new path of prosperity… and wait for impressions to come to you.

As soon as you've gotten some impressions, wait for a moment in which you feel that the inflow of messages would not be interrupted, and then start doing some automatic writing to record the inflow of impressions. The notes that you take via automatic writing are extremely important, as we will use them in later meditational processes to devise a Plan of action.

You will probably have to do the meditation, and particularly this last part of the meditation, many times, before the vision of your Ideal Lifeplan, along with all of its elements including the avenues for the inflow of prosperity into your life, will form into a cohesive and specific vision. And that's ok, since you'll probably enjoy doing this meditation and basking in the Light of your Soul.

Also keep in mind that even if you are an advanced meditator, we are all human right now. So sometimes you'll get into the purest Soul consciousness right away and get very clear answers, while at other times, if you've got a lot of here-now stresses in your life and you are not doing any meditations or practices to dissolve that stress and elevate your spirit, it may take some effort to let go of all the brainfucking that comes up as you sit and start meditating, and you may not get high enough into Soul consciousness to get clear answers. And if that's where you're at in a particular time in your life, than that is part of your process, and you need to honor it: keep doing some of the meditations of Chapters 3 and 4; keep practicing kindness-to-self as we'll discuss in *A Lifestyle Prosperity From Your Soul;* and keep doing Zohar Breath Meditation on its own, until you do get into a mode of truly connecting with your Soul Self and feeling the stillness-peace-Love-Light-clarity-hope that are the hallmarks of dwelling in Soul consciousness. Then, when you are truly connecting, come back and do this meditation until you get not only clear answers that just feel right in every fiber of your being, but also a cohesive and complete vision of your Ideal Life.

Your Ideal Daily Routine Internal Experience

This is the meditation to bring everything into crystal clear focus. You are going to bring into meditationally focus the smallest details of your Ideal Life, for two purposes: The first is to check your Ideal Life vision against the highest Truth of your Soul. That is, to ensure that internally dwelling in the reality of your Ideal Life does indeed bring you love and joy. If it does, than it means that what you are internally experiencing as your Ideal Life is indorsed by your highest life purpose to bring you prosperity from your Soul. But if you do the meditation and your Internal Experience does not make you feel joyous, loved, safe, and absolutely fulfilled, than might I suggest that the "ideal life" that you are envisioning is not Truly your Ideal Lifeplan, because it is not based on your Soul's plan for your Ideal Life. In that case, you'd need to go back to the previous meditation, until you get an Ideal Life vision that feels absolutely joyous when you internally dwell in it. Joy here is a telltale that what you are experiencing internally is indeed the Lifepath that your Soul has signed you up for, which is guaranteed success.

The second purpose of this meditation is to have a complete Internal Experience—engaging all of your senses—that is so joyous that it adjusts your energetic vibration into likeness with the life that you envision, creating a mutual resonance that magnetizes it into manifestation as your life.

So, select a quiet place in which you would be uninterrupted for the duration of this meditation. Cleanse, and protect your space as you've learnt to do in Chapter 1. Bless your space with the specific intents for a Zohar Breath Meditation. Specially set the intent for Angelic help in facilitating an especially strong connection with the wisdom of your Soul and with the information available through your Akashic records. You may light a candle that you've blessed, or incense that evokes feelings of personal power, hope, and single-minded Divine purity. Put on relaxing non-verbal music that brings about your deepest connection with your Soul Self.

The Meditation:

Sit on your meditation cushion, in your most comfortable meditation pose, with your spine loosely erect, your shoulders relaxed down, your chest slightly out, and your chin slightly tucked in. Close your eyes, and start gradually deepening your breath… Start Zohar Breath Meditation—inhaling Divine white Light into the back of your heart chakra… envisioning (or setting the intent that) this Light engulf and nurture your entire being… and exhaling the Divine White Light out of the front of your heart chakra. Go past the point of cleansing your mind, and get to the point of absolute stillness and peace, basking in the Light of your Soul for a while…

Now let the observer in you bring into mind your vision of your Ideal Lifeplan that you have perfected in the previous meditations. By now, you should have done enough Ideal Life Meditations that bringing your awareness to it should not be an effort of your human mind, but a natural place your Soul wants you to dwell in, and thus, a pleasant internal experience of you. Indulge in every fantasy that stem from this vision… just allow this vision of your Ideal Life to indulge you like a daydream of a perfectly "guilty" pleasure. Gradually start directing your attention now to the smallest details of the day-to-day routine of your Ideal Life.

Without veering from the peaceful consciousness of your Soul or from the vision of your Ideal Life, have your here-now self ask your Soul:

☯ When you co-Create your Ideal Lifepath, how does your daily routine look like?

Now as you delve into the details of your Ideal Life vision, start directing your attention to deeply experiencing your wishes as manifest integral parts of your life. Use all of your senses to internally feel engulfed and surrounded by every element of this co-Creation—like a perfectly lucid daydream that feels so real that you could swear you are really living it! Start tuning into all the activities that would be a part of your daily routine once you manifest your Ideal Life into reality. For example, if it is financial prosperity that you wish for, let your Soul's wisdom show you the daily activities of your occupation, position, business, project, or investment. If it's a romantic soulmate relationship you wish for, you may concentrate on the sensations, feelings, scents, visions, and activities that you would experience when you manifest this relationship into your life. But do all this without losing the perspective of your Soul Self. Whenever you catch your logical mind kicking in and starting its normal brainfucking, just go back to Zohar Breath to get back into your Soul's consciousness. Continue dwelling in the experience of your Ideal Life.

As you see-experience yourself living your Ideal Life, without veering from your Soul's consciousness, ask your Soul to show you:

- ☯ What daily activities do you see yourself engaging in during the course of your Ideal Life? What do you see yourself doing on weekdays? What do you see yourself doing on weekends? Are all those activities enjoyable?

- ☯ What natural talents of yours come into full expression in the daily activities of your Ideal Life?

- ☯ What deep passions of yours find their expression daily in this Ideal Life?

- ☯ How does your body feel while busy with these daily activities? Light and vitalized? Or tired and heavy? This is a great telltale. If you see your body feeling light and vitalized, fully tune into that feeling and dwell in for a few moments…

- ☯ Engage your sense of vision – what are some of the sights that you see in your daily life, when you live your Ideal Life? Beautiful views? Beautiful designs? An office? A store? A nature environment? Your Soulmate/family? The happy smiles of all the people you've helped?

- ☯ Who are the people that you see on an every day basis? Co-workers? Your many clients? People you help? Your new family? The smiling bank clerk that receives your large daily deposits? Keep envisioning and fully dwelling in the experiences of who/what you see during your Ideal daily Life.

- ☯ Engage your internal sense of touch: what are some of the pleasant things that you touch during the daily routine of your Ideal Life (besides money)? The pleasant fabrics of your new clothes? The hug of your soulmate? The kind handshakes of supportive people you meet throughout your day?... This is your time to feel sensual about the fulfillment of your dream, like a new vitality that you would feel when your dream life is fulfilled. I find this to be a tremendously helpful step towards becoming the Ideal-me and stepping into who I am to become, in order to reclaim my Ideal Lifepath of prosperity.

- ☯ What are the fragrances in your life? Are you surrounded by a natural environment and smell cedar and flowers blooming? Are you smelling delicious bakery smells every day? Are you engulfed in the perfumes of the many people that frequent your new successful business/job/endeavor? Is it the aftershave/perfume of your soulmate?

- What are the tastes of your Ideal Life? Are you eating gourmet foods? Are you eating holistically healthy foods? Are you going to many lucrative luncheons? Are you having plenty of romantic dinner with your soulmate? Is success so palpable that you can taste it?

- How is your general feeling? Are you calm, yet excited and joyous? Or are you stressed (hopefully not)? Do you have a deep sense of content? Do you feel fully supported by the Universe, your Soul, and the people and circumstances in your life?

- How does being in-shape/successful/married to your soulmate (or whatever your Ideal Life may be) make you feel? Do you feel the weight of responsibility? Or do you feel the peace that comes from life agreeing with you?

- Regarding your Ideal Lifework: How do you feel about making such a positive difference for the many people that your occupation helps?

- Does this Ideal Life bring a new vitality and joy into your life?

If it is a loving relationship you wish for ~

- Tune into how you feels when you are in your Soulmate's presence
- Tune into how you feel waking up together
- Smell his/her breath… his/her shampoo… his aftershave or perfume
- Feel his/her touch… nurturing… loving…
- How does making love to your Soulmate feel differently from having sex with other lovers you've had in the past? Allow yourself to feel it internally.
- Feel the safety of walking through life together
- Feel as beautiful as he/she would make you feel
- Feel your inner cell of God-likeness connecting with his/hers

If it is health that you wish for ~

- Tune into how you feels when you get in shape/healthy/light as you wish to be…
- How does your body feel when you reclaim your Ideal health?
- What are some of the activities you enjoy doing with this healthy body? Fully indulge in that internal experience…
- What are the main foods that you enjoy now with your healthy body?
- What are some of the choices that You see yourself making in order to get to this healthy state?

In this meditation again, after you pose each question, or after each time that you actively direct your attention to a particular aspect of your Ideal Life's daily routine, go back and do more Zohar Breaths to climb back up to the consciousness of your Soul. Then, retaining your Soul's perspective, allow yourself to fully dwell in the feeling and internal experience of that aspect of your Ideal daily routine.

After you allow yourself to fully delve into this as a complete Internal Experience, do some automatic writing to record the impressions of your Ideal Daily Routine. You will use this list of impressions in the final meditation of this chapter, when you devise a specific plan of action to bring your Ideal Life into reality. So the more detailed your automatic writing notes, the better.

Also, let me reiterate that not all days are alike. On some days it might be easy for you to reach meditational heights, while on other days your mind is preoccupied and does not easily let go of the mundane. That's OK. You can repeat this meditation as many times as you need to, until you get to a complete Internal Experience of your Ideal Life and daily routine that involves all of your senses. The idea is to have a lucid, vivid daydream that feels real, in which you internally use all of your senses: you smell the smells, taste the tastes, see the sights, hear the sounds, and feel the textures and feelings that are a part of your desired manifestation. The more real your Internal Experience is, and the more joy and love you feel deeply resonating within you as you experience it, the more powerfully you will attract this manifestation into your actual life (by creating an attractive mutual resonance with it).

Inventory of Your Life Meditation

We are now at the beginning of the bridge between your "now" reality and your Ideal Lifepath. Before we can step onto the bridge, though, it is necessary for you to take inventory of your current life, so that you can ascertain for yourself which elements within it already are in alignment with your Ideal Lifeplan, and which elements need to change.

Remember the Serenity Prayer? "God, please give me the serenity to accept the things I cannot change, the courage to change the things I can change, and the wisdom to know the difference." While the Universe does indeed conspire to help you manifest everything that you Truly desire, every manifestation and blessing must come to you in its perfect Divine timing. Recall the discussion of the perfect mosaic of your life in *Prosperity From Your Soul*. There are many gifts awaiting you during the treasure hunt of your life. Some of them are intended for immediate manifestation, and others are meant for you to discover after you've walked further along your path and acquired more wisdom. The secret to finding all the treasures lies in the perfect balance between asserting your free will in a way that dwells in the wisdom and Light of your Soul, and trusting that the gifts that are intended for you will fall into your lap at the most auspicious moment, guided by the perfect flow of your life. So the wisdom of the Serenity Prayer is knowing that reconciling the Ideal and the now really is about knowing which parts of your Ideal Life are achievable now, and which parts you must trust the Universe to bring to you. That is a great steppingstone towards constructing a well thought out plan to bring your Ideal Life into your current reality.

By the end of this chapter, you'll get more specific about what part of Your (Soul's) Ideal Lifeplan lies in your (here-now self's) hands, and what part of it should you leave for the Universe to bring you. But first, let's count some of the things we already know are your responsibilities: It is your job to keep yourself clear of any lower vibrational energies; it is your job to remain in a state of joy, kindness, gratitude and generosity, which reflect your True essence; it is your job to keep actively tuned into the essence of whom you Truly are; it is your job to hold within the flame of your heart the vision and love resonance with your Ideal Life; *and it is your job to live your life in a way that is inspired by those profound inner Truths.*

Humbly, if I may put my own twist on the Serenity Prayer: at this juncture of your becoming a conscious co-Creator of your life, the objective is to differentiate between elements in your life that are already in accordance with your Ideal Life, which you are happy about; and elements that no longer serve your highest wellbeing, and are therefore going to change. Now the change here might be just a change in attitude towards that element—seeing it as a blessing in disguise; it might be a physical change of that element; or it might be a little of both. The only one who's fully qualified to advise you on that is your Soul.

While this meditation is made more powerful when combined with the processes, guidance, reiki empowerment, and group consciousness of the *Level 1 Prosperity From Your Soul Course*, it can also be very powerful when you do it on your own, provided you do it earnestly and set crystal clear intent.

Prepare for the Meditation:

Before you get into a fully meditative mode, sit at your desk, or otherwise in a quiet place in which you would find enough peace of mind to do some Soul-searching as you do all this writing. This is not yet your meditation space; this preparation is a partially cognitive step.

Take a large sheet of paper, and at the top part of it write all the themes and circumstances in your life that you are happy about. Then, divide the rest of the page into two columns. On the left column, list all the themes in yourself and in your present life circumstances that you perceive as negative or unpleasant—things you'd like to change. It could be a lack of something, past events that etched a scar deep inside you, or anything else that's weighing on you. No one but you needs to ever see this paper, so don't be bashful. Write down all comes to your mind. Once you start the meditation, you'll be writing in the right column the blessings (Soul lessons) hidden in conditions that are in your life to stay, as well as Soul directives of how to change the things that are meant for you to change as you reclaim your Ideal Lifepath. So write everything very spaciously, so that there is enough room for the answers/insights that are going to be written on the right column parallel the elements written on the left. (See Appendix A for a worksheet for this meditation.)

Now prepare your meditational space. Find a quiet time and place in which you would be undisturbed during this meditation. Cleanse and protect your space as you've learnt to do in Chapter 1. Bless your space with the specific blessings for Zohar Breath Meditation. Put on inspiring non-verbal music that can send you deep within. You may want to light a candle or incense that you have blessed.

Put the page that you have prepared and some writing utensils by the side of your meditation cushion. You may hold it between your hands and pray/set the intent that highest Divine insights will come to you during the meditation, to complete this page in the most harmonious way that is in alignment with your Ideal Lifeplan.

The Meditation:

Sit comfortably on your meditation cushion (which should be a tired old cushion by now… just kidding), with your spine loosely erect, your chin slightly tucked in, and your shoulders relaxed down. Close your eyes, and start gradually deepening your breath…

Start doing some Zohar Breaths—inhale Divine white Light into the back of your heart space… exhale white Light out of your front heart chakra… Let everything else go. Just breathe the Divine white Light in and out of your heart space, and bask in the Light of your Soul. Now that you are proficient at tuning into your Soul's blissful presence, you'll probably get blissed out more easily and profoundly. Go high and deep with this and allow yourself to soar and be carried by the supreme stillness-peace-Light-Love-nurturing of your Soul for a while.

Without veering from the consciousness of your Soul, have your here-now self read each "negative" point, and ask your Soul:

- ☯ Despite the discomfort, did this situation/condition help redirect your life to a more positive direction? If so, how?
- ☯ Did it give you the drive to strive higher for yourself?
- ☯ Did it teach you anything?
- ☯ If the answer is "No" to all of the above questions, than ask: Could this situation be dissolved by using some of the practices/meditations detailed in Chapters 3 or 4?
- ☯ If the answer is "Yes," what was the opportunity for growth afforded by this experience? Or, What were the benefits you've gained from it?
- ☯ Does this situation/condition still serve your highest purpose? This is the question that will help you determine which situations/conditions are here to stay and be made lemonade from, and which should be changed to reclaim your Ideal Lifepath.
- ☯ If the situation/condition no longer serves your highest purpose, what the Ideal way to let it go, change it, circumnavigate it, or rise above it, in order to facilitate reclaiming the health, happiness and prosperity of your Ideal Lifepath.

By the end of this meditation, you should have a page full of positive points! The points at the top of the page were positive to begin with. The few "negative" points that are in your life to stay are no longer negative, since your Soul have shown you the hidden blessings or growth they afford, which should help you change your attitude and feelings towards them. And since the majority of the "negative" situations/conditions will probably be things that no longer serve your highest purpose, your Soul will have instructed you to take specific actions to solve them, and drive your life towards your Ideal one. After this meditation, you will know what the variables are. In other words, when you devise a plan of action to reclaim your Ideal Lifepath, you wouldn't be taking any steps to change the things that you are happy about.

For example, during my Ideal Life meditations, I saw myself co-Creating a spiritual retreat that would help people of all walks of life. During my Ideal Daily Routine Internal Experience, I saw all the details of this retreat as if it already existed. I was actually surprised by the detail of the information that came to me. I internally experienced my daily routine of this Ideal Life, and it was very blissful—reverberated harmoniously in every fiber of my being. So here is how my Inventory of My Life meditation went: At the top of my page, my list of the things that already were in alignment with my Ideal Life was pretty short, and contained: my good heart that sees the goodness in each person and genuinely wants to help him/her realize their Ideal Life, leadership skills (having been an airline captain), intelligence and ability to pay attention to details, being a reiki master, and having been Given the knowledge of these books, the unique massage modality of Rezossage, and RezoDance to teach in retreats. However, my list of "negative" themes on the bottom of the page was so long that when I made the list, before starting my meditation, I perceived that there were obstacles there I couldn't overcome: obesity and migraines were physiological things I didn't think I could overcome; stubbornness and impatience are personality traits I was born with; lack of business education; and of course I lacked the appropriate funds to sponsor the establishment of the resort retreat that I've seen in my meditations. Surprisingly, during the meditation, I was Given an antidote to each one of the negative points: I was told that my obesity and migraines would fall away and disappear gradually but very quickly once I finish writing the books and start taking the steps towards teaching the retreat. I received the insight that my stubbornness and impatience really are my oomph—the fire underneath my toosh that would give me the courage to make it all happen. I was also instructed to do something kind and joyful "just-for-me" each day, as joy would help me tame my impatience and flow with the synchronistic flow of the Universe better. With regards to lack of business knowhow and investment capital for the retreat, since I did this meditation many times before I actually trusted the reassurances that Soul sent me meditationally, I was Guided again and again to trust that once I finish the initial stages, the business advisors and the funds to make it all happen will show up in my life synchronistically—with no efforts on my part. And since I had never written a book before, and had no intention or chasing publishers, than by virtue of the fact that you are reading this book, you know that at least the publisher has found me by the synchronistic flow of the Universe. So from this very personal example, you can see how profound this meditation can be within the process of reclaiming/co-Creating your Ideal Life. It gave me the confidence to move forward, and showed me how.

One thing to keep in mind as a result of this meditation is that these things that you are happy about are your non-negotiables. For example, my own non-negotiables are: no matter what happens to the business aspect of things, I will never stop doing reiki, meditating, and yearning for Divine Light and Oneness. And no matter how disappointed I am with people, I will never stop loving them and holding space within my heart for them to be happier, kinder and more loving. I know that sounds naïve, but that's who I am. You too need to know what are the core things about yourself that are a part of your True essence, and therefore are non-negotiable. And this meditation helps you put order into things.

Now putting aside both the non-negotiable top of the page, and lemon-turned-lemonades in your life, the bottom part of the page also contains specific instructions from your Soul on how to leave behind some of the limiting conditions and disharmonious themes, and shift your life into a success. If you recall the Serenity Prayer again, than in this meditation, your Soul has given you the wisdom to know the difference between the things that you cannot change and the things you *can* change. It has also given you the serenity to accept the things that you cannot change by showing you the blessings hidden in those conditions/situations. But most of all, your Soul has actively told you specifically how to change the things that you *can* change, and by knowing exactly how, has also given you the courage to do so. Pretty neat, ha?

Meditation to Devise a Plan of Action

I know that this is going to make you giggle, but remember the old way of making To Do lists? Well, it's time to make one! To be clear, this is not an "off the top of your head" kind of a To Do list; it's a special, meditationally derived, auspicious To Do list, which will start you walking the A-B-C of your Ideal Lifepath (see Chapter 8 of *Prosperity From Your Soul*), to navigate your way to your rendezvous point where the Universe is meeting you to assist or carry you the rest of the way.

So how shall we approach making such an important list? Well, if you look back at all the profound meditations that you've done, and the high-level of information that you derived from them, you'll realize that you already have all the background information required to start your auspicious To Do list: You already know what your mission in life is; you already have a complete vision of what your most Ideal Lifepath can look like; and you have a detailed list of all the activities, talents, and passions that are part of this Ideal Life. More than that, you even have a list of specific actions that your Soul has instructed you to take from the last meditation. What's left to do is make a To Do list.

So the specific actions that your Soul has instructed you to take, during the last meditation, in order to change negative situations into positive ones should be the first to go on your To Do list. The rest of the items that should go into your auspicious To Do list need some explaining:

Within the many details that compose your Ideal Life and Ideal Daily Routine, as your Soul has helped you envision and internally experience them, some things are out of your immediate control, or at least out of the immediate control of your here-now self. Those are the spaces in your Plan where your Soul will fill in the gaps later, as the Universe meets you to help you fulfill these parts of your Plan. But if you look carefully at all the notes of your automatic writings, which you've done during previous meditations, I'm sure you'll notice that there are many aspects of your Ideal Life and Ideal Daily Routine that are absolutely achievable in your life right now. And all of those things that meditationally came from your Soul are important to fulfill, even if they do not yet seem directly related to the manifestation of financial prosperity. And here is why:

The items that should go into your auspicious To Do list aren't necessarily only logical business steps to take to achieve prosperity. That will come later in the game, as you repeat this meditation again and again as time goes by, and as your here-now logical self helps anchor the insights from your Soul into a logical plan, after the Universe has introduced some auspicious synchronicities into your path. The initial job of your meditationally derived To Do list at this stage is to help bring your vibrational essence into resonance with the life that you want, and thus send a vibrational signal into the Universe that you are ready to receive its manifestation. For example, one of the most important components of my Ideal Life is the reunification and happy life with my twin-flame. But as far as this endeavor, there are many things that I do not control: I cannot control when or how I meet him. That Divine time-space is up to the free will of both our Soul Selves, within the mosaic of our lives. But there are a few things that I can control to that end: I can do things in my everyday life to feel beautiful and worthy of love, and more importantly, I can do my best to live my everyday life by the Light of my Soul, which is going to send out a vibrational resonance to attract him. For the closer two soulmates are to their individual Soul Selves, the stronger the magnetic attraction that will actually pull them together in their here-now reality. So to that effect, my auspicious To Do list includes items like, "meditate," "be kind to myself," "do something joyful every day," "swim and do activities that make me feel beautiful and in touch with my body," and other activities designed to get me into a vibrational mode of feeling beautiful, worthy and attractive. Another thing that I can control which relates to vibrationally attracting my twin-flame is acquiring the skills for the activities I meditationally "see" myself doing with him during our lives together. For example, my Ideal Life vision includes going sailing with my soulmate, hiking with him, and taking a trip to Italy while being able to speak Italian. So I have added on my auspicious To Do list items like "learn to sail," "learn to speak Italian," "get in better hiking shape." Now if you look at my list of activities, in and of themselves, they seem trivial. Nowhere in my list does it say anything like, "go online dating." The steps that I included here are not logical steps to achieving what I want. They only become important manifestation tools when you consider that these are the things that bring my vibrational essence into resonance with my Soul Self, the Ideal-me, and with whom I will reclaim being when I am with him, thus strengthening our vibrational magnetic pull on each other. I used a soulmate as my first example, exactly because it is not something you can logically manifest – just poof! So it's easy to see in this example how the items on this auspicious To Do list are related to the goal that you're trying to manifest – vibrationally, not logically.

When you think of financial prosperity, people tend to mistake this To Do list with a business plan, and that is not the intent here (not yet, anyways). Remember that the prosperity of your Ideal Life may not be a logical progression from where your life is right now, but is given to you by Grace, for the purpose of helping your Soul fulfill Its mission for this earthly life. So for example, when I was first channeling the wisdom for this book series, I had no idea that it was going to amount to three books. Ideas just used to come flooding into me from Source, usually at the most inconvenient time of 3am, and when I was done with the automatic writing, I had no idea of the contents of what had been written through me. Even later when I was transcribing my notes into the computer and they started shaping into a book, I had no idea who was going to want to publish or read it. But I trusted the Divine message that kept telling me that if I listened to the dictation that God was giving me, the publisher would find me, and everything would flow easily. Years before I started to receive the information for the books, I had a vision of creating a spiritual resort-retreat that would help people reclaim their Higher Selves and live happier, more successful lives. And for years, I ignored that vision, even though it came in full details—as if I'd already been there and seen it, simply because I logically "knew" that at the time, I did not have the business knowhow or the funds to make this retreat a reality. But the vision kept coming, clear as daylight, and the only answer I was given during my meditations was that I was to write all the information coming to me as if the funds and business knowhow were already there, and that those would come into my life at the right moment in the process.

A few years later, when it came to doing my own auspicious To Do list, the items pertaining to financial abundance on my initial list contained included nothing more than to finish channeling the information that was coming through me (for these books, for retreats curriculums, for RezoDance, and for Rezossage), and organize them in some logical way. Of course, that didn't make any sense to my logical here-now self, since nobody actually makes money out of writing books, and as wonderful and powerful as I knew RezoDance and Rezossage were, I had no idea how to start marketing them. I mean, I knew beyond doubt that these new modalities that have come through me can help people: I've done Rezossage on clients with knots, ropes, and even trigger points in their muscles, and was able to alleviate them easily without inflicting pain (conventional deep tissue massage is usually painful); and my clients felt nurtured in their whole being. I also instructed and facilitated RezoDance for small groups, and even for some atheists, and they felt healed, very well balanced, and happy. My mother—the biggest atheist I know— RezoDanced with me one day, and by the end of it her face was glowing like she'd just swallowed a light bulb, at least had a facial. So I knew I had been Given something valuable that could help people a great deal. I just had no idea what to do to bring those fabulous tools to the people yet. But since it felt right to do so, I followed the advice of my Soul anyway—I went on to write all the information that was coming through me.

But all that time, since my logical (skeptical) here-now self was still nagging me, I kept meditating to periodically ask my Soul and my Spirit Guides and Angels for clarification on the plan for my life, and on how it was going to support me in the real world. Months later, as I meditated again to tweak my auspicious To Do list, I received more clarification and even some logical steps to follow, to make my dream of Soul Path Retreat a reality. As I kept meditating, little by little, more information come from my Soul Self, which was more specific on how to proceed… until my auspicious To Do list actually became a detailed step-by-step Plan to follow. When I thought about the steps later, they actually made business sense. My Soul had broken the process down for me into three steps: first, I was to teach retreats in other locations that host spiritual retreats; then I was to plan to open a studio similar to a yoga studio in which I would teach these retreats; and then open Soul Path Retreat in a resort location. My Soul has even given me the sub-steps to follow to finish organizing the materials into a form I could teach to others. However, with all the logical steps and sub-steps of my Plan, my Soul and Spirit Guide kept telling me to be prepared to skip steps one and two—to keep my mind and heart open, because the investors and my soulmate were probably all going to come into my life before I complete some of my logical steps. As I kept meditating periodically and asking for more clarity on the process, my To Do list added a few more items, such as "learn to, and write a business plan," "research location," "research marketing plan," etc. I think the reason that my Soul and Spirit Guide were leading me through these logical steps, even though my rendezvous point with the Universe was much closer than I realized at the time, was to appease my analytical mind—so that I can feel at peace with following the Plan, without my overly logical mind brainfucking me out of my Ideal Lifepath. It's kind of like the Bedouin Arabs say: "Trust in Allah, but tie your camel anyway so it doesn't run away." Despite how logical this plan now seemed, it took my skeptical here-now self a long time to actually trust my Soul's guidance and to get serious about writing all of this stuff. But once I did, everything really did flow synchronistically.

And the same (or better) will happen to you. So some of the items on your special To Do list should be the items from the last meditation, when your Soul has instructed you to do to change negative themes in your life into positive ones. New items that you are adding to the list during this meditation should have two characteristics: they should be the items out of your Ideal Life and Ideal Daily Routine, which you can fulfill right now, and which will have a vibrational effect on bringing your energy into likeness and resonance with what you want. It doesn't have to make business sense yet. It will come together into a plan that makes here-now sense later. But the first time you do this meditation, your auspicious To Do list should just contain items that elevate your vibrational essence and start your inspired action along the A-B-C of your Lifeplan (see Chapter 8 of *Prosperity From Your Soul).* As you start walking the path of a conscious co-Creator (Stage 7), you should periodically repeat this meditation, to tweak and add items to your list as you feel inspired to… until you get to a point on your path where you can actually see the bridge between your 'now' reality and your Ideal Lifepath.

But it's ok if your auspicious To Do list is initially pretty sketchy, and not necessarily seems related to actual manifestation of prosperity. Write in it all the items that you feel inspired to write, as the logical connection between it and your Ideal Lifepath will become apparent later. As time goes by, and as you start walking the initial steps with full trust in your Soul's directives, some synchronistic events and developments will happen in your life, at which point you'll repeat the meditation again, and receive directives from your Soul to add new items to your auspicious To Do list… By the time you've done the meditation again and again, as time goes by, it'll start looking more and more like an actual cohesive Plan that you can follow, which makes multidimensional sense, and you will get to the point from which you can actually see the bridge from the 'now' to your Ideal Lifepath.

The reason that your Soul is deliberately hiding from you some of the later steps of your auspicious To Do list is that It doesn't want to overwhelm you. This is similar to a parent teaching their kids about reading: as a parent, you wouldn't tell your six-year old that she/he must learn to read Shakespeare and the philosophy of Plato; you would tell him/her that he/she must learn to read, so she/he can read simple bedtime stories for themselves. You deliberately hide the fact that this reading skill is to serve their higher education later, because you don't want to overwhelm your child with unnecessary worries and responsibilities. Your child, though, trusts that if he/she follows your instructions, everything will fall into place perfectly, and life will be great. The relationship with your Soul is the same, your Soul being the parent, and you being the child.

When you make your list, remember to include in it items from all the aspects of your life: health, prosperity, happiness, a meaningful relationship… and everything in between.

Prepare Your Space for the Meditation:

Find a quiet time and place in which you would be undisturbed for the duration of this meditation. Cleanse, protect, and bless your space as you've learnt to do in Chapter 1. Specially bless your space and set the intents for Zohar Breath Meditation. Put on some inspiring non-verbal music. Bless and light a candle.

The Meditation:

Sit comfortably on your meditation cushion, with your spine loosely erect, close your eyes, your chest slightly out, your chin slightly tucked in, and your shoulders relaxed down. Start gradually deepening your breath. Start Zohar Breath Meditation… until you get to the point of absolute stillness-peace-Love-Light and nurturing feeling of your Soul's presence.

Now bring forth the complete vision of your Ideal Life, including the details of the your Ideal Life Daily Routine Internal Experience. Allow yourself some time to dwell in the bliss of your Soul's healing presence for a while. When you get deeper and more peacefully in the presence of your Soul and its wisdom, without veering form the consciousness of your Soul, ask your Soul:

- ☯ Which of the details of your Ideal Life is achievable right now, in your present reality?
- ☯ What steps can you take right now, that will tilt the balance, and direct your life towards the manifestation of your Ideal Lifepath? (These may not necessarily be actual items on your Ideal Life list, but things leading to them, like my example of studying Italian)
- ☯ Which of these achievable steps will make you feel healthy, beloved, prosperous, accomplished, or whatever is necessary to bring your energetic vibration into resonance with what you want in your Ideal Life?
- ☯ What actions can you take in order to shift your perspective into the new paradigm of your Ideal Lifepath?
- ☯ What actions can you take right now to fulfill parts of your Ideal Life? (These are actual steps, like my example of planning to teach retreats in other locations before opening an actual resort. They could either be parts/aspects/bits of your Ideal Life, or they could be early versions leading up to the full manifestation of your Ideal Life in all of its riches.)
- ☯ Is there a certain amount of time that should pass, or are there any pre-conditions that should be fulfilled before you could fully merge with your Ideal Lifepath? (As in my example of finishing the channeling of the information before proceeding with any business planning)
- ☯ What is your "starting gun?" Is there a specific sign that should tell you that it's time to start taking physical action?

As we have done before, after each question that your here-now self asks, bring your attention back into the Zohar Breaths, and persist with your concentration on the Divine white Light coming in and out of your heart space as you deeply breathe… until you get to the stillness-clarity-peace-Love-Light of your Soul again. Then be still and receptive, and wait patiently for the your Soul's answer…

Be aware here again that the answer of your Soul will always be high vibrational, and that it may reflect a direction that your logical here-now self could not have thought of. If this answer is indeed given by your Soul Self, than the message will be very clear and consistent with your previous Soul meditations, and you will feel a profound peace with it. When you get an answer that resonates with you deeply, do some automatic writing to record it, as you may not remember it later when you snap back to here-now wakefulness. This automatic writing is not yet your To Do list. It is just the impressions and higher ideas communicated to you by your Soul during the meditation.

Now do a few more Zohar Breaths, and recall your impressions of the Ideal-you that you have merged in The Ideal-you Meditation (Chapter 6)… Bring forth the image, feeling, and vibration of the Ideal-you, and briefly repeat the merging with the Ideal-you. This shouldn't take that long, since you have already merged with the Ideal-you several times, so that its image and feeling should just flash into your consciousness. Remember that the consciousness of the Ideal-you is the you that your Soul is holding space for your here-now self to become, so it is somewhere between your Soul's vibration, and your here-now self's vibration, which is the perfect place to be in for the next stage.

Now that you are somewhat grounded, but yet the messages you received during your meditation are still very vivid in your mind, organize your notes and impressions into your auspicious To Do list. If the impressions start to fade and you feel like the well of your inspiration fades, you may either repeat the process of the meditation right away, or you may go back and do it again on a different day. As discussed above, it's good to repeat this meditation periodically as you merge with your Ideal Lifepath.

When you're done with the meditation on a particular day, add at the bottom of your list the words "this or better." And this is actually something that you should add to all of the notes that you take during all of these important meditations, especially your Ideal Life and your Ideal Daily Routine meditations. Keeping in mind that your Soul deliberately tells/shows you only the part of the picture that It thinks you can handle; and taking into account our human limitations of not always being able to tune into the highest Soul consciousness; realize that your meditational visions and impressions may not be the final movie of how your life is going to go. So you should always leave room for the Universe to manifest for you something that is better for your highest wellbeing than what you were able to tune into in any particular meditation.

After you've done the meditation enough times, and you feel like your auspicious To Do list is shaping up into real Plan, you may want to do an intentful ceremony to express your free will. For example, you may wish to copy it onto parchment paper, bless it, and put it in a meaningful place in your personal space, like under a crystal that you've blessed, or in your personal alter if you have one. Usually the intent behind this type of ceremony is to assert your free will that this list will lead to the manifestation of your Ideal Life. Another type of ceremony that some people like to do is to actually burn the parchment paper containing your list (under the full moon), as a way of expressing that you are setting your vision free (an important manifestation concept that we'll discuss in the next chapter), and trusting the Universe to manifest it (or better) for you.

One thing that I would like to put in context for you here is being kind to yourself as you embark on your journey of achieving all the items on your To Do list. Initially, while your list only contains two or three leisurely items, you'll just add those activities to your normal weekly schedule. But as your list beefs up into a real Plan, it will probably contain many more items, all of which can take additional time out of your already busy schedule. Remember that to magnetize prosperity into your life, you must live in a vibration of joy. In *A Lifestyle of Prosperity From Your Soul*, we will talk extensively about how to organize your lifestyle to make room in it for the new activities, while still dwelling in the vibration of joy and kindness-to-self, to magnetize prosperity to you. But for now, just keep in mind that you must arrange all the new activities in your list on your calendar such that your life is balanced, and you have plenty of time not only for work and chores, but also for play, leisure, meditation, fun physical activity, sleep, and recreation. For even activities dictated by your Soul Self as part of your Plan must be dipped in Love and joy, in order to send you on the magnificent journey of manifesting your most Ideal Lifepath, and reclaiming all that you Truly are.

Having done your Ideal Life and Ideal Daily Routine meditations, you've probably had some good visions and Internal Experiences of your Ideal Lifepath. And having started your auspicious To Do list, you probably have an idea about your first few steps to merge your "now" reality with your Ideal one. But if we equate your Ideal Lifepath to a building, than even though you've glanced at the finished building and have seen a partial blueprint of it, you still don't know where building materials are to come from, and exactly how to erect the full building. At this point, you probably only have a partial blueprint, and the first few steps that that you must do to start building, such as digging a ditch and building the frame. Especially if your Ideal Lifepath seems far removed from where your life is right now, it is very likely that you have no idea how the humble steps of your To Do list would help you build your empire. And that's OK. Even though you've seen-experienced the vision of your Ideal Lifeplan, your plan to bring it into here-now reality is not complete yet. As we've been discussing throughout this chapter, over the next few weeks and months as you start walking the initial steps of your Plan and as you live your everyday while dwelling in the Light of your Soul, some auspicious synchronicities will start happening. And then when you repeat the last meditation periodically, more steps and information will keep coming to you to beef up your auspicious To Do list into a real plan, and as you follow those dwelling in the Balance of Grace (see next chapter), more auspicious synchronicities will happen that will lead your life closer to your Ideal… until at some point, you'll start seeing your Ideal reality as a natural extension of your 'now' reality.

What is important to realize is that having seen your Ideal Life meditationally, and more than that, having experienced it as an internal reality, mean that this reality in which you are living your Ideal Life already exists at some realm (see Chapter 6 of *Prosperity From Your Soul*), and is therefore possible for you to magnetize to you, or more accurately, to merge your current life with. It is up to you to do so, by trusting in your Soul's loving plan for your life, following the inspired steps that your Soul has given you, and by generally walking the path of a conscious co-Creator.

The next chapter—Walking the Path of a Conscious co-Creator—will guide you to find the balance, in your everyday life, between proactively taking steps to co-Create your Ideal Lifeplan and being receptive to gifts from the Universe, while staying in a joyful, prosperity-magnetizing vibration, and navigating your life towards your Ideal one.

Chapter 8

Walking the Path of a Conscious Co-Creator

Congratulations on all the Soul searching that you have done, and on the profound understandings that you've reached through your meditations.

At this point of our journey together, the metaphysical understandings of the first *Prosperity From Your Soul* book are probably not so esoteric for you any more, since the meditations of this book have allowed you to experientially internalized their wisdoms and make them your own. And by now, you probably have at least a sketch of a plan to reclaim your Ideal Lifepath. But as discussed in Chapter 8 of *Prosperity From Your Soul*, walking the A-B-C of your plan does not necessarily mean that you know how steps X or even J will come about. You probably have a perfectly clear vision of your Ideal Life, and an idea of what steps A through G of your plan would require you to do. Of course it's possible that as you started to implement your first few steps, the Universe suddenly revealed to you all the rest of the steps—you've synchronistically met your investors, business partners, new boss, Soulmate, teacher… and you are confidently already walking the path of your Ideal Life. But if you've just finished doing the meditations of the last chapter, than most likely, the Universe has just started drizzling auspicious synchronicities into your path, and has probably not quite gotten around to meeting you halfway yet. And in order to manifest all that you once thought was impossible but now know is part of your Ideal Lifeplan, the Universe does have to meet you halfway, doesn't it? So the sixty-four-thousand-dollar question now is: What should you do now to make sure that the Universe meets you halfway, and that you navigate your life to that rendezvous point where the Universe is meeting you?

And the short answer is: even if you do not yet know how to get from point G to point X of your plan—even if you're expecting the Universe to meet you at point G and transport, or at least assist you in getting to point X, you still have to live every moment of your life *as the conscious co-Creator that you now are.* And if you are to live every moment of your life as a conscious co-Creator, than we need to define what that would require of you: what does it mean to walk the path of a conscious co-Creator? That is what this chapter is about: to give you some practices that will help you walk the path of a conscious co-Creator, so as to ensure that you make it to the rendezvous point where the Universe is absolutely going to meet you.

The first prerequisite to making it to the rendezvous point is keeping your energetic apparatus clear and bright, so that your Mental Body is continuously receptive to clues from your Soul Self, and can foster ideas and plans of action with clarity; your Astral (emotional) Body facilitates lighthearted upbeat feelings that enable you to take the actions inspired by your Plan, and to be receptive to gifts from the Universe; and your Etheric and physical bodies are clear of any debris and illness, and reflect the radiant energy of lightness, freedom, happiness, and health that is now coming from your Soul. In this way, your entire aura and energetic apparatus facilitates the pouring of Creative energy from the Divine into your physical reality through your Infinite Funnel of Abundance. In chapters 3 and 4, you have done tremendous work on yourself removing blocks, and actively restoring your Infinite Funnel of Abundance. You can't afford now to let any new energetic debris re-block your Infinite Funnel of Abundance. And here is the reason why you can't afford to let yourself harbor any negative thoughts or feelings: Since you have already been to the height of meditation, and have dwelled in the Light of your Soul, your vibratory rate has increased. And the more connected you are to the Light of your Soul, the higher your vibratory rate, the more powerfully you resonate with the reality in which your thoughts and feelings are manifested, and thus the faster you merge with those realities. This essentially means that the more spiritual you are, the faster you'll manifest your thoughts and feelings into reality. You might have already started to feel this lately: you think of a parking spot in a certain place, and there it is; you have a feeling that your vacation plans will change a certain way, and it happens; you intuit that an auspicious opportunity will soon find you, and it does… It goes without saying that now that you are more potently co-Creating your life, you want to keep the flow of manifestation positive and in accordance with what you Truly want.

The first step of making sure that the co-Creative intents that you transmit into the Universe are positive and in accordance with your True wishes is to become aware of the continuous tape of your subconscious beliefs, attitudes, thoughts, and words in your mind. An integral part of this awareness is to shift any self-defeating thoughts, beliefs and attitudes about yourself into positive ones of self-worthiness, and an internal knowing that your wishes are about to manifest. This is what the first part of this chapter will help you do – the internal work that will help you stay vibrationally connected to the Infinite Funnel of Abundance on a daily basis.

Vibrationally staying connected to the Infinite Funnel of Abundance on an everyday basis is a huge part of ensuring that you make it to your rendezvous point where the Universe is meeting you to fulfill your dreams. But this vibrational alignment is induced not just by positive cognitive thoughts, beliefs and attitudes. Remember that the biggest bulldozers that move our energetic vibrations are feelings. So in the second part of this chapter, we'll discuss the Balance of Grace, which is the most potent tool that I can to help you stay in a positive vibration of magnetizing success to you on an everyday basis.

The third aspect of making sure that you make it to the rendezvous point with the Universe is to actually navigate your life towards your Ideal Life that you've meditationally seen, which requires finding a delicate balance between on the one hand, taking inspired action, seizing opportunities, and being proactive bringing your ideas into fruition, and on the other hand, being *receptive* to Universal guidance, and *allowing* the Universe to bring you gifts effortlessly. This state of fine balance between doing and receiving is something that you need to find every day. So the last section of this chapter, called *Setting Your Vision Free*, will give you some conceptual tools to assist you in finding this delicate balance. But really and truly, the one that can most skillfully guide you to find it is your very own Soul.

Positive Thoughts-Words for Positive Manifestations

As you already know, words and thoughts are very powerful tools for co-Creating your reality. So the first level of staying in a prosperity-magnetizing positive vibration is choosing your words and thoughts positively. On a simple psychological level, since you are your own constant audience, your words and thoughts have a more profound effect on you than they do on others. And you want your words to be good self-fulfilling prophecies, not bad ones. Further, as you have come to understand in *Prosperity From Your Soul*, words have a certain co-Creative power. Your thoughts (subtle words) can beef up into feelings; and your feelings have a tremendous effect on your energetic vibration, which seeps out into the Universe and creates a mutual resonance that magnetizes what you say, think, and feel to come to you.

So saying or thinking, "oh, I'll never lose that weight, I'll never be able to get in shape again" actually keeps you in a loop of continuing to co-Create an overweight, out-of-shape condition. But if you say instead, "I crave only healthy lean foods; I enjoy physical activity; I'm getting leaner and lighter every day; I am in the best shape of my life," than as soon as you internalize those statements into your subconscious and start gathering appropriate positive feelings around them, you will start magnetizing to you a reality in which your statements are true. In the same way, statements such as, "Oh, I'll never be successful," "I'll always be poor," "I'm a failure," and the like, cause you to feel and therefore energetically vibrate as the essence of lack and failure, thereby continuing to magnetize those conditions into your life. In Chapter 8 of *Prosperity From Your Soul*, we've talked about some of the internal monologues relating to our preconceptions about money, which do not serve our highest path to success. And the first level of uprooting those unconscious beliefs that do not serve your Ideal Lifepath is simply gaining the awareness that they exist, and having some realizations regarding the possible affects of those non-serving subconscious beliefs on you specifically, all of which you've probably done when you read that chapter.

The first step towards shifting your internal dialogue into one that supports co-Creation of prosperity is to catch yourself whenever you are thinking self-defeating thoughts, or are about to say something self-defecating, and replace those thoughts and words with positive, more hopeful ones.

The second step is to become aware of your thoughts throughout your day, and whenever your internal monologue is reinforcing any non-serving beliefs, you can interrupt them and alter the course of your mind and feelings. So for example, if you catch yourself internally saying, "I'm going to fail," or "I'll never succeed in this kind of endeavor," immediately command your mind: "Stop! Cancel! Delete!" According to various New Age psychologists, this effectively stops all thought (conscious and unconscious) for a few seconds, and therefore stops the self-defeating tape. In those few seconds, your conscious mind has a narrow window of opportunity to implant some reinforcing, positive beliefs, such as: "I am successful. I deserve success. I succeed in everything I do…" And you do deserve success, love, health, happiness, prosperity, and every good thing… by virtue of who you Truly are.

Now, let me explain that even though the particular antidote affirmation that you use may not exactly be true in the here-now moment of your life, they are ultimately not untrue. And here is why: as long as a better situation exists within the deep yearning of your heart, than its reality already exists in a parallel reality (recall Chapter 6 of *Prosperity From Your Soul*), and you are already destined to merge with it. It is true that from your here-now perspective, the positive situation you dream of exists in a reality that you perceive as future. But since at the level of your Soul, time doesn't really exist, this favorable parallel reality is already an integral part of your expanded Self. In fact, the very yearning for this better situation was implanted in you by your very own Soul. So when you affirm to yourself "I am wealthy. Success and prosperity flow into my life easily and abundantly…" even if at present moment your bank statement shows overdraft, you are not lying. You are merely reminding yourself of your True potential, and of the reality that awaits you (if you reclaim it). So get in a habit of telling yourself good things, think positive, and find joy, beauty, and love in every task. Love yourself. Love your life. And reaffirm positive things at every chance you get.

Reprograming Your Subconscious Tape:

In Chapter 4, you've taken some meditational steps to deeply deprogram childhood traumas, and remove energetic blocks from yourself. But let's go a step further. Let's talk about deprograming self-defeating beliefs and attitudes from your subconscious mind, and replacing them with positive ones.

Most people tend to think (or have been convinced by modern psychologists) that to deprogram deep unconscious beliefs, one must undergo a lengthy process of psychoanalysis, psychotherapy, and the like, or at least buy an expensive series of tapes with subliminal affirmations to help the process. But from a spiritual perspective, no psychologist or spiritual guru can know you as deeply as you know yourself, I don't care how well trained or enlightened they are. And no one on this planet can have a stronger, more convincing influence on your mind—conscious or unconscious—than you yourself. And reprograming your subconscious mind with positive beliefs and attitudes is actually simpler than you might have thought.

Each occasion in which your body is still, and your mind is peaceful yet active, has the potential to reach your subconscious, especially if you split your consciousness into the observer and the observed and reach a self-hypnotic state. And you've done that in each one of the meditations that you did in this book: there was a part of your mind that was conscious, awake, and able to direct the meditation; and there was the other part that was either digging up junk from your brainfucking noise, or soaring into the bliss of your Soul consciousness.

The potential to reach your subconscious is even more potent every time you start drifting off to sleep at night, and each morning when you're just starting to wake up—in the space between wakefulness and sleep. In the morning, when you first start being aware that you are dreaming, and are just in the very initial stages of waking up, you are in affect tuned into your subconscious. And if you can get your higher consciousness to kick in and affirm some positive beliefs and attitudes during that time when you are still kind of dreaming, than they would reach your subconscious. And if the affirmations you now input into your mind contradict some existing negative programs, than they will effectively deprogram the old non-serving beliefs, and instill the new positive ones. So for example, if you dreamed that you were poor and alone—a dream that probably came from a subconscious tape saying, "I don't deserve love and success," and during your in-between phase (before fully awakening), your higher consciousness intervened and affirmed, "I am radiant child of God. I deserve to be loved. I am ready to receive love. I deserve success. I am successful in everything I do…" than over time, you will have effectively deprogramed your self-defeating subconscious program, and instilled a new positive belief system in your mind, which will help the co-Creative endeavors of your wakeful life.

In the same way, when we go to sleep, there is a point in which our minds just go through the worries and concerns that are still troubling us, or the movie we've seen. And beyond that point, our consciousness just drifts off into an undecipherable mindless jumble of thoughts. As we gradually drift off, we detach from outside stimuli (sounds and light around the room), and turn our mind inward, until at some point we switch off to dreamland. Now, if you can control your relaxation-to-sleep process like a meditation—if your higher consciousness can conduct the process in a controlled way, allowing the brainfucking noise to surface, letting it go, and redirecting your consciousness into some positive thought, than when you get to the stage of switching off outside noises, you'll be in a state of total peace, while retaining continuity of consciousness, and listening only to your inner mind. This is the point when you can internally listen to the tape of your subconscious beliefs and attitudes, and have an opportunity to interject positive affirmations to contradict any negative beliefs.

You can also record yourself saying the affirmations that you think are appropriate, and play that tape for yourself as you are falling asleep, and set it as your alarm clock. You can even record yourself saying the affirmation in a soft voice, while peaceful music plays in the background. This is easy to do on your smartphone, and it's easy to set that track that you've recorded as your alarm. And the affirmations that you record in your own voice have an advantage over affirmations spoken by anything else in the world. Since it is you yourself speaking, your subconscious would accept it as true more easily than the voice of any shrink or guru.

Affirmations done during those in-between stages are the most effective, since they not only probe the subconscious, but also have the power to influence and reprogram your internal dialogue and belief system into ones that support your path as a conscious co-Creator.

How to Phrase Your Positive Affirmations:

When communicating with your subconscious, you have to realize whom you are addressing. In most cases, the part of you that formed any self-defeating programs was either a young child (your child self), or it could even be your reptilian-brain—the part of your brain in charge of primal survival. Therefore, even if you are a smart executive or have an advanced degree from an Ivy League university, the aspect of your subconscious that is playing the self-defeating tape in your mind has the intelligence and the understanding of a young child at best. And if you think about it, young children do not really understand long phrases with complicated words; they don't really have a good concept of the future; they don't understand double negative phrasing; and they don't get it when you allude to things in a metaphoric indirect way. They understand specifics, and know what is, and affects them directly, right now.

For that reason, the affirmations that you use should be phrased in a manner that is:

- Specific to what you want to achieve, to your specific issues, and to the particular programs that you might be running in the back of your mind. "~~Everything is alright~~" is not specific enough. Use instead affirmations that are specific and related to the issues at hand, such as: "I am wealthy" or "I am in perfect health," depending on what your issue actually is.
- Worded in a short and concise manner that any three-year-old could understand, so that your subconscious lower mind could comprehend. A statement like "~~The projection of my financial portfolio is in to top ten percentile~~" is completely ineffective as an affirmation, because your subconscious child self cannot understand it. A much better affirmation is: "Money come to me easily and abundantly," or "I'm successful in everything I do…"
- State things in a positive way. "~~I am going to stop feeling unworthy~~" is a double negative. Change it to: "I am worthy."
- In present tense: "~~I will be prosperous~~" should change to: "I <u>am</u> prosperous"

<u>Examples of affirmations effective in bringing about financial prosperity</u> –

- My life is abundant in every positive way.
- I am living my Ideal Lifepath
- I am worthy of receiving an abundance of money
- Money comes to me easily and abundantly
- It is easy to manifest money
- Money is good and spiritual
- I am worthy of success
- Everything I do is successful
- I am successful and wealthy
- I am becoming more successful every day
- I am becoming wealthier every day
- I am open to the Infinite Funnel of Abundance
- I am open to receiving prosperity through all positive channels/avenues
- I trust in the Divine to bring me True prosperity
- My [dream endeavor] is successful

<u>Examples of affirmations effective for love</u> –

- I am beloved
- I am worthy of being loved
- I love myself

- ❧ I am fabulous
- ❧ I am beautiful
- ❧ I am loving, warm, smart, fun-loving (whatever your positive attributes actually are, as you'd put them in a dating profile, repeat them to yourself)... I am a catch!
- ❧ I am ready to receive love
- ❧ I am ready to give my love openly and freely to others
- ❧ I am a Universal channel for Love
- ❧ I am Divine Love
- ❧ I surrender to my Soul's plan of bringing a fulfilling loving relationship into my life
- ❧ I trust my Soul completely

Examples of affirmations effective in facilitating health and diet –

- ❧ I am becoming healthier every day
- ❧ I enjoy fresh vegetables, fruit and wholesome foods
- ❧ I love engaging in Joyful Physical Activity (see *A Lifestyle of Prosperity From Your Soul)*
- ❧ I am in great shape
- ❧ I am full of youth and zest of life
- ❧ My body lets go of access fat quickly and easily
- ❧ Fresh healthy food is always available and abundant (I don't need to store it as fat in my body)
- ❧ It is safe to let go of access fat in my body
- ❧ I ground the enormity of my Soul's energy as personal power, health, prosperity, and happiness (not as physical body size)
- ❧ My aura is radiant and strong (so I do not need to enlarge my physical body through overeating)
- ❧ I am totally nurtured by the Universe (so I do not need to over-nurture myself with comfort food)
- ❧ I am the Balance of Grace

Another practice that may help you start each day in an upbeat tone is to remind yourself of all that you Truly are. I mean, it's more than ok to seek to improve yourself and have a better life. That's what these *Prosperity From Your Soul* books are all about. But the best daily motivator for reclaiming your True Self and your Ideal Lifepath is giving yourself credit for all that you are and all that have achieved so far. So when you get up in the morning, look yourself in the mirror, and say – "I'm going to have a fantastic day." "I'm beautiful." "I am a beloved child of God." "I am wealthy and successful." "I am happy." "I am in perfect health." "I am beloved." Whatever the need is in your life at that moment, get in a habit of affirming to yourself every day that your prayer is already answered, and that the answer is about to come to the surface of observable reality and manifest physically in your life. And when something good happens in your life, make it a point to affirm: "Of course this good thing happened to me, because I deserve it!"

At the end of each day, rather than beat yourself up over all the things that you didn't quite manage to achieve yet, give yourself credit for all the ones that you have achieved, love yourself for whom you are, and honor where you are in your process at that present moment. In *A Lifestyle of Prosperity From Your Soul*, I will give you some specific practices that should help you put the worries and hyped-up energies of the day behind, relax, reconnect with your True Self, and settle into a very peaceful night sleep. But for now, just make it a point to take some time each evening to honor whom you are at that moment in life, and give yourself some credit for all that you have achieved that day, even if it's just one humble task.

The Beloved Face in the Mirror

Self-love is a springboard for loving others, as well as for staying in a vibrational resonance that attracts the prosperity you seek. But what exactly do I mean by self-love, and how should this self-love be expressed?

To help you ascertain the answer to these questions for yourself, let me ask you: If you were caring for a precious child that you love dearly, what would you do for him/her? What would you do for this precious child out of your deep love for him/her? (And even if you are not a parent, take a moment here to really think about the answers.)

Would you…

- ♥ Create a clean nurturing environment for him/her?
- ♥ Cook healthy and nutritious meals for him/her?
- ♥ Groom him/her well?
- ♥ Dress him/her comfortably and nicely?
- ♥ Take him/her on nice walks in some beautiful place?
- ♥ Forgive him/her any shortcomings and faults (objective or self-perceived)?
- ♥ Really listen to all of his/her thoughts, worries, dreams, and plans for the future, non-judgmentally?
- ♥ Soothe his/her fears, encourage, and reassure him/her?
- ♥ Be kind, compassionate, and loving to him/her, no matter what?
- ♥ Hug him/her with the true love that's in your heart?
- ♥ Bring him/her a present every now and then?
- ♥ Suggest daily joyful things to do?
- ♥ Help him/her find the Balance of Grace daily (more on that balance in a little bit)?
- ♥ Bring him/her joy regularly?
- ♥ Be a dependable friend to him/her, no matter what?
- ♥ Regularly tell him/her how much you love him/her, and patiently help him/her let go of any barriers to receiving your love?
- ♥ Remind him/her of his/her own greatness?

And if you would do all that for someone else, why wouldn't you do the same things for the precious child within you? Now understand that your Soul regards you (your here-now self) as

Its precious child, therefore It Loves you unconditionally—a Love that has similar characteristics to those listed above. The only obstacle to really loving yourself this way comes from your here-now, human self.

Now stand in front of the mirror, and do a few Zohar Breaths to go into your Soul's consciousness, until you feel the Love-Light-peace of your Soul. Now open your eyes into an off focus gaze, and hazily look at this person looking at you in the mirror… Tune into the Love that your Soul has for this human persona that's looking at you back from the mirror. It might take some time to get used to this concept. So spend a few moments getting into that mode. You may go back to closing your eyes and taking as many Zohar Breaths as you need, to help you tune into your Soul's mode of unconditional Love. Then, partially open your eyes, and look at this person in the mirror some more, but out of a total space of Love. At first, it may be easier to just delve deeply into looking into your own eyes—the mirrors of the Soul. But then, with this off-focus view, allow yourself to catch view of some of the details of your face and body… and feel the Love that your Soul has for this precious child. Let that feeling of total love flood over your entire being.

The first time I actually did this practice, it was a little disorienting: my physical eyes saw my actual physical body, which was overweight at that time; but my spiritual eyes, which were tuned into Soul consciousness, saw an ethereal image of a thin, happy, and radiant me, superimposed on this physical persona. Also, the physical person looking at me back from the mirror looked alien—like it was a stranger, not me, but some kind of a golem. It was only the ethereal image of me that felt real. This discombobulated me a little bit the first time. It took several practices for me to be able to go deeper into Soul consciousness and feel the Love that my Soul has for this human persona. One time I was even able to tune into the reasoning why my Soul's chose this particular physical body shape through which to experience this incarnation, which was a bit illumination that shed light on many things in my life at the time.

So when you start doing this practice, realize that this person that's looking at you back from the mirror the vessel that your Soul has chosen for the experience of this lifetime. It therefore has all the backing and support of your powerful Soul. The you that you see—whether that's the physical image reflected back at you, or an ethereal Ideal-you superimposed over the physical (as I saw), is indeed a precious child who is unique, and has many wonderful qualities. Take a few minutes at the end of the meditation to appreciate your inner qualities, your uniqueness, your honesty, integrity, courage, kindness, and other good qualities with which you live your life every day. Appreciate all that you have achieved so far in your life, in terms of who you have become. And give yourself extra brownie points for the lessons that you've learnt, and the karma you've overcome so far.

Just spend a few minutes each day deeply looking at yourself in the mirror, tuning into the Love that your Soul has for you, and contemplating which action from the above list (or perhaps an action of self-love that I haven't listed here) you are going to do today to feel and express your love for this precious child that's looking at you back from the mirror. You should implement at least five self-love actions each day. Finish this practice by saying to your inner child "I love you."

Finding the Balance of Grace Daily

Beyond affirmations, beyond all the quite literally Soul searching meditations that we have done so far, and even beyond guiding you to tune into to your Ideal Lifeplan, the most profound tool that I can give you is to guide you to find your Balance of Grace daily. The importance of finding the Balance of Grace cannot be overemphasized! Because beyond the meditations, visions, and plans, the one thing that keeps you on a positive upbeat path of manifesting your plans most fabulously is reclaiming your Balance of Grace daily.

When you lose your Balance of Grace, you might feel "stuck" again; you might despair and conclude that the whole plan was just a pipedream; you might even sink into depression, and become oblivious to the fact that beneath the surface of your observable reality, the Universe has already begun to manifest your wishes for you. And if you let yourself sink into that negative vibration, you detach yourself from the Infinite Funnel of Abundance and from the auspicious synchronistic flow of the Universe. It is the Balance of Grace that continuously keeps you in a vibrational resonance that attracts to you the prosperity you seek.

So what exactly is the Balance of Grace? Simply put, the Balance of Grace is what you feel when you bring the bliss of your Soul into this existence. It is a subtle feeling about life, yet it is deep and profound. It is also when you, most naturally, vibrate in an attractive resonance to the prosperity that you seek. To try and pinpoint what it is more specifically, the Balance of Grace is the happy and harmonious balance between:

- The peace of dwelling in the bliss and radiance of your meditations – and the vitality and youth of being zestfully alive in this here-now reality…
- Being optimistic – and being realistic…
- Taking active steps to bring about my Ideal Lifepath – yet leaving room for the Universe to step in, surprise you, and manifest things *for you* in a better, easier, more harmonious way than you've imagined possible…
- Being empathic towards others – yet Setting healthy boundaries…
- Your Soul Self – and your here-now self.

When you find that balance, it leads to a vibration of pure joy, and a very alive feeling, in which all colors are extra vivid, all sounds, smells, touches and tastes are more harmoniously acute, and everything is just extra beautiful. The balance of Grace really is the balance of all parts of you. It is the you that is perfectly zestful, youthful, vital, and very alive; and yet it dwells in the perfect heavenly peace of knowing that you are fabulous just as you are, that you don't have to do anything but authentically be you to validate your existence, that all that you need and deeply want is absolutely going to be given, and that everything is ok in the greater sense. In most of our adult life, this could be a pretty elusive feeling. Sometimes it is almost like having once caught a glimpse of a heavenly picture, but not being able to clearly recall it.

But the Balance of Grace is not as elusive as it might seem, since it is an integral and deep part of you—dormant within you. It is essentially what I've called the Ideal-you in Chapter

6— who you're meant to be, and the version of you that your Soul is still holding space for you to reclaim being.

Living the Balance of Grace really is accentuating the you that is tightly connected to your Soul Self, yet at the same time is very grounded, ready to face the practical challenges of life in a joyful lighthearted way. It is the you that has found the perfect balance between the angelic Grace of your Soul, and being anchored into this here-now reality—the you that has strength of both your Heavenly and Earthly sides to go forward and reclaim your Ideal Lifepath, as well as the grace to be content in each moment. This is why I've capitalized the "G" in the Balance of Grace: because the Grace here is coming from the part of you that is a very natural extension of your Soul, which is of course, Divine.

For me, I sometimes achieve this Balance of Grace after a long meditative walk on the beach, on one of those warm afternoons, when the sun is sparkling on the water like millions of diamonds; seagulls are soaring up high; and I'm listening to, say Bach's Great toccata in C major, or a Chopin piano concerto… I mean after that combo—the diamonds on the ocean, the smell of a spring ocean breeze, the most beautiful pieces of music ever written, and the freedom to take them all into the heart and enjoy them, one simply must contemplate beauty, love, and joy, which leads to the elusive Balance of Grace.

One way to look at the Balance of Grace is as the feeling that, "it's ok to just be me." And really and truly, isn't that what it's all about? Recall from *Prosperity From Your Soul* that manifesting prosperity is all about being your most authentic Self—grounding as much of your Soul Self and Its natural Divine Abundance into this physical existence as possible. After all, the whole point in this life is for your Soul lessons and experiences to mold you into all that you *can* become—a bigger, brighter, more experienced Soul. The specific mission that you were given to complete in this lifetime (which you've meditationally perceived in Chapters 6 and 7) is simply the path that is best suited to get you there. So for example, say your life mission is to build a healing and rehab center for "at risk" youth. Building the center is not your destiny. Your destiny, or destination, is the same as all our destinations: to re-merge with the Divine in blissful Oneness, merging into Oneness the brighter, more advanced Soul that you've become. That is retirement in the Truest, most blissful sense of the word. Your life mission is the specific Lifepath (laid out by your very own Soul) that's going to get you there in the most efficient way, while achieving the Soul growth you'd set out to achieve. It is true that if you build that healing-rehab center (or whatever your life mission is), it would benefit humanity. And *it is also true that when you walk your Ideal Lifepath, monetary prosperity is a natural, and very welcome byproduct*, which is given to you to support your life mission. But since your life mission is designed to achieve Soul growth, it is intricately connected with whom you Truly are. So to get there, you must dwell in the perfect harmonious balance that integrates all parts of you—the Heavenly and the Earthly. And since the financial prosperity that you seek is a natural *byproduct* of integrating your Soul into this reality in a perfect balance, you understand why the Balance of Grace is so monumentally important in being a prosperous co-Creator of your life, don't you?

That being said, the chaos of life will never stop. There are always challenges that you must rise to meet. That is simply the nature of this "physical" existence. It isn't that you do one meditation or even a retreat, and you'll be sitting blissfully on a mountaintop under your Bodhi tree, being fed grapes by Antonio Banderas (or Sharon Stone) dressed in loin cloth, and gold coins will be dropping all around you from the skies like manna. When you return to the True HOME of your Soul (and may you live a long and happy life until that transition), you will indeed feel fed, nurtured and Loved without having to do anything but receive. But as long as you are living in this "physical" existence, the Balance of Grace is something that has to be reclaimed on a day-by-day, moment-to-moment basis, by whatever means can help you recapture that elusive feeling. And trust me when I say that it can take a lifelong to capture that, even for the holiest of persons. But it is in those precious moments in which you do achieve the Balance of Grace that you tap into the Infinite Funnel of Abundance and powerfully pull its blessings to manifest in your life.

There are many ways that can lead you to experience the Balance of Grace. The practices contained in this chapter are only some of them. The next book, *A Lifestyle of Prosperity from Your Soul,* will more closely guide you to shift your lifestyle into one that is conducive to capturing the Balance of Grace more consistently every day. I hope, though, that these practices will be the doorway that leads you to tap into your considerable inner wisdom, so that you may find many more practices leading to more and more moments in which you dwell in the blissful Balance of Grace.

How To Achieve The Balance of Grace:

1. Find balance, time-wise, amongst all the elements of your daily life: sleep (getting a good night sleep, but not oversleeping), meditation, Me Time, downtime, play, joyful physical activity, socializing, work, and all other positive elements in your life. This is also an important manifestation tool, since it will help you make room in your life for the new activities related to your Ideal Lifepath. More about balancing your lifestyle to facilitate your new path as a conscious co-Creator in *A Lifestyle of Prosperity From Your Soul*.

2. Find balance in your body between sleep-relaxation time and joyful physical activities. Practice nutritional kindness-to-self through the Zohar Kindness Diet (see *A Lifestyle of Prosperity From Your Soul*). This step alone can help eliminate physiological stress, and allow the free flow of Spirit within your body-temple to restore the real You. It is also a huge manifestation tool: your body-vessel is the vessel through which your Soul experiences this lifetime. So keeping it healthy and balanced will help you tap into the Infinite Funnel of Abundance more consistently.

3. Meditate daily to –
   Cleanse the mind from the brainfucking noise and let go of stress
   Cleanse your energetic apparatus
   Keep yourself tuned into your Soul's consciousness and vibration

4. Be kind to yourself! Allow yourself to feel fabulous with who you are and with life, even if you haven't yet captured the pie in the skies. Feel perfectly validated in everything you feel and are at each moment. And remember the Balance of Kindness. Realize that sometimes the Balance of Kindness means forcing yourself to brush off negative feelings,

cleansing yourself and your environment from any negative influences, and reclaiming your natural happy state. Other times, when deep negative feelings are a reoccurring theme in your life, the Balance of Kindness actually means that you should allow yourself to temporarily fully feel them, so you can get to the bottom of why you feel this way, solve the issue, and purge out these themes at their root cause, so that you never have to feel that way again. When your Balance of Kindness tilts towards having to experience things deeply, don't judge yourself. Forgive your human shortcomings. But by the same token, when you finish feeling/exorcising the discord, engage in an activity that restores your natural feeling of fabulousness. Let your Soul Self guide you in finding that balance.

5. Dwelling in your True Self means measuring everything you feel, think, and do, against the God Meter. Remember: joy is the one thing that both your Soul Self and your here-now self agree on. So true and deep joy—the kind that makes you wiggle your toes with pleasure—should be your most valuable tool for finding the Balance of Grace in every thought, feeling, and action, in every moment of your life. In addition to the joys that you find in the small moments of your life, you should do something fabulous – "just for me, because I'm fabulous" each day—something that reminds you of your fabulousness, and helps instill joy.

Defining Your Own Terms

In the same way that I've defined terms like, "The Balance of Grace," "The Infinite Funnel of Abundance," and other terms in this book series, you too can define your own terms. By the power of free will vested in you by the Universe, you have the power to make the terms you define work as your pre-agreement with the Universe. Once you define a term, then whenever you speak it, you invokes the definition in your mind, feelings, and in your energetic-vibrational resonance with the Universe. Because they have now function as a pre-agreement with the Creative force of the Universe, then when you speak your term, if you so defined it, it can also invoke the assistance of your Angels, Spirit Guides, and/or any deities that you invoked in your definition.

For example, I energetically protect and bless my space every night before I go to sleep, using the reiki symbols, the power of the spoken word, and sometimes lighting an incense or a candle. After a while doing this, listing each night all the things that I wish to let go of, dissolve, and be protected from, became a long and cumbersome process. So one night, I was guided to define the term: "all that does not serve my Soul Self." I used to use the definition that I'd heard many New Age thinkers call "all that no longer serves," until that night, when I received guidance explaining that some thoughts, feelings and energies have and will never serve my Soul Self, and thus the term "no longer" is not appropriate. The guidance also explained that I needed to define which part of me it should serve – here-now self, or Soul Self? So here is the definition that I spoke into existence as my contract with the Universe: "Whenever I say, 'I now let go of all that does not serve my Soul Self,' I am automatically invoking the help of Archangel Michael, my guardian Angels, and other Light beings to assist me in letting go, dissolving, and protecting from all low-vibrational energy, all low-vibrational life-forms and entities, all ill-will towards me, all energetic entanglement cords, all negative self-defeating programs, all road blocks, and any other negativities that do not serve my Soul Self and my Ideal Lifepath. I ask to fend off and dissolve any hungry or needy energy directed at me by others, and replace it with generosity and abundance energy flowing into my life. As I will this, so must it be. Thank you. Thank you. Thank you." And ever since I've defined this term, it has become an agreement between me, my subconscious mind, my Soul Self, Archangel Michael, my guardian Angels, and the other Angels and Light-beings who respond to my affirmation/plea. So now I don't have to list all of these things every time I want to cleanse myself and my space energetically. I just say, "I now let go of all the does not serve my Soul Self" and it is all done.

In the same way, you may define terms as agreements that serve you and your life. You can even make up words, such as "my fabulousity," to evoke feelings of self-fabulousness in you, or even gibberish mantras that helps you recap the feeling of your True Self. The point is, defining your own terms is a tool that you can use to assert your free will to manifest or un-manifest something, as you co-Create your life.

Setting Your Vision Free

Setting the vision free was the hardest concept for me to understand for the longest time, especially since most New Age circles call it, "letting your vision go." Now with the understandings that I have received when I was channeling the wisdom for these books, I can tell you that setting your vision free does not actually mean that you let go of your dreams and yearnings, as those should always be kept in the innermost, sacred chamber of your heart.

So what does setting your vision free really mean, and how does one set one's vision free? To start with, let's first understand that setting your vision free really stems from a perfect trust that the Divine plan is going to work for you.

It is wonderful to get to know your Soul Self, and live by Its guidance. It is important to know what your True gifts are, and what makes your heart sing with joy. And it was necessary for you to tune into your Ideal Lifeplan, and to chart some preliminary steps to take towards its co-Creation. But remember that these steps that you've charted are kind of like a blueprint. Remember that in order not to overwhelm you or burden you with daunting responsibility, your Soul only gives you a few steps at a time—perhaps only the A through F of your Plan to start with. The Universe is still supposed to meet you halfway. And you don't yet know what form this meeting is going to take in the reality of your life. So you need to leave room for this meeting, and for your actual Lifepath to vary somewhat from what you've perceived. Because ultimately, if you find the Balance of Grace each day, your Soul will lead you to the path that is best suited for you, from an unbiased, purest perspective of seeing the whole picture. And this path may be better than the one you have preliminarily tuned into. Maybe you wanted to marry a good person, but God has intended for you to marry a great person; maybe you wished to be a good employee, but your Soul is pushing you towards a position or business that accentuates your True gifts and makes you happy; maybe you were planning to take a bank loan to bring your new business idea into reality, but God has already sent you a like-minded investor, or even a philanthropist, who shares your vision and wants to take your business National. The point is, don't hold the Universe back from giving you something greater than what you have charted for yourself. Be open and receptive to the gifts that the Universe wants to precipitate upon you.

This takes a high degree of trust. An integral part of this level of trust is not to obsess about the fact that you don't yet know how you'll get form point G to point X of your Plan. Keep reminding yourself the Universe is meeting you at point F to carry you and help you the rest of the way. Once you've had an Ideal Life vision that resonates musically in every bell inside you, you should walk the path with confidence and trust.

Now about that trust, what is it that you are really trusting? Trust that everything that you Truly desire it's already co-Created, is coming, and is in fact already on its way to you. It is this trust that gives you the peace to enjoy the preparation time. It's like preparing to go on a hot date. If one didn't absolutely know the date is already lined up, one wouldn't enjoy the preparation. A woman might begrudge the pain of waxing her legs, and the time she has to spend fixing her eyebrows, her nails and her hair. A man might begrudge the hard work he's putting into the gym to blow the steam of stress of anticipation; having to carefully pick the restaurant; having to shave extra close; or worrying about how to impress the woman. We only enjoy the preparation for the date when we know that the other person wouldn't call in the last minute to cancel or stand us up; that the date is happening; and that it has a hot potential! You too have a hot date with the Universe! You have a date with your Ideal Lifepath, and your desired co-Creation already manifest in it! So enjoy your preparation time—do whatever you need to do to get yourself to trust that the Universe is already begun to Create and send you your desired manifestation.

While you wait, use that time to prepare for your manifestation to come, like a someone whose already got a hot date lined up, and is so happy about it, that she is absolutely enjoying every minute of waxing her legs and eyebrows, and fixing her nails; or he is taking extra joy researching and booking up the restaurant, choosing what to wear, and figuring out how to impress the woman. The point is to enjoy not only the date itself, but also time of getting ready for it. So while you wait for the Universe to do Its part, get your ducks all lined up in a row: write a business plan, take care of all the loose ends, and do all the things you set out for yourself to do in your auspicious To Do list that you wrote down at the end of chapter 7. Get yourself ready for your date with your most prosperous Lifepath, and *make sure you have a good time doing it!*

One reason that this is so important is free will. Remember that Creation is based on free will, and that actions speak louder than words. So your actions effectively speak your intent— your free will. When it comes to co-Creative endeavors, on the one hand, it is true that you need to take action inspired by your Soul, to tell the Universe that you trust Its Divine plan for you so completely that you have already started to walk the steps of the plan. On the other hand, if you are constantly in an overdrive of doing too much, than the vibe that you are sending out to the Universe is that you want to *do* everything, meaning that you are not leaving room for the Universe to help you in your manifestation endeavors, which asserts your free will not to allow the Universe to help you. So it becomes obvious that to set your vision free, you need to achieve a balance of some sort, between taking actions that are actually inspired by your Soul, and leaving room for the Universe to meet and assist you.

Metaphysically speaking, the vibration of joy and trust helps you stay in a peaceful vibration that more harmoniously resonates with, and therefore attracts, your desired manifestation. But if you're obsessing about a project and are constantly thinking, "Oh, I've got to make that project happen! I simply have to make it happen!! How can I make it happen?" than you are not really trusting that it's coming, are you? What you are doing in that case is sending out into the Universe a vibe that is tainted with an undertone of desperation and mistrust, which pushes that manifestation away and prevents it from coming into your life. It may already be co-Created out there in the ethers, or perhaps even in physical form. But the undertone of mistrust in the vibe that you are sending out into the Universe creates a discord, which interrupts the mutual resonance that was supposed to pull it into physical manifestation into your life. This could be likened to a woman who comes on to a guy too strongly, or to a man who's coming onto a woman too desperately, and even before their first date says, "I love you, I love you, I want to marry you, let's have sex tonight, please, please, pretty please!" You understand that in this example, the man or woman who is the object of the desperation will never show up, and the date will never happen.

Think of a funnel that's supposed to collect rainwater into a vessel. Rain may be extremely abundant, but if at the bottom of the funnel you have a pump powerfully pumping high-pressured salt water up through the funnel, than no fresh rainwater would be collected, because the pressure of the salt water will prevent the rainwater from coming in. In the same way, any obsessed, hyper-strong energy that you keep sending out is of a different vibrational frequency, which does not *allow* for a *harmonious* attractive mutual resonance to sustain, and therefore doesn't allow you to vacuum the object of your desire into your life, so to speak.

The type of energy that does allow an attractive mutual resonance to sustain is a peaceful and harmonious one—the type that comes with the peace of knowing beyond doubt that your desire is already on its way to manifest in your life. This is kind of like me writing these books without a publisher in mind, trusting completely that if God gave me this wisdom, She-He must want this knowledge disseminated to help people, so She-He will absolutely send me the appropriate publisher without any effort on my part. It is from this level of peace and trust that the ability to set the vision free comes. You see, as I write these lines, on the one hand, I want them to help people with all my heart; but on the other hand, I am not too attached to how the dissemination of this knowledge will happen. I know that the Divine has given this knowledge through me for the reason of helping people, so I know-feel beyond doubt that the Universe will absolutely find a way to get it to reach you and other readers. You see, on the one hand, I'm devoting years, and hundreds of hours of my life to channeling the knowledge and editing it; on the other hand, I'm not attached to how, why, or when. The balance—setting my vision free in this case is in the form of enjoying every inspired moment of being a conduit for the Light; having many moments in which I can just "see" you and other readers finding your True Selves and the prosperity that stems form It with the help of these books. This is an example of finding the balance between doing all the necessary stuff to prepare for your manifestation to come, and at the same time not being too attached to the "how," the "when," or the "from where/who" of it, thus setting it free to resonate with the Universe, and come back to you in fully manifested form.

This brings us back to gratitude: It was too early to talk about this concept in Chapter 3 of *Prosperity From Your Soul*. But knowing what you know now, part of what you've been grateful for all along was the future manifestation of your desires. That is, you know so deeply within your heart that your desire has already been co-Created, and that it's on its way to physical manifestation in your life, that you already feel happy and grateful. This is not just a meditational Internal Experience. It is when your meditational Internal Experience has already crystalized into deep internal knowing that it is so. That is the level of trust and internal knowing that keeps you in a joyful, light, and therefore harmonious vibrational resonance, which cannot help but attract True and all-inclusive prosperity into your life.

We have walked together a profound path. And I feel privileged to have inspired you, even in the smallest bit, to know your magnificent Soul, and to discover your Ideal Lifepath. But as profound a path as we've already walked, the real work begins now, as you start implementing the steps of your Plan, and as you start walking the path of a conscious co-Creator.

For at this point of our journey together, we are at the end of Stage 6—Devising a Plan of Action, and the beginning of Stage 7—Walking the Path of a Conscious co-Creator. The initial part of Stage 6 happened during the meditational processes of the last chapter, when you meditated on your Ideal Life, had a complete Internal Experience of it, and meditatively devised your auspicious To Do list. But as we have discussed, your auspicious To Do list initially outlined just the first few steps—the blueprint of your Plan, and is therefore not complete yet. It will become more complete throughout Stage 7, as you continue to walk the path of a conscious co-Creator daily.

You see: the Infinite Funnel of Abundance, most likely, will not hit you like thunder on a bright summer day. Your life will merge with it gradually. Of course, it is different for everyone; it could even be different for you in different times in your life. But the Infinite Funnel of Abundance doesn't necessarily mean that you'd suddenly win the grand lottery prize, or that your desire would just suddenly appear on your doorstep one day—poof! More often than not, the Infinite Funnel of Abundance shows up in one's life gradually and continuously.

As you continue to affirm high-vibrational thoughts, feelings, and actions, and become better able to find the Balance of Grace daily, you will be continuously opening yourself up and tapping into the Infinite Funnel of Abundance. As you live in the Balance of Grace, the Infinite Funnel of Abundance may show up in your life as additional inspired ideas that you get, as people that you meet who would help facilitate your dream, and other auspicious synchronistic events directing you to fulfill your dream in unexpected ways. With time, your auspicious To Do list, which may have only had ten items when you first wrote it, will beef up into a full-scale life Plan, as the Universe continues to meet you halfway in your everyday life, and as you keep getting inspired ideas, bumping into supportive people, and experiencing auspicious synchronicities. And as you keep joyfully walking this path, incorporating the steps of your Plan, and enjoying the

Universe's support, you will be subtly navigating your life towards your Ideal Lifepath. And as you keep setting your vision free on an everyday basis, with full confidence and inner knowing that your desired manifestation is already on its way to you, the circumstances of your life will start gradually shifting for the better… until one day, you will look back at the goals and dreams that you had written, and see that you're there—you're living your Ideal Lifepath.

Since Stage 7 is the stage that you'll be in the longest, and since it is so monumentally important in bringing your Plan into fruition, book 3 in the series—*A Lifestyle of Prosperity From Your Soul* will help you shift your lifestyle into one that facilitates continuously maintaining the Balance of Grace and setting your vision free. It will give you practices that will help your physical body achieve the strength necessary for the activities of your new Plan; bring your body-vessel to vibrationally match your new prosperous life, thereby helping you bring the Infinite Funnel of Abundance through into physical dimensions; and guide you to arrange your lifestyle in ways that leave room in it for the manifestation of the new Universal abundance.

Throughout your path as a conscious co-Creator, one thing to remember and try to internalize into a deep feeling is: You are fabulous! You are perfectly validated just for being you! You are a unique and tremendously beloved child of your Creator. Your Soul, as an integral part of the Infinite One—has the power to co-Create for you all that you Truly want. Therefore as you continue to merge with your radiant Soul, you become better and better able of bring forth into manifestation in your life all that your heart desires.

As I continue to pass along to you the Guidance that I have received, I am with you in my prayers, lovingly holding space for you to co-Create and manifest the most fabulous life that makes your heart sing with joy in each of its moments.

Appendix A

Meditation Worksheets

My Ideal Life Meditation Worksheet

Step 1:

From the highest perspective of your Soul, what is your life's mission for this human lifetime?

In broad strokes, what was the Ideal Plan that your Soul has laid out for you to best fulfill that mission?

Step 2:

What True passions did your Soul plant in you, specifically to help guide you towards fulfillment of your life mission?

What talents and gifts did your Soul give you to help facilitate your mission in this life?

From your Soul's perspective, what is the most Ideal way to let those talents and desires come into play in your here-now existence? What activities do you "see" yourself engaging in on a daily basis, which serve your Truest passions and are served by your Truest gifts in your Ideal Life?

If the Ideal-you could live an Ideal Life right now, without any constraints or limitations (if money was no object, and there were no physical/objective limitations), what would that life look-feel like?

In what ways does the Ideal Life that you've perceived so far make you feel fulfilled? How does it bring your natural talents, hopes, dreams, and earnest-most desires into a lifestyle of happiness and fulfillment?

Does this Ideal Life that you "see" right now make you feel the same as you felt when you were tuned into the Essence of Your Soul's Vision Meditation? The 'you' that you see in this Ideal Life vision, is it the Ideal-you that you've merged with in the Ideal-you Meditation? Or is it different?

If you were living this Ideal Life, would it better the people around you? Would it better your community? The world?

Step 3:

Within your Ideal Lifeplan, if you reclaim being the Ideal-you, how does your Soul intend for you to capitalize on your Truest talents and passions?

What is your Ideal Lifework? What were you meant to do in this lifetime, because you do it so well naturally, and because you derive so much joy out of it?

How can your Ideal Lifework be translated into an occupation, vocation, profession, position, an investment, a business, or another moneymaking endeavor?

My Ideal Daily Routine Meditation Worksheet

The daily activities of your Ideal Life:

Enjoyable: Not enjoyable:

Your natural talents/gifts that find their expression in the daily activities of your Ideal Life...

Your deep passions that find their expression in the daily activities of your Ideal Life...

Your body feelings during the daily routine of your Ideal Life...

Enjoyable: Not enjoyable:

Emotional feelings you regularly have during the daily routine of your Ideal Life...

Enjoyable: Not enjoyable:

Sight, sound, touch, smell & taste sensations you experience as part of the daily routine of your Ideal Life...

Enjoyable: Not enjoyable:

Inventory Of My Life Worksheet

Things & Circumstances In My Life That I'm Happy About:

_____

_____

_____

_____

_____

_____

_____

Pre-Existing Conditions, Things & Circumstances That I'm Unhappy About	Lit by the Light of your Soul, What growth was gained from the condition? Is its negativity still necessary in your life?

Bibliography

Chapter 1

1. Shutes, Jade. *Aromatherapy 101: Foundations.* East-West School of Herbal & Aromatic Studies. Willow Springs, NC: Author self publishing, year unknown.
2. *Field Of Dreams.* Dir. Phil Alden Robinson. Producers: Lawrence Gordon & Charles Gordon. Story by: W. P. Kinsella. Universal Pictures, 1989.
3. Howells, Harvey. *Dowsing For Everyone, Adventures and Instruction in the Art of Modern Dowsing.* Place of publication unknown: The Stephen Greene Press, 1979, pg. 11.
4. Hall, Judy. *The Crystal Bible.* Cincinnati, Ohio: Walking Sticks Press, 2004.

Chapter 2

1. Brown, R.P. MD and Gerbarg, PL. "Richard P. Brown Biographical Outline." *Have A Healthy Mind.* 2013. Jan. 2014. <http://www.haveahealthymind.com/brown-bio.html>
2. Brown, R.P. MD and Gerbarg, PL. "Patricia L. Gerber, MD Biographical Outline." *Have A Healthy Mind.* 2013. Jan. 2014. <http://www.haveahealthymind.com/gerbarg-bio.html≥
3. "Psychology Color." *The Oracle Educational Foundation.* Publication date unknown. Jan 2014. <http://library.thinkquest.org/27066/psychology/nlcolorpsych.html>

Chapter 3

1. "Stress: The Different Kinds Of Stress." *American Psychology Association.* Article is said to have been "adapted from The Stress Solution by Lyle H. Miller, PhD, and Alma Dell Smith, PhD." <http://www.apa.org/helpcenter/stress-kinds.aspx>
2. Loux, Renée. *The Balanced Plate.* New York, NY: Rodale Inc., 2006.

Chapter 5

1. "Pocket K No. 25: Biotech Plants For Bioremediation." *International Service For The Acquisition of Agri-Biotech Applications.* Nov. 2006. Jan. 2014. <http://www.isaaa.org/resources/publications/pocketk/25/default.asp>

Printed in the United States
By Bookmasters